The Third and Only Way

The Third and Only Way

REFLECTIONS ON STAYING ALIVE

Helen Bevington

DUKE UNIVERSITY PRESS   DURHAM AND LONDON   1996

© 1996 Duke University Press   All rights reserved   Printed in the United States of America on acid-free paper ∞   Library of Congress Cataloging-in-Publication Data appear on the last printed page of this book.

The following reviews originally appeared in the *New York Times Book Review* and are reprinted here by permission: "*A History of the Writings of Beatrix Potter,* by Leslie Linder" (July 18, 1971); "*A Thousand Pardons,* by Katinka Loeser" (October 3, 1982); "*Lorelei Two, My Life with Conrad Aiken,* by Clarissa Lorenz" (May 22, 1983); "*The Letters of John Middleton Murry to Katherine Mansfield,* selected and edited by C. A. Hankin" (November 13, 1983); "*To the Is-Land,* autobiography by Janet Frame" and "*An Angel at My Table* autobiography by Janet Frame book two" (October 7, 1984); "*What Are People For?* essays by Wendell Berry" (April 15, 1990); "*The Mind of the Traveler, from Gilgamesh to Global Tourism,* by Eric J. Leed" (1991).

"Anecdote of a Jar," from *Collected Poems* by Wallace Stevens, © 1923 and renewed 1951 by Wallace Stevens is reprinted here by permission of Alfred A. Knopf, Inc.

for David, with love

Must I leave the words unsaid
(Then what are words for?)
Hold my tongue, play dead, unheave my breast,
Spin cobwebs in my head,
Forget the rest?
Not bloody likely.

Contents

I

The Third Way

≼ The date is November 1980. As it happens I'm writing just now, in this particular month and year, for a reader who has shown a passing interest in my life and admits to being doubtful as to how it will turn out—the reader being myself. B., my husband, used to laugh at me for never failing to ask "What happened next?" after he had told whatever was on his mind, say, about running into the provost in the A & P and discussing the price of peaches.

"*Nothing* happened! That's it," B. would groan and shake his head. "Why do you always ask one question too many?"

"Did the provost buy the peaches?"

"I don't know. He went his way and I went mine."

"Good. I like to know how a story ends."

Having written three volumes of autobiography, I see it's high time to wind things up. Leonard Woolf is an example of a man who was still winding them up at eighty-eight in his fifth volume of memoirs. Garrulous by then, forgetful, repetitive, he went blindly on to record a singular lack of events, and no conclusions.

My first volume, *Charley Smith's Girl,* ended with the words "There must be a third way." Two other ways were my mother's and my father's, the way they lived and died. My mother, Lizzie, divorced from Charley when I was two and unaware that I had a father, lived alone from the time I left for college and a life of my own. She lived strong and valiant in her solitude till nearly ninety, seeming to confirm the claim that life is worth living. Granted longevity, she wore a pink rose in her hat and didn't consider herself old. She survived without lament, not happy but acceptant, when it was clear there was no other way. I said once, "You have courage," and she replied, "It takes courage." I thought that wasn't enough.

I blamed her that her friends fell away when in fact they died, that she had few resources beyond a little gardening, a little music; and like Hetty Green hoarded her money against the day fast approaching when time would topple her. It seemed to me a poor choice of survival, as if she had a choice. "My soul and body!" she would cry. "What more can I do?"

My father, Charley, gave up his life and died in despair, affirming the need to despair. Though he lived not alone but with his son Boyce, one morning he turned his face to the wall and, beyond human reach, never spoke or left his bed again. Charley's way was suicide, slow suicide. Four years earlier his beloved second wife, Boyce's mother, had died. Charley struggled with grief, trying alcohol then drugs, till finding this earth without her unacceptable, he refused to live, he willed himself to die. It was a cold message to leave behind.

To escape both destinies, I meant to find a third way, of neither solitude nor despair. An obligation to myself was to be happy, or not to be un-happy; I would use my wits to take the way neither Lizzie nor Charley had found. Why did I think that I alone would escape? Instead, against my will I am solitary like my mother and suicidal like my father, both the one and the other. Without having found it or knowing where to look, I still believe there must be a third way.

For a while I thought it was the knack of saying like Robert Herrick, "Tumble me down and I will sit upon my ruins (smiling yet)." Herrick defied fortune from his fallen state, which, as the future tense of the poem clearly shows, he hadn't yet tumbled into — and indeed never did. In some 1,400 poems, he wrote of love, the pleasures of love, the need for love, yet lived comfortably a bachelor all his life. When I surveyed what ruins I might sit upon — my house and five acres, my typewriter, my Oldsmobile, my bank account — I could see that a smile of undefeat would be bold but probably ironic. Besides, would it be possible to smile?

It was the idea of sitting alone on anything that baffled me. How do you accept aloneness, the kind without reprieve? Camus said, in the opening words of *The Myth of Sisyphus,* "There is only one philosophical problem which is truly serious: it is suicide." In an alien world where man's condition is absurd, why shouldn't he seek to escape? Finally Camus rejected suicide, with its stark answer, when he realized he wasn't alone as he rolled his heavy stone again and again to the top of the mountain. Though the senseless toil would never end, it was shared, the absurdity of it was shared. Hell was at least sociable, with plenty of company in the brotherhood of the damned. Camus reflected, oddly enough, "One must imagine Sisyphus happy" — happy, that is, to be alive. Five years later at only forty-seven, Camus was killed in an automobile accident.

George Herbert wrote, "By all means use sometimes to be alone. Salute thyself." The catch there is in the word "sometimes." Change it to "always," to Chaucer's "allone withouten any compaignye," and you end the celebration. Wordsworth knew "the bliss of solitude" surrounded by four adoring women: his wife Mary, sister Dorothy, daughter Dora, sister-in-law Sara. Keats found the highest bliss (he says in "Solitude") "When to thy haunts *two* kindred spirits flee." Or as Cummings sang, "We're wonderful one times one."

Yet the men I most admire — Thoreau, Gilbert White of Selborne, Montaigne — were solitary. Thoreau lost no opportunity to crow about it: "I thrive best on solitude," "I love to be alone." He lived to himself companionable and free, not recluse but rebel, and the world pleased him the better for being simplified. Mr. White of Selborne took in Mrs. Snooke's tortoise for company and made a list of 120 birds visible and audible in his Hampshire countryside. Montaigne climbed to his tower, surrounded himself with a thousand books, and wrote, in his essay "Of Solitude," "The greatest thing in the world is to know how to belong to yourself." Though he had considered suicide, his solution finally lay in acceptance. There was no martyrdom in it, no resignation. On the contrary, there was contentment and, as Thoreau said, "an immense appetite for solitude." Each man found the answer in himself.

When I was nine years old my father Charley told me what I had to do. On one of the few occasions that we were together and he took time to give any thought to my future, he handed me the key to happiness that he admitted had been of no use to him. It would make my fortune, be my inheritance, bring me thriving and content. "Be lucky," he said. "That's the whole secret. Just keep in mind what you want and latch on to it. Be smart, have it your own way. That's the trick, my girl. Be *lucky*."

Well, Charley, what do you think of your daughter's luck now? Am I going to swing it any better than you did?

The obligation not to be unhappy—it makes sense as a provident way, not found by chance or available for the asking. There are the nights of sweating panic when tomorrow can't be imagined, and you wait it out till daylight to begin another day. You marvel at the terror of existence.

My son Philip telephoned from the Cleveland Clinic Hospital early one night last August, and he said quietly, "The pain is unbearable." He had said it before, whispered it, "terrible, terrible," the same words. "May I come?" I asked, as I always asked, but this time he answered, "No, not yet." During the past months and years I had been with him often, as often as he would allow—staying at the Park Plaza across from the hospital for four weeks in July, watching him as he fought to live. Unable to work or read or write, he was losing ground. I talked with his doctors, who refused to make a prognosis. After a series of operations, tests, experiments with new drugs, consultations, blood transfusions, the doctors told Phil his life expectancy was unknown: he could die at any time—in an hour, in a day—or he could live for years. One of them said to me, "Phil meets life with honor, in a class of heroes by himself. He conquers on his own terms." This time it was too late. He was without expectancy. And so was I.

We talked every night by phone; his voice was all I had, not even the letters he wrote in his mind to tell me how it was. This night I said, as I always said, "I love you," and he said, "I love you too," and the connection was broken. He may have broken it himself. I called him back immediately and he answered, "Phil Bevington."

"I just wanted to say goodnight. I love you, Phil Bevington."

"I love you," he said, and his voice was calm. Shortly afterward he took the overdose of Seconal. The suicide notes were dated Sunday, the day before. They revealed nothing.

He left, and I do not know what it cost him, alone in a hospital room. I only know he was finally destroyed. It was a senseless automobile accident. As a graduate student at Duke he had accepted a ride home in a friend's new Volkswagen after a lecture. The little car had gone out of control, swerved, and crashed into a tree. From the impact Phil's back was broken. He was barely breathing with, they figured at the emergency room at Duke Hospital, about five minutes left to live. He was twenty-two.

Yet he survived for more than twenty years, fighting an extraordinary battle — an indestructible man. By that time he had his work as a nuclear physicist and professor at Case Western Reserve, he had his family, he held on. His work was his life. Though he did lose in the end, it is the suffering that is unthinkable. The doctors called it intractable pain, the kind they had no skill to lessen. He was brave, he was my son, he was destroyed. No one speaks in his voice, he does not exist. The words I wrote at the time of the accident, "He will live!" proved to be wrong, an intolerable lie. His death makes the thought of survival a mockery.

But one does survive. To go on living thereafter hardly beckons — it looms. At this moment the only survival I know is through words, with their insufficiency, their imprecision; the distraction of words, other people's words and my own concerning their fate and mine. My three solitaries — Thoreau, Mr. White of Selborne, Montaigne — were word men, givers of testimony. None wrote for the world's opinion, but they were sedulous in keeping journals to note their grounds for existing. They had only the time being to set it down, and they did. In the end it may depend on a blank piece of paper.

Enid Bagnold, who wrote her autobiography at eighty, drew a picture of a writer in old age sitting alone at a table lost in her game of solitaire. She goes on carefully piling word on word till, with a faint smile on her lips, she falls dead face down on her pack of words.

Solitude is cured by love, work, death, these alone. There are those who choose work as the least unrewarding of the three and become the great practitioners. "Leonardo, why do you give yourself so much *trouble?*" he was asked. The only time Pliny the Elder didn't work was while taking a bath. At his meals a servant read to him as he made copious notes on stars, wind, rain, trees, plants, fish, birds, beasts, insects, and mankind. Working all night, wearing mittens for warmth, he claimed to have gathered twenty thousand facts from some two thousand volumes, freely combining the false with the true since he believed everything he read and his love of the marvelous spurred him on. From tireless research Pliny recorded the existence of mermaids and centaurs, of men with dog's heads who bark. He noted the magic power of turnips to cure cold feet, thistles boiled in water to bring about male children, the carrot to induce lust. He learned that a head cold clears up if you kiss a mule's muzzle, that none among mortals is happy, though fortune deals lavishly with the man *who* is *not unhappy*. His curiosity cost Pliny his life. He died with a pillow tied round his head, suffocated by falling ashes while studiously observing Vesuvius erupt at Pompeii. He had no information in his notes about love.

In his *Italian Journey* Goethe said he was a person who lived in order to work. Violently seasick on the voyage there, he lay in his cabin and polished off the first two acts of *Tasso*. In his diary Max Frisch wrote, "Work is the only thing that preserves me from terror." In her diary Virginia Woolf defined the worthlessness of work except as refuge, a means to keep the worker alive. Katherine Mansfield wrote in her journal, "Life without work—I would commit suicide."

I too have a bottle of Seconal beside my bed. I said I wouldn't live if he didn't, I would die when he did. But I didn't die, I was left behind (weep for the dead, my father and my son. And for me in between). Nightmares follow me like the Eumenides lest I imagine I can escape. In a dream I compose a suicide note asking forgiveness, but no one is there to forgive. My reason is simple, it is grief, but does one die of it? Charley did.

Yeats said he would be content to live it all again in this "frog-spawn of a blind man's ditch." I write his words knowing they are not mine. For these months I've tried, but I have lost accommodation, I am running out of choices. How can I *not* give up?

He died three months ago, and August becomes November. The precipice is there, available if one is obliged to look for it. Seneca said to the unhappy slave, "Do you see the precipice?"

Suicide is deeper than any hurt, devastating to the lives of others. People are quick to call it cowardice: "One doesn't *do* that sort of thing," they said of Hedda Gabler when she shot herself. Yet it can become a necessary choice. I understand that. I can't wish him alive; for him death was a rational decision finally arrived at. It was the only way. In my dream he is on his feet, dressed in a business suit, saying, "I have to go now. Hang in there, Helen."

For me, if there is another way I must find it alone. Or is the third way Philip's way?

We are the love seekers. Auden wrote a great line: "We must love one another or die," and then said he didn't mean it. I wonder that the three solitaries got along so well without it, flourished and rejoiced. "Do what you love," Thoreau said. "Pursue your life." But he didn't say the pursuit might be of love itself. White of Selborne stayed celibate, unmarried. In his naturalist's journal he kept the entries on love to the amorous dalliance of greenfinches, bees pollinating his cucumbers, rams paying court to the ewes under an August moon.

Nature lovers appear able simply to love nature and call that love enough. (Wordsworth: "Nature to me was all in all.") Thoreau preferred otters, woodchucks, and loons to the company of men: "I love nature partly because she is not man, but a retreat from him." When W. H. Hudson read White's *Selborne* at fifteen and began a journal inspired by White, he spent solitary days on the Argentine pampas putting into words the rapturous experience of hearing birdsong. (In *Green Mansions,* Rima chirped like a bird.) Already at fifteen he was amazed by his intense feeling for nature, which was a mystery to me, especially at certain moments, when it would come upon me with a sudden rush. So powerful it was, so unaccountable, I was actually afraid of it, yet I would go out of my way to seek it. . . . And I would ask myself: what does it mean?

To discover what it meant became the work of his life. "I imagine that Thoreau was such a one," he said.

Montaigne—the third solitary—clung to his dearest friend, La Boétie, suicidal at his death "which is the death of me." For wife and daughter there are no expressions in his essays of affection or longing. His marriage was dull. He had no son. He forgot how many children he had lost, "two or three" (of six daughters only Léonor lived). He advised cutting loose from the painful ties that bind us to others—"I try to have no express need of anyone"—and sought detachment lest he be made inconsolable by loss. He chose instead to love life and cultivate it. Life was his affair of the heart, not the love of another whom one must always lose. But is it enough to love *only* life? *only* nature? to give up people entirely? Shake your head, Montaigne.

I don't believe in celibacy. By the evidence, love and work are a necessary combination. Yeats said it in "Adam's Curse," written to Maud Gonne when he was thirty-seven and hopelessly in love. In the poem he reminds her of a night at summer's end when he, Maud, and her sister Kathleen ("That beautiful mild woman, your close friend") sat talking together. Yeats had just said a little bitterly what hard work poetry is, though one must pretend it comes spontaneous and easy. You might better get down on your knees and scrub floors or break stones for a living,

> For to articulate sweet sounds together
> Is to work harder than all these, and yet
> Be thought an idler by the noisy set.

Then that beautiful mild woman, Kathleen, said the same was true of being a woman—you worked hard at being beautiful. Yeats replied that everything since Eden, through Adam's curse, was hard work, even love.

Love itself was labor, an art requiring high courtesy and learning, unappreciated these days and made to seem idle enough.

And they were silent, gazing at the fragile shell of a moon. Maud Gonne said nothing, her thoughts perhaps as sad as his own. In the labor of love he had failed, but so had she. She, who was called the most beautiful woman in Ireland, would go on being beautiful, he would go on writing poems to her, but in the third way they had grown weary-hearted. At the end he speaks only to her, the unattainable:

> I had a thought for no one's but your ears:
> That you were beautiful, and that I strove
> To love you in the old high way of love;
> That it had all seemed happy, and yet we'd grown
> As weary-hearted as that hollow moon.

(The next year, 1903, she married John MacBride, whom Yeats called "a drunken, vainglorious lout." He himself married a plain girl at fifty-two.)

So far I haven't asked a woman about the way she took, in the light of whose life I might measure my own — Jane Austen, say — for a clue. She never married or had a real love affair, but neither did she live alone or sleep alone. Cassandra, her sister, her other self, shared her life ("I tell you everything") and suffered her death.

Madame de Sévigné, 1,555 of whose letters survive, had too much solitude on her hands, too much need of her child for whom her love knew no limits. She wished her heart were as warm toward God as it was toward Françoise. When Françoise became the Comtesse de Grignan and left Paris to live in Provence, her mother, standing at a window watching the carriage depart, wanted to throw herself to her death. She sobbed for five hours. "It requires more courage than I possess," she wrote, "to bow to this tragic destiny."

Colette, from her own acquaintance with love, tried to do without it. As a child she was secure in her mother's love, told by her "You are my golden sun." But marriage with Willy taught her there are no certainties; she learned to despise herself for being a deceived, rejected wife. "To endure without happiness and not to droop, not to pine, is a pursuit in itself, you might almost say a profession." It helped to have an orderly mind, a sense of discipline, tenacity in a makeshift world. On her own she made painful experiments in love affairs with both sexes. She hated to write and said so, but writing freed her from reliance on other people. "The freedom to live untied to others" — Colette wanted that.

Yeats called it tragic joy that says life is absurd and accepts the tragedy. At least it's better than Rimbaud's "I believe myself in hell; hence I am there."

The obligation not to be unhappy: F. L. Lucas, writer and lecturer at Cambridge University, had the curiosity to try, in the essay "Happiness," to locate the elusive thing. He began with those in the past who were miserable, who claimed toil and care as their lot. Dr. Johnson (though he said it's the business of a wise man to be happy) wouldn't live one week of his life over again "in a world bursting with sin and sorrow." Coleridge at thirty said, "I do not know what it is to have one happy moment." Tolstoy counted fewer than fourteen happy days, Anatole France denied having *une heure, un jour.* Poor Stendhal cried, "Happy, I would have been charming."

Such confessions Lucas found astounding and dismal. Why is happiness so difficult to come by? The lament is always in the air, a persistent echo from Ecclesiastes to Lear. No one can exaggerate the suffering man has known, yet surprisingly scant is reliable testimony as to how much happiness exists.

What are the causes, Lucas asked, the sources of happiness? What makes one happy? He never found out. After a search doomed to defeat he only suggests ways of being happier than not:

Health — a first requirement.
A calmly balanced imperturbability — not a cause but a condition.
Freedom from fear — not a source but a proviso.
Vitality. An excess of stamina, a kind of thriving: "There are distinct advantages in being tough."
The ability to accept the way things are, the mind not tormenting itself.

Activity. Always to have some work at hand.

Love, if you can get it: "One truth is the unreality of many human relationships. It is perilous to risk one's heart on a single person."

Last of all, laughter. Like Montaigne, who said "I do nothing without gaiety." Like Sydney Smith, who, though he never recovered from the death of his son, chose laughter over tears, advocating "Short views, for God's sake, short views."

Horace defined a happy man:

Happy the man, and happy he alone,
He, who can call today his own:
He who, secure within, can say,
Tomorrow do thy worst, for I have lived today.
Be fair, or foul, or rain, or shine,
The joys I have possessed, in spite of fate, are mine.

So did Matthew Arnold (writing about Goethe):

And he was happy, if to know
Causes of things, and far below
His feet to see the lurid flow
Of terror, and insane distress,
And headlong fate, be happiness.

"Happy is the man," said Wordsworth,

Who only misses what I missed, who falls
No lower than I fell.

What am I saying? There is really no escape. The writers I quote are dead, yesterday's people, silent before such words as Auden left behind: "There is nothing to say. There never has been. There is no way out. There never was." (When her disciples asked the Cumean sibyl, given eternal life and shriveled to nothing in a glass, "Sibyl, what do you want?" she answered, "I want to die.")

In the meantime
There are the bills to be paid.

In the meantime, in the isolation of the countryside I write not to redeem the time but to cancel it. Writing is work, a way of lifting a finger, and nothing is more solitary. I've written it before: the dogwoods, mockingbirds, white house on the hill, the life with B., the life with two sons till they went off to Exeter and Harvard and found their wives and found their professions. Except that now I'm not living my life, I'm recording it. "Whom do I tell when I tell a blank page?" asked Virginia Woolf in her diary. I'm not good at making sense of it, the way one falters, circumscribed by loss, wrestling with words for something one no longer wants to say, words to shut out the silence.

"It was not," said Eliot, "what one had expected." It was not "the long hoped for calm, the autumnal serenity." The serenity becomes the turmoil as the seasons change. And there is, it seems to me, a limited value in living with yesterdays when the persistent, ineradicable memory is of loss, and the time is always now with its bewilderment and pain.

Lying awake, calculating the future,
Trying to unweave, unwind, unravel
And piece together the past and the future,
Between midnight and dawn, when the past is all deception,
The future futureless.

("I was much further out than you thought," wrote the poet Stevie Smith. "And not waving but drowning.")

Once years ago B. and I went to Europe for six months leaving the front door unlocked. When we returned, there was a sheet of paper taped to the door that said, "I came in Saturday night and took a bath because my well was out of prime," signed by a neighbor. Since then, as the countryside has turned criminal along with other communities, the doors are locked and bolted, each house a fort with alarm systems, watchdogs, gun, each occupant a target—not a world to face alone. After four break-ins, after being threatened one night at gunpoint, I am warned by Detective Atkins in the kindliest way, "I strongly urge you to sell your house and move into town. It isn't safe out here, you're too vulnerable, too isolated. I don't want your life on my conscience."

Staying alive becomes a predicament in an age of fear when the planet itself appears bent on suicide, and survival comes to mean survival of the human race. Can one even *choose* to live or die in a nuclear age when we have the power to destroy the world in an hour, as Hiroshima was leveled in nine seconds? One's plight is everyman's; death is the death of mankind. F. O. Matthiessen wrote in a note that he left in his hotel room before he jumped to his death, "How much the state of the world has to do with my state of mind I do not know." Before his death Saint-Exupéry wrote, "I hate my own time with all my heart." "Why was I born," asked Shaw, "with such contemporaries?"

It is harder than before to count the benevolences and mercies, to notice *things* before the eyes, customary things, focus the mind on them. In a gallery of exhibits one is distracted by racing thoughts, losing sight of what one lives by. William Carlos Williams could write about a glass of parsley, the plums in the icebox, the cat in the flowerpot (and say confidently of Emily Dickinson, "I was a better poet"). Nothing he encountered was too familiar or too nasty for notation. "No ideas but in things," he said:

> Things and things unmentionable,
> the sink with the waste farina in it and
> lumps of rancid meat, milk-bottle tops: have
> here a tranquility and loveliness.

Emily Dickinson never wrote like that! Wouldn't it be funny if she had? Williams said he dealt with the particular to get at the universal, just as she did, but her selection was more fastidious. Still, an unworthy object like a mud puddle appealed to Cummings, who wrote of childhood "when the world was puddle-wonderful." Wordsworth had a puddle of his own that he carefully measured from side to side: "Tis three feet long and two feet wide."

How much curiosity does it take? How much interest in puffballs? W. H. Hudson watched a London sparrow so closely he knew it from every other sparrow when it hopped by. The immediacy of a thing recommends it, if one will stop to look. Today I saw a copperhead slither across the lawn with a bird in its mouth. Other sightings included a dead bee, a bluebottle fly—minor distractions, not main events. I said I wanted a living tree for company in my living room. A generous man, overhearing, potted and brought me a leafy bamboo that reaches to the ceiling. Now I need a panda, by nature solitary, to come and live with me. Pandas love bamboo.

I might look more steadfastly at human beings (instead of exclusively at dead writers) to concentrate the mind. People are what they seem to be. On television they are pictures talking. When I watch on Masterpiece Theatre Henry James's *The Golden Bowl*, I see four reserved people conquering each circumstance as it appears. In that steady tale nobody dies or breaks his heart, and I make a memorandum of it. That is not to say Henry James knew entirely what life and love were about. His desk at Lamb House had a secret compartment that, when he died, was found to contain a prescription for eyeglasses and a remedy for gout.

When I watch *War and Peace*, Andrei says, "To be happy one must believe in the possibility of happiness." "Meanwhile my life drifts on," Pierre tells himself. "There's nothing left to happen."

Le coeur oublie: no, I don't believe the heart forgets. The most one can hope is to take heart again. I've gone so far as to join a class in aerobic dancing—to which I returned a week after Philip died—to take heart, so to speak, by counting heartbeats between spurts of dancing to rev up the pulse, keep in touch with the cardiovascular system. Our instructor Beverly shows you how high you can leap if you try. With her we perform the Cha-Cha and the Teaberry Shuffle in a romp to shake off age, heft, heartache, a tendency to list and droop. Beverly believes in the heart's resilience.

I must remind you I am talking about staying alive.

Then he stood the cans on the bunkroom table and started opening them. "As far as I'm concerned," he said, "the purpose of life is to stay alive and to keep on staying alive as long as you possibly can." (Joseph Mitchell, "The Fishermen")

So that's it. The reason for staying alive is that you have the habit. But is it reason enough? Whatever I do, I can't turn into a placid old person in a rocking chair or a retirement home. If I could I would live seasonably, without fear or panic in a state approaching calm; but the idea of calm exists in a sitting cat.

It is a question, now
Of final belief. So, say that final belief
Must be a fiction. It is time to choose.

In this world, "this invented world," Wallace Stevens said, "we live by our ability to create the necessary fictions." He illustrated his meaning by such phrases as the fiction of the leaves, the moonlight fiction, the fiction of the mind, the fiction of an absolute. "The final belief," he said, "is to believe in a fiction, which you know to be a fiction, there being nothing else." To him poetry was a supreme fiction. So was God.

Final beliefs or fictions:

It is an illusion that we were ever alive, / Lived in the houses of mothers. — Stevens

The main thing is to know how to endure. — Chekhov

One is born, and one dies. And always there are people enough. — Karel Čapek

And appraisals:

That the strategy of survival may be to recover the attainable things, like equilibrium; to learn acceptance, accommodate grief, give it house-room, let it rage itself out; to try gradually to back off from the preci-pice.

That each grief is absolute. There is no preparation in having been hurt before. Each loss starts with an incredulous *NO!*

That one's sorrow is not the world's sorrow, or the neighbors'. The world is of necessity indifferent. (Mr. Zuss: "Oh, there's always *someone* play-ing Job. Anyone can play that part.")

That living is a hazardous enterprise. Nobody is unique in finding it threatening, even fatal.

Believe that there are compensations in being alone.

But it is better to belong to someone.

Take note of the smell of grass, and by such improvisation seek the dis-traction of things. (Gilbert White in his journal: "Clouds fly different ways." "Green woodpecker laughs at all the world.")

Believe that tomorrow is a day also. Tomorrow and tomorrow.

It is late to store up admonitions. Yet without them one may as well ab-dicate altogether. Tonight on television I tuned in to somebody saying to his friend Sheila, "Don't worry, Sheila. You're alive, you're alive." I switched channels to a man deep in a harangue about rules of behavior. You must make no mistakes, he was saying. You must maintain perfect accuracy of judgment. You must exert your authority or you fail. Turned out he was talking about playing a bagpipe.

It is late to seek definitions. On April 20, 1904, two months before he died, Chekhov wrote to his wife Olga: "You ask what is life? That is just the same as asking what is a carrot. A carrot is a carrot, and nothing more is known about it."

Before his life became unendurable, Philip wrote me a letter that said, "I seem to be ready for another try at survival. I like that word, it's par-ticularly appropriate for our time, that and peace. The best word of all, though, is love."

I know now that the third way is Philip's way, which is to stay alive as long as one can, to survive as well as one can. The third way is *the courage to live and the courage to die.*

"Whoever is alone will stay alone," wrote Rilke. "Will sit, read, write long letters through the evening."

And here I am, here I am.

Chekhov's Way

Chekhov, so soon to die, stayed a happy man. The letters he wrote, some four thousand that survive, show him cheerful, basically a man who liked wine, pretty women, and the sound of church bells. In the end, church bells were all that remained of his faith.

You would call his life hard. He wrote, "There was no childhood in my childhood"—a time of poverty with beatings from a harsh father, son of a serf. Chekhov had his first hemorrhage at twenty-four, the year he graduated in medicine from Moscow University. He died of tuberculosis at forty-four, three years after marrying the actress Olga Knipper of the Moscow Art Theatre, from whom he lived apart, forced to seek a warm climate in the Crimea. From his thousand stories and five plays of Russian life, one is easily deceived into thinking him melancholy, depressed by life and despairing of the people in it. Tolstoy told him, "As you know I detest Shakespeare. Well, your plays are worse than his." Chekhov laughed. Aware of the pathos of existence, the loneliness, the boredom, he said, "I only wished to tell people honestly, 'Look at yourselves, see how badly and boringly you live!'" His story "Happiness," a favorite of his, says there is happiness enough in the world if you know how to find it.

In the country, where he loved to stay, he would announce, "I am a man who enjoys life," "I am thriving to the marrow of my bones." The birds sang indefatigably, the smell of freshly cut hay intoxicated him: "One has only to sit beside a haystack in order to imagine oneself in the embraces of a naked woman." In his thirties he bought a rundown estate of 675 acres in Melikhovo to escape an apartment in Moscow and the solitude he hated. ("When I'm alone, for some reason I become terrified.") Here he brought his parents, brothers, beloved sister Masha, and endless guests; here he planted cherry trees, felt joy: "At moments I am so happy that I pull myself up and remind myself of my creditors." But he spent his nights coughing.

Chekhov loved the theater, the characters in his plays and the actors who portrayed them: "So I, after dining with the star, was aware of a halo round my head for two days afterward." His wit never failed him, his love of laughter that saved him from despair. Much as he believed in the necessity of work ("You must work, you know, and never stop your whole life through"), he would drop it for a party, gathering a company of revelers round him. "When I become rich," he wrote, "I shall have a harem in which I shall keep fat naked women, with their buttocks painted green."

He had no intention of marrying, kept hidden the fact that he was coughing up blood. In 1899 he was condemned to stay most of the year in Yalta, from which with the success of *The Seagull* he wrote, "If I did not have to live in Yalta, this winter would be the happiest of my life." He knew he had not long to live: "My friend, you forget I'm a doctor." When he relented and became the husband of Olga Knipper, he addressed her in hundreds of letters, pouring out endearments to my unusual wife, my exquisite missus, my sweet delightful Knippschitz. "And you, why are you depressed?" he asked her. "What are you depressed about? You are living, working, hoping, drinking. . . . What more do you want?"

Chekhov's last play, *The Cherry Orchard,* written in 1904 while he struggled to stay alive, was performed as a tragedy of empty, trivial lives, a fact that hurt him, a misinterpretation of its meaning: "I call the play a comedy, in places even a farce" (though he also cried, "One must not live such a life!") An hour before his death he improvised a story that made Olga laugh heartily. The doctor came in and ordered champagne. "Ich sterbe," he whispered to the doctor. To Olga he said smiling, "It's a long while since I have drunk champagne," drained his glass to the last drop, lay back in his bed, and died.

The Happy Life

Martial, the things that do attain
The happy life be these, I find:

The riches left, not got with pain;
The fruitful ground, the quiet mind,
The equal friend, no grudge, no strife;
No charge of rule nor governance;
Without disease the healthy life;
The household of continuance,
The mean diet, no delicate fare;
True wisdom joined with simpleness;
The night discharged of all care,
Where wine the wit may not oppress;
The chaste wife, wise, without debate;
Such sleep as may beguile the night;
Contented with thine own estate,
Nor wish for death nor fear his might. — Surrey

Henry Howard, proud, haughty, fiery-tempered Earl of Surrey — not a word of this beautiful poem fitted his tragic life. As a translation of Martial, who wrote in favor of the simple life (and in disgust with Rome retired at forty-eight to the country), it corrects Martial's stoical epigram XLVII, "Ad Seipsum," reminding him that the joys of such a life include the possession of a chaste wife, which Martial almost certainly never had.

An aristocrat of royal blood who was intended to marry Princess Mary, future queen of England, Surrey was more elegant than simple, more arrogant than wise, "the most foolish and proud boy that is in England." As courtier he witnessed the downfall of his cousin Anne Boleyn, Henry VIII's second wife; saw his other cousin Catherine Howard, Henry VIII's fifth wife, put to death; and with reason trembled for his own fate. ("Too dearly had I bought my green and youthful years.") The powerful family of Henry's third wife, Jane Seymour, whom Surrey treated as vulgar upstarts, successfully plotted his downfall as another victim of the king's wrath. Before he was thirty he was trapped among enemies in court intrigue that, through his hauteur and pride, caused his death. On frivolous, trumped-up charges — that he favored Catholics, that he had eaten meat during Lent, that he had recklessly broken windows in London—he was imprisoned in the Tower, accused of a plot to murder the king, tried for high treason, and condemned to be hanged, drawn, and quartered at Tyburn. Finally, in a more honorable kind of death which befitted his rank, he was beheaded on Tower Hill.

In 1557, ten years after his death, forty of Surrey's love songs and sonnets, including this poem, "The Happy Life," were published in *Tottel's Miscellany* "to the honor of the English tongue." "We resteth here," he wrote, "that quick could never rest."

Saint Francis of Assisi. Maybe because it's April, now eight months since Philip's death, I think of this man. He was happy, the Poverello, so in love with life that the legends surrounding him ought to be true. One story has him singing duets with a nightingale. The bird would trill a phrase and he would repeat it, two *jongleurs de Dieu* lifting their voices antiphonally till Francis ran out of breath. A nightingale can outsing a saint.

Born eight hundred years ago, he was a little man with black eyes who wore bells on his ankles to warn crickets to avoid being stepped on. He talked to stones and trod on them with care, removed the worms from his path and set them by the wayside, ordered honey and wine for the bees to see them through the winter, invited a cicada into his cell and chirped to encourage her. A lamb followed him to church and together they heard the Mass.

The quality of courtesy in Saint Francis was not strained. Because he loved fire, he wouldn't extinguish a candle. He showed marked civility toward all things great and small: people, animals, trees, flowers, stones, the wind and the rain. He exhorted the cornfields and vineyards to love God. He taught Sister Cow to genuflect. He preached to the sparrows of Alviano; Giotto painted him informing the birds of the gospel of love.

He reproved the Wolf of Gubbio for eating people. "Come to me, Brother Wolf," he said; and the hungry wolf that had terrorized the town of Gubbio (near Assisi) lay down at his feet, put its paw in his hand, and solemnly promised to behave itself and become a Christian. J. R. H.

Moorman says in his book *Saint Francis of Assisi,* "What could be more convincing than the story of the Wolf of Gubbio?"

The Confessions. I wonder what Wallace Stevens meant when he said, "I would sacrifice a great deal to be a Saint Augustine." My own reason for revering this man is that he asked God in the days before his conversion, "Make me chaste and continent, but not yet." Till now I'd never read *The Confessions* or known the extent of his dallying—this bishop of Hippo, church father and saint, who hadn't wanted to give up the flesh too soon.

He was born in 354 in a Roman town, Tagaste, when the Roman Empire had become officially Christian under the mighty Constantine. The days of persecution were over and his mother Monica was a practicing Christian, his father a pagan baptized on his deathbed. In this story of his sensuality and his penitence, written when he was about forty-five, Augustine wants you to believe that at sixteen he was already a sinner, wild and licentious and free, who looked at the girls and, my goodness, "boiled over" and "seethed as does the sea" with wanton desire. Moreover, he was a thief who once stole some pears from an orchard. He recalls with shame how, late one night in Tagaste, he and his friends invaded a nearby orchard and plucked the fruit, not to eat but to throw at the swine merely for the fun of it.

Then, he continues, "to Carthage I came, where a cauldron of unholy loves bubbled up all around me." Augustine's father sent him at seventeen to school in Carthage to study rhetoric. There, "inflated with arrogance and the madness of lust," he sought to learn about love, going to stage plays which only added to the fire of his passions when the lovers displayed their own. "Such was my life!" he cries of it, one spent in ungodly yearnings, "in love with loving." He took a mistress, and they unintentionally had a son whom he named Adeodatus, meaning "by God given." For fifteen years he lived with her unwed, and the insistent need "to love and be loved was sweet to me." Meanwhile he taught rhetoric and eloquence in Carthage, in Rome, and in Milan. It was in Milan that the miracle of conversion happened when, deeply troubled, one day in the year 387 at thirty-three, Augustine rushed into the garden, flung himself under a fig tree, and, in a passion of weeping, poured out his guilty heart to God: "But thou, O Lord, how long? How long, Lord? wilt thou be angry forever?"

And a voice said to him, "Take up and read." And he took up and read the letter of Paul to the Romans (13:13–14): "Not in rioting and drunkenness, not in chambering and wantonness, not in strife and envying, put on the Lord Jesus Christ, and make no provision for the flesh to gratify its lusts."

The endearing part is that it took him so long.

Marcus Aurelius. He will tell me. The end to seek in life is not happiness, he said. It is peace of mind. Years ago when I came across the *Meditations*, I copied out passages that made sense to me. They make sense to me now. He wrote his one book, not in Latin but in Greek and called it *To Myself*—a strangely detached yet intimate diary for man or emperor to keep, to remind himself, "Let it be in no man's power to say that in you there is no simplicity and no goodness. Make it a lie for anyone to think this of you, for who can hinder you from being both simple and good?"

Though he adhered throughout his days to the Stoic doctrine—one of reason, impassivity, restraint, self-discipline—Marcus Aurelius kept intact a belief in the essential goodness of life. In a time of universal corruption he was virtuous, with a sense of decency that led him to be indulgent of the lack of it in others. He rid himself of anger. So real was his tolerance, so sparing of rebuke, that he blamed himself for his own indignation. "Why am I troubled in spirit?" he asked. "Why should I be indignant?"

Forbearance carried him far toward an insolent wife, Faustina, a wanton who disgraced him openly with her lusts and infidelities (while in his book he thanked the gods for so obedient and faithful a wife). Toward Commodus, his incurably vicious son, he was too forgiving, too indulgent. According to Lemprière, Commodus in his degenerate youth corrupted his own sisters and, as emperor at nineteen upon his father's death in 180 A.D., "kept three hundred women, and as many boys, for his licentious pleasures." "The intervals of lust," said Gibbon, "were filled up with the basest amusements." When his debauchery and drunkenness led to insanity, Commodus proclaimed himself Hercules the god, carried a club, and wore a lion's skin over his purple and gold-embroidered robes. He fought gladiators and killed wild beasts in the Roman arena. Herodian of Antioch, who in his history of Rome asserts that he was an eyewitness, claims that Commodus killed one hundred lions with one hundred javelins, never missing a throw. He walked naked in public to the shame and horror of his people, becoming so hated for his demented antics and cruelty that his sister Lucilla conspired with a group of senators to assassinate him—a plot that failed. At thirty-one Commodus was poisoned by Marcia, the favorite of his mistresses, then strangled to death by a wrestler of the court. His reign of thirteen terrible years began the decline and fall of the Roman Empire.

Yet Marcus Aurelius's diary is without complaint of his bestial son (whom possibly he may not have fathered). Instead it is a record of a man's philosophy, concerned with his inner life and filled with communings to steady himself to be the way he wanted to be. They are his day-to-day thoughts hastily noted for his study and reflection, often on the battlefield during the years spent fighting the barbaric Germanic tribes who attacked the frontiers. He hated war and loved peace. He sought understanding of others with compassion in his heart, a modest man to whom goodness was simply a matter of obeying reason. He has been likened to Saint Francis of Assisi. But Francis lived with God. Matthew Arnold called Marcus Aurelius "perhaps the most beautiful figure in history." John Stuart Mill likened him to Jesus Christ—a dubious comparison that made Marcus seem holy, a very god, as he was not, and a Christian when in fact he disliked Christians. He was born a century after Christ was crucified.

Withal, in spite of his charity he was not a saint, not blind to the ways of the world and the people in it, who, he once wrote, are like little dogs biting one another. "Every morning repeat to yourself, today I shall meet with a talebearer, an ingrate, and a bully; with treachery, envy, and selfishness. It is no surprise men are like this. How can any of them harm me? For none can involve me in shame save myself."

Short is the time that remains to you of life, he told himself—a mere hairbreadth of time before you are dust, without hope of eternal life after death, consigned to nothingness, to oblivion. Therefore, always take the short way, for the way of nature is short. Live as on a mountain, it matters not whether here or there. Nothing can make you think what is false or do what is wrong. And if the forces of evil finally become too many and too imperious so that you are not free, "kill yourself," he said. "No one can prevent that."

"Very little," he wrote, as if to give himself more assurance, "very little is needed to make a happy life."

Happy Pepys. Three hundred years ago Pepys was a man who played the flageolet and lute, took physic, took a bribe, had a boil under his chin, buried his pet canary, fondled the girls, kissed Mary Mercer and Bagwell the carpenter's pretty wife, dreamed of Lady Castlemaine in his arms, sang madrigals, and wrote, "I think I may reckon myself as happy a man as any is in the world."

Hospitable, too. For breakfast one New Year's Day, he gave his guests "a barrel of oysters, a dish of neat's tongues, a dish of anchovies, wine of all sorts and Northdown ale. And now, I am in good esteem with everybody, I think!" He got nits in his periwig, caught cold from having his ears washed, lived through the bubonic plague ("God preserve us all!") and the Great Fire, which reached his lane and singed the cat. Dalliance with the housemaid Deb Willet, for which his little wife came at him with a poker, caused "the greatest sorrow to me that ever I knew in this world." As one who hated to be unquiet at home, he sometimes wished himself single, and sorely regretted the time he blacked his wife's eye.

Having made peace with her and acquired a leather coach with coachman and two black horses, gained prosperity plus a worrisome pain in his eyes, on May 31, 1669, aged thirty-six, Pepys closed his book halfway through his life, closing a door on the rest of life and death still left to tell. A world of his own disappeared from view. Elizabeth died the following

November—the pretty French girl he married when she was fifteen, he twenty-two, penniless and in love. She died six months after he stopped taking note of her teasing, her jealous fury, her pies and tarts in the house in Seething Lane. And he never told his grief.

When I remarked to the librarian of Magdalene College, Cambridge—Pepys's college where the six volumes of his diary and his three thousand books are kept in his own carved bookcases—that I had been coming to this room off and on since 1936, he said in surprise, "Is there something you are looking for?"

"I don't know," I said. "Whatever it is, I always find it." And Pepys as well.

2 🦅

Ways to Love

Love and work, I said, these alone . . . And so it has to be. The third way becomes inevitably a search for love—that being the way of the world. Yet all the while the question remains, where do you look for something you can no longer define, that by now seems like a youthful illusion? Is it really the flesh that continues to matter most, or does one settle finally for something called the mind? The body or the soul? Poetry itself could never exist without its passionate involvement in such a predicament. As Campion reminded us,

> Never love unless you can
> Bear with all the faults of man.

Andrew Marvell was a man whose passion was for gardens, so obsessed by the color green that he would reduce the world to it, "Annihilating all that's made / To a green thought in a green shade." He was a solitary man who chose "to live in Paradise alone" without a wife, without a love affair; an invisible man of few words who believed prudently "not to write at all is much the safer course in life." The best choice was to sit idle at home and not be laughed at. Little is known of his private life. The son of a Yorkshire parson, he became Milton's assistant in the Commonwealth, was elected to Parliament, and died in London at fifty-seven. His poems, a handful of lyrics found among his effects, were published three years later, apparently by his landlady. Milton knew him for more than twenty years and said he was a man of singular desert; he didn't say Marvell was a poet.

But the other Marvell, the poet, had a head full of couplets, a heart fastened on love "begotten by despair / Upon impossibility." "To His Coy

Mistress" is a poem of sexual desire so urgent, explicit, direct, witty that it's impossible not to wish him luck in seducing her, to wonder why she has hesitated this long. In our time, his plea would be "To His Girl Who Holds Out instead of Going to Bed with Him." But if she is reluctant, Marvell is a patient lover; he would prolong the wooing to the end of time:

> I would
> Love you ten years before the Flood,
> And you should if you please refuse
> Till the conversion of the Jews.

She deserves to be possessed at such a rate, and he's the man to do it. She is worth waiting for. But there isn't time; her body and his lust will not survive the grave. Soon worms will end that long-preserved virginity, it will be too late for love in the vast eternity ahead.

If his simple logic persuades her, there's nothing to worry about. Marvell doesn't chide or beg or threaten to kill himself. He is playful but impassioned, sincere in wanting her now, trying to win her through laughter. And laughing, as she must, no doubt she will agree. Together they will outwit time and the tomb—two splendid lovers, still young in all their beauty and strength.

But I wish I knew the man who wrote that love poem. And the girl too—if in fact she ever existed.

Like Marvell's "To His Coy Mistress," John Crowe Ransom's poem "The Equilibrists" is witty and frustrated by love. Both describe a familiar problem of trying to get a girl into bed, though Marvell is himself the yearning lover, Ransom the concerned bystander.

Ransom's couple are rapturously in love, lusting for each other. Wherever the lover goes he is obsessed by longing for her body's fragrance, its whiteness and beauty inviting his embrace. Her mouth is a "quaint orifice" from which come hot kisses, accompanied by the cold forbidding words spiraling down like gray doves from the ivory tower of her mind, an officious tower that says N O. Her body is a lily field beseeching him to pluck and bruise and wear the lilies. Her eyes speak love, saying pay no heed to the cruel words, take the lilies. But again the gaunt mind releases the doves crying honor, honor, telling him go away, leave me alone, let us never meet again.

A terrible predicament. You expect honor among thieves, but honor between lovers, keeping them apart? In anger the poet steps into the poem to consider this "torture of equilibrium," which seems to him deplorable:

> Ah, the strict lovers, they are ruined now!
> I cried in anger.

Unable to give each other up or yield to their passion, they stay suspended halfway between — two acrobats, equilibrists on a tightrope, balanced precariously. Observing them, perplexed by their plight, the poet resolves to intervene and force them to a decision to escape this gallows where they hang, asking with a "puddled brow," *which* do you want, heaven or hell? Is it honor in heaven, spiritual union and a bodiless marriage? Or dishonor in hell, rending each other's flesh, insatiable, unsatisfied? Great lovers choose hell. Either choice is wrong; each means the loss of something precious, the body or the soul.

In the end he is convinced that the lovers are right, the conflict is unresolvable. As he watches them twirling each in his orbit, he sees with new tolerance and insight how beautifully they are balanced, radiant in their hot lust and cold honor, a splendid achievement. Don't judge them, let them be. So he fashions their tomb, to which they will come unchanged, and writes an epitaph in their praise: Go on spinning forever as you are. Keep the strict balance between fire and ice, body and soul, passion and honor, heaven and hell:

> Equilibrists lie here; stranger, tread light;
> Close, but untouching in each other's sight;
> Mouldered the lips and ashy the tall skull,
> Let them lie perilous and beautiful.

Yet when all is said, it is *her* mouth that means yes, *her* skull that says no; his mind has been more receptive. Marvell and Ransom are perfect gentlemen, though Ransom isn't the one tempted. It's the lady who raises all the fuss.

Richard Wilbur's poem "Love Calls Us To the Things of This World" is another love story with a problem, its title from Saint Augustine. A man is roused in his apartment early one morning by the sound of straining pulleys of a clothes line. He opens his eyes and falls back to sleep, while his astounded soul, spirited awake, hangs in the air briefly suspended from his body. Through the window the soul sees, high in the air, the washing on the line:

> Outside the open window
> The morning air is all awash with angels.

In the clean clothes with no bodies in them, the soul is aware of angels like itself, some in bedsheets, some in blouses, some in smocks. They swell in the breeze, rising and swaying, flying in place. The wind makes them breathe and fills the clothing with joy. They move and stay, like white pure water.

But the body is about to wake up. The soul shrinks from what it must face united with the flesh, when its purity will be defiled by the rape of everyday, its innocence punctually ravished. The soul has other needs. It prefers the angelic state, to be clean and good. It cries, "Oh, let there be nothing on earth but laundry."

As the day begins, the soul accepts the impure state and descends once more to join the body, by "bitter love" called to the things of this world. The man wakes, yawns, rises. He speaks in a loud imperative voice: Take down the clothes from the line, let them be filled with bodies, let the angels become men. Even thieves wear clean linen, for we all go clothed in our immortal souls. Lovers go sweetly dressed to be betrayed by love. Nuns, wearing the habits of faith, strive to keep the difficult balance between body and soul.

Yeats wrote of the same conflict in "A Dialogue of Self and Soul," where at first the dominant soul has the better of the argument, summoning the body to climb the penitential stair and withdraw to the tower of the spirit:

> I summon to the winding ancient stair;
> Set all your mind upon the steep ascent.

But the obstinate self chooses to stay where it is, in the midst of life, holding fast to an ancient sword wrapped in a piece of silk dress — emblems of love and war. The soul is incredulous that the imagination of a man long past his prime should cling to the flesh when he is promised deliverance from the crime of birth and death, sexuality, the sins of the world. What the soul is offering is heavenly glory.

All pretense of debate is dropped; the self meditates alone on the "crime" of mortality that the soul would save him from. He doesn't want deliverance. He asserts the right to live, to suffer and endure, and in a sickening review — from the ignominy of boyhood to the man among his enemies — faces the failure, the malice, the hate, the loss of love that life contains. Without hesitation the self elects not heaven but earth as the only choice:

> I am content to follow to its source
> Every event in action or in thought;
> Measure the lot; forgive myself the lot!
> When such as I cast out remorse
> So great a sweetness flows into the breast
> We must laugh and we must sing,
> We are blest by everything,
> Everything we look upon is blest.

Triumphantly he accepts every event and casts out all shame or guilt for his part in it. Quick to claim the flesh, to be alive, the victorious self is in a state of blessedness. Soul has lost the debate.

And yet, said John Donne, what is the problem? The conflict of body and soul *is* resolvable. In "The Ecstasy" he shows what love finally is, why there is no need to choose between them since both are mortal. Love is oneness, achieved when two lovers become one body and one soul.

In a dialogue of one, Donne reminds his beloved what has happened to them — of a day of ecstasy when they sat and then lay on a bank of violets, gripping hands, gazing into each other's eyes. So complete was their union that their souls were suspended between them, equal and identical. If a bystander who understood the language of love were listening, he wouldn't know which soul spoke. In one voice the lovers said,

> This ecstasy doth unperplex
> (We said) and tell us what we love

At that moment they knew it wasn't sex (or sex alone) that had changed them into one. When their bodies had become one body, their souls became one soul, like a violet multiplied and grown in size. They knew finally what love is; they were indivisible, nothing could separate them, they would never be lonely again.

But, he tells her, let's not forget to thank our bodies since they were the first to unite us:

> We owe them thanks, because they thus
> Did us, to us, at first convey.

Only through the body's passion could the soul respond. The flesh is the teacher. The body is the book. Therefore, any lover listening now wouldn't note a change in us when again we make love. It is the same either way, the union of body and soul.

(I remember one student's dazed interpretation of "The Ecstasy": "Holding hands is fine, but sex is not all there is to love.")

I'm puzzled, though, as an onlooker myself. In "The Equilibrists" Ransom never says why his two lovers can't have it both ways, body and soul, but must stop halfway between heaven and hell, deprived of both. As a poet he appears to know less of hell than Dante, less of heaven than Milton.

In *Paradise Lost,* when Adam talks in Eden with the resplendent archangel Raphael, whose six wings are downy gold, he learns a lot about angels while Raphael, admitting he is hungry, eats his lunch "with keen dispatch." Angels, it appears, have real bodies, real appetites. Differing from man only in wearing wings, "they hear, see, smell, touch, taste, digest, assimilate." And fight wars. When Adam asks how they express their love, "by looks only, or do they mix / Irradiance?" Raphael, blushing rosy red, answers, "Let it suffice thee that thou know'st / Us happy, and without love no happiness know'st." What of the body you enjoy, he tells Adam, we enjoy, "and obstacle find none / Of membrane, joint, or limb, exclusive bars." Angels embrace and "total they mix," flesh with flesh, soul with soul.

Ransom tells his lovers otherwise, assuring them that there is no love-making in heaven. In hell, on the other hand, lovers feed upon the body, "infatuate of the flesh upon the bones." Rending each other when they kiss, "the pieces kiss again — no end to this."

Dante had a better acquaintance with hell. In Canto 5 of the *Inferno* he tells the love story of Paolo and Francesca. As he descends the levels of hell, Dante finds the two together in the second circle, where carnal lovers are punished in an eternal tempest, blown by hurricane winds as strong as their passions. A whirling multitude of lovers sweeps by (including Cleopatra, Helen of Troy, Dido, Paris, Tristan of Lyonesse) and among them Dante recognizes two figures fluttering in the wind whose tragic death he knows well. Francesca, the daughter of the lord of Ravenna, was married to Giovanni Malatesta of Rimini, a hunchback ugly and deformed. On a day in 1285, when Dante was twenty, Giovanni found his wife with his handsome younger brother Paolo and in a rage stabbed them to death. As Dante wrote the poem the murderer was still alive.

In the name of love, Dante asks for their story. Francesca speaks, while the wind is quieted and Paolo, silent beside her, weeps. She tells how "love led us to one death." They were alone without fear of discovery, reading together a tale of the guilty love of Lancelot and Guinevere. As Lancelot kissed his loved one, then Paolo, whose name she never speaks aloud,

Then he whom naught can sever from me now
Forever, kissed my mouth, all quivering.
Upon that day we read no more therein.

The book revealed their love to them and brought them to damnation. Dante, a living man among the dead, is so moved to pity by the sight of the grieving lovers that he faints, collapsing in a swoon like death, heart-struck at the pain and power of love.

In Dante's hell all sinners are bodiless, mere shades or wraiths casting no shadow. For eternal punishment the lovers remember and know bodily desire. They feel the same love as before but they cannot make it. There is, says Francesca da Rimini, "no greater pain."

In his unfinished sculpture, *The Gate of Hell,* Rodin originally had Dante sitting at hell's gate (who as *The Thinker* now sits alone in Rodin's Parisian garden). In the sculpture Dante is deep in thought, studying the two figures, Paolo and Francesca, wrapped nakedly in a sensual embrace (who are now the lovers in his celebrated statue *The Kiss*). If Rodin read Dante, he must have preferred to show his lovers happy in the flesh.

3 🖎

Uncommon Women and Their Ways

Joyce Carol Oates, appearing on television in an interview, presents herself as a thin, unsmiling writer, pale and wan as a Dickens waif. "We can't be judged by our appearance," she says, adding she doesn't have sex appeal and makes no effort to charm. Her voice trails off, no louder than a falling leaf.

All of which has little to do with her writing or her habit of reporting the murderousness of people's lives in tales of violence, suicide, madness, even cannibalism. She merely reminds me of my theory, wisely abandoned as short on evidence, about the female in literature, that odd women become writers or that writing causes women to become oddly out of focus. I used to tot up the recluses and spinsters of Victoria's time —Emily Brontë, Christina Rossetti, Emily Dickinson—and deplore the fact they hadn't become wives and mothers, healthy and well-adjusted. The talented ones in our time too seemed out of sync, retiring souls living sheltered and unwed in a Southern town, like Eudora Welty; spinsters monstrous fat like Amy Lowell, fey like Marianne Moore, flaky like Edith Sitwell, mad like Gertrude Stein; women embattled like Mary McCarthy, oversexed like Erica Jong, suicidal like Virginia Woolf, Sylvia Plath, Anne Sexton.

It's clear I needed to make in a more charitable spirit a new list of uncommon women, odd no doubt (not necessarily writers), who have themselves found a way to live and to die. I wanted to know the way each went and how it turned out. Was it a good life, as good as any? "One isn't born a woman," said Simone de Beauvoir. "One becomes a woman."

There isn't a false Cressida among them, or a Dolores whose sins were seventy times seven. Yet all, being human, were hard beset. Being female, they reveal the size of the predicament, even how to survive it. "Dear

Christopher," wrote Freya Stark to a sympathetic friend, "I always wonder why it should be derogatory to behave like a woman when one is one."

But in saying so I seem to forget a more urgent reason for writing about these uncommon women and their lives—and about other people and other lives—the reason for writing at all. It's the only way I know to escape the solitude that attacks me, the fear of being without occupation, the terror of living for a lifetime alone. Through the company of others, but most of all through books and more books—always books to banish the clouds—you can begin to look more closely at someone else's life, where it is going and finally how it ends.

At thirty-eight, Montaigne retired to the isolation of his tower, surrounded himself with a thousand books, then discovered that just reading them passively, or scribbling notes in the margin, was never enough. He had to put into his own words and apply to his own life what these figures he met—from Socrates to Seneca—revealed and what sense they made: such as how to deal with solitude, how to live appropriately, or how not to live at all. He read books too about love—Rabelais, Catullus, the *Decameron*, the *Kisses* of Johannes Secundus—and it was altogether a haphazard plan. It was a random search without method, fragmentary and piecemeal, to find his own way by asking the way of others, quoting from them, speaking their minds "to speak my own mind better." Some of his essays, he said, were off the mark, went roaming and made less sense than he intended. Some of them "smelled a little foreign," as if left wholly to chance, as if he had carelessly lost his way and strayed from his subject. But in the end all led to the same conclusion. Montaigne's own book that resulted contained the words, "It is myself that I portray."

Flannery O'Connor. Her father died of lupus when she was fifteen, after which she and her mother Regina moved to Milledgeville, Georgia, where she went to high school and college for a "sorry" education that didn't teach her to spell or use a dictionary: "I never sense I am spelling something incorrectly and so don't look up the words"—

like Hemmenway, teasespoon, champaine, Phillopino — or the grammar, "I have done forgot." At twenty-five she became ill with lupus, and her mother moved the two of them to a dairy farm a few miles outside of town. Flannery kept thirty peacocks, got around on crutches, and in 1964 at thirty-nine died. She never had a love affair. "There won't be any biographies of me," she said, "because lives spent between the house and the chicken yard do not make exciting copy."

You write, she said, what you can. She wrote, not out of experience, with little available, but out of a bizarre imagination. "All my stories are about the action of grace on a character who is not very willing to support it, but most people think of these stories as hard, hopeless, brutal, etc." Hard, hopeless, brutal they are, dealing with psychopaths and freaks — violent, grotesque, and invented. The distortion, she said, is intentional. Set in the rural South, they end usually in a shattering death, as if no other solution occurred to her.

One of her best stories, "A Good Man is Hard to Find," tells of the terrorizing and slaughter of a stupid but harmless family of six — father, mother, grandmother, two children, and the baby — casually killed on their way to Florida because they happen to be where an escaped murderer, the Misfit, runs into them. (The cat survives.) After wiping them out one by one he says, "It's no real pleasure in life." But to portray this mass murderer as gaining, at that moment, an insight into his own nature and his rejection of Christ is too easy. Nor is his terrified victim the grandmother allowed time to experience the supposed mercy at the hand of God that redeems her soul before she is shot. The disturbing story is fiction, contrived and implausible (even if such crimes do occur in real life) — the picking off of a family in meaningless deaths. Flannery O'Connor intended it to fit her belief in divine clemency and grace. As a devout Catholic she meant to tell in her horror stories the relation of a person to God, and the meaning of suffering and redemption. The peacocks that "wallowed" in her mother's flower beds became a Christ symbol. But she was a victim of circumstance, unable to use her talent to write of encounters she never had. It's a great loss. Her personal letters are better informed about the real world she lived in, outspoken about her own plight. In them a warm and honest woman finds the words to explain and accept who she is, not ever having to invent.

Mary McCarthy. She said she believed in indignation as an indispensable trait of character. She believed in wit, lucidity, and a capacity for being outraged. Quick to lay about her, Mary McCarthy tended to skewer people and flay them. The very thought of Lillian Hellman annoyed her. "I said once," she told Dick Cavett in a famous interview, "that every word she writes is a lie, including *and* and *the.*" Her disparaging word for John Mitchell, Nixon's attorney general, was *turnipy.* At various times she had it in for J. D. Salinger, Truman Capote, and God. She didn't believe in the hereafter, in marriage (though married four times), Women's Lib, or the Kennedys. She was totally against being born again. That's how vexed she was, fit to be tied. Katherine Anne Porter said she was "the worst-tempered woman in American letters."

Her willingness to expose people, show them up, pay them back, meant she hurt them deliberately. The eight girls of the Class of 1933 (her own class) at Vassar who found themselves portrayed in her novel *The Group* had reason to resent and hate her for the damaging revelations she made about their private lives after graduation. She dealt freely with their marriages, their contraceptive devices and sexual involvements — the deflowering of Dottie, the impotence of somebody's husband, the lesbianism of Lakey, the suicide of Kay. It wasn't only her wicked tongue that betrayed her, it was her lack of compassion. Mary McCarthy was obsessed with what she called "the integrity of sheer fact," with telling the whole truth regardless of the harm it did. With her reckless candor in giving the facts, she revealed more facts than were pertinent, more than one wanted to know. She ignored the need in life and letters for selectivity.

In her last book, *Intellectual Memoirs,* a thin piece of autobiography concerned with two years spent in Greenwich Village, from 1936 to 1938, and not published till after her death of lung cancer in 1989, she says, "I was forthright and fearless, and I was gaining a certain renown for it." What a bashing it is to leave behind: a jumble of forgotten names and seedy relationships, of collisions, bruises, pricks, stabs, blows, and bleeding encounters. Hard to believe is that in her seventies, terminally ill and close to death, Mary McCarthy was still angry and resentful; that she found such scarifying details worth telling. These are the messy love affairs of fifty years ago, the drinking bouts, the squabbles spitefully reported, the failed unions with Philip Rahv and Edmund Wilson (who did become her second husband), the infidelities, the promiscuity.

"It was getting rather alarming," she wrote. "I realized one day that in twenty-four hours I had slept with three different men. Though slightly scared by what things were coming to, I did not *feel* promiscuous. . . . None of my partners, the reader will be relieved to hear, had a venereal disease."

This to be remembered by.

Lorelei Two is the title of the book, the name Conrad Aiken gave the second of his three wives in his memoir *Ushant*. The others were Lorelei One and Lorelei Three. What he began in *Ushant* ("You shan't" or "Thou shalt not") as an obcure account of himself as the character D., a Ulysses on a steamer voyage threatened by sirens and shipwreck, becomes in the present volume an explicit story of a real shipwreck—his second marriage as told by Lorelei Two. The nickname wasn't playful or teasing; he meant that women are sirens who trap men.

Clarissa Lorenz, her real name, reveals to any in doubt how harrowing it is to live with a genius, especially a dedicated poet. She had heard praise of perfect wives, such as Dostoyevski's and Carl Sandburg's, who sublimated themselves to their mates. When she met George Bernard Shaw and listened to his monologue, she marveled at Charlotte's silence, at the inner turmoil a wife must suffer in a famed man's shadow. Face to face with Thomas Hardy's widow, she wondered why so many literary men's wives have limp handshakes. "Unfortunately," she says, "artists have a domestic streak and long for family life. That's the hitch."

The two met in 1926 when she interviewed him for the *Boston Evening Transcript*, what Aiken called "the fatal interview," from which she walked away that foggy night telling herself "I'm in love." She didn't know he was married and the father of three young children, whom he would abandon for her. Nor did she know, and he didn't tell her, of the tragedy of his childhood that traumatized his life, bringing terror, guilt, despair. It happened one night in Savannah — Aiken was eleven — when he heard his mother's half-stifled scream, the sound of his father's voice counting to three, and two loud shots. Alone he tiptoed into the dark room "where the two bodies lay motionless and apart, and, finding them dead, found himself possessed of them forever."

Clarissa asks herself why, after a stormy three-year "courtship through a wringer," she consented to marry him. When she became pregnant, he arranged against her will for an abortion. In jealous rages similar to his father's he accused her of promiscuity, a siren by whom, he wrote, "I shall be driven to murder." After his divorce they were married in Rutherford, New Jersey, with William Carlos Williams and his wife as witnesses. At the marriage license window, Aiken explained to the clerk that he was an adulterer. "Hell, aren't we all?" said the clerk.

They moved to England, where without consulting her Aiken leased Jeake's House, Sussex, the same house where he had lived with his first wife and eventually would live with Lorelei Three. The place was damp and cold, deathwatch beetles ticked in the wood, yet he allowed nothing to be changed. "I intend to run this marriage. Is that clear?" "Crystal clear," she said. Malcolm Lowry turned up from Cambridge University to spend vacations as a paying guest — Aiken's protégé and drinking companion with whom Clarissa associated sprees and catastrophe, though Aiken told her all good writers drink. By the second year of their marriage he said, "I don't really need you any more" — a shy austere man whom, unaccountably to herself, she truly loved.

In the turbulent summer of 1932 he feared he was going mad: "My father's death should have freed me, but it didn't. I've been dreaming again and again of killing myself. I shouldn't really be alive." On a night when tensions mounted, she escaped the house and went to a movie. Halfway through the picture she had a premonition of danger, in panic ran all the way home to find he had turned on the gas and was lying unconscious on the kitchen floor. In *Ushant* he narrates the attempted suicide differently. Lorelei having gone to the cinema, he says, D. sat down to read an article by Wyndham Lewis, which he found excruciatingly funny, and with the gas rings and oven fizzing behind him awaited the end, perfectly serene. She appeared in the nick of time, he says, only because she had already seen the second feature.

"Why had I hung on so long?" Clarissa asks. The man who fell in love with her was the poet who found marriage intolerable: "I could never reconcile the tyrant with the poet who wrote 'Senlin' and 'Punch.'" (But did she remember Punch's sad cry, "Was there in all this wide world never / One woman I might love for ever?")

She fled to America alone in 1936. Nearly fifty years later, after Conrad Aiken's death in 1973, she wrote this story from the wounding evidence in her diary. She says she wrote for clarification, to admit her share of the guilt. His parting shot had been, "It's all your fault, and you know it."

Yet I wonder why she chose to keep the pain of memory alive — or why confessional writing deals so exclusively with hurts given and received. Aiken in a veiled fashion had elected to tell the unhappy tale himself, though it happened, he says in *Ushant,* "Far away, and long ago. And so many ships between, so many ships between."

Simone de Beauvoir. Writing is the loneliest occupation, she believed. "Solitude is a form of death." In her last years she lived a recluse with hands constantly clenched, *la malheureuse,* alone in a Paris apartment with her collection of dolls. Unfriendly critics called her the "Grande Sartreuse," who wrote in four volumes her claim to an exalted life with Sartre. For fifty years till his death at seventy-four, they worked, talked, loved, traveled together, and she told herself, "I was not in his class." In *The Prime of Life* she traces their history when existence was shaped by her love for him, his dominance over her, their times spent in endless talk at the Deux Magots and Café de Flore. Brought up a strict Catholic, she turned from God to Sartre, accepting his values, the conditions he imposed: the freedom to love others, the obligation to be honest and conceal nothing. Theirs would be a necessary love, he said, with other affairs contingent to it. They would take out "two-year leases," after which each would go his own way for two years, then return for another two-year union. The arrangement caused her heartbreak and terror but she never gave up. She would keep him at any cost. "My trust in him was so complete that he supplied me with the sort of absolute unfailing security that I had once had from my parents, or from God." There was no word of regret that she never had a child.

Arthur Koestler said his walleyed friend Sartre looked like "a malevolent goblin or gargoyle," with goggling eyes and misshapen body. He also said, "The tragic end was the falling out of Sartre with Simone before his death."

Six years later in 1986, she died, "in a cloud of depression, alcohol and Valium," according to a piece in the *Times Literary Supplement*. It said that the image of Sartre and her as lifelong lovers was one she largely created herself: "There is no evidence of his ever having given up anything for her, not his time, not his work, and most certainly never a woman." During his countless love affairs he was indifferent to her, sometimes openly cruel. People remember her sitting alone in a Paris café, drinking and weeping without him. The image she created was a facade, the pretense of a happy love.

Sartre's famous play *No Exit* must have hurt her with its definition of what he thought hell to be: other people ("L'enfer, c'est les autres"). Hell is a room with no exit, a cheap bare hotel room where a cowardly man is condemned to spend forever in the company of two jarring, hateful, threatening women — never to escape through all eternity, never for a moment to be alone.

His autobiographical volume, *Words,* ends, "My sole concern has been to save myself."

Virginia Woolf. In 1953 Leonard Woolf published her *Writer's Diary* in one discreet volume. Twenty-five years later, the real diary began to appear in five volumes, edited with exhaustive footnotes and a formidable index. She called herself a diariser and didn't intend it to be published: "Who's going to read all this scribble?" Quentin Bell's introduction praises it as a major work of historical importance, a masterpiece: "It is, in fact, one of the great diaries of the world." It isn't.

Such copious details of daily living — the servant problem, bursting waterpipes, reports of the weather — don't transform her into a self-revealer. To be a great diary like Pepys's, whatever it has to say must be entire, concealing nothing. Mrs. Woolf at thirty-three, three years married, revealed of her life only its surfaces. She stayed, as was her nature, private and invisible even to herself. The diary begins January 1, 1915, and stops abruptly after six weeks because of a severe mental breakdown, to be resumed the following October. Two years before, she had tried to kill herself, then starve herself to death. Her grave illness in 1915 was her third attack of madness, second attempt at suicide. No hint of these depths appears in her hasty entries, though she says, "I intend to keep full notes of my ups and downs." She records small happenings, the fact her watch stopped, she broke her spectacles, "I began today to treat my corn" and fifteen days later, "My corn is cured." Volume 1 ends: "We [Leonard and I] think we now deserve some good luck. Yet I daresay we're the happiest couple in England." How happy does she mean? She was a frigid wife who abhorred sex, far from willing to confess it, who had told him when they married in 1912, "I feel no physical attraction to you."

Throughout the five volumes there is her enormous curiosity about people — friend, acquaintance, passerby — of whom she writes with little mercy. Her love of gossip is inquisitive, devaluing, malicious. Some called it "obsessive malice" toward her fellow writers. Clive Bell is intolerably dull, David Garnett an over-educated prig, Max Beerbohm a Cheshire cat, Rose Macaulay "lean as a rake, wispy, and frittered," E. M. Forster "milder than the breath of a cow." T. S. Eliot is muffin-faced. Harold Nicolson has a mind that bounces when he drops it. Edith Sitwell, grown very fat, powders herself thickly, wears a turban and looks like an ivory elephant.

"How many friends have I got?" she asks; the number of her "undeluded" friends is very small. Lytton Strachey occurs to her, but he hasn't an interesting mind, she isn't interested in what he writes. "I am alarmed by my own cruelty to my friends" (even more by her friends' cruelty to her, especially when she published a book: "It occurs to me how I'm disliked, how I'm laughed at").

On May 18, 1933, on a visit to Italy, Virginia Woolf wrote in her diary of sitting by an open window overlooking the Bay of Spezia in which Shelley was drowned: "Mrs. Shelley and Jane Williams walked up and down the balcony of the house next door waiting while Shelley's body rolled round with pearls — it is the best deathbed place I've ever seen."

Eight years later she found her own deathbed in the Ouse River near her home.

Beatrix Potter. Today I bought a Peter Rabbit book to give to a child because it occurred to me that Beatrix Potter was said to think as a child, to know all her life what it was like to be five years old. She was five 125 years ago. I wondered if Peter Rabbit was holding his own these days with Bugs Bunny, Mickey Mouse, Snoopy, Kermit the Frog, and Miss Piggy. Beatrix Potter wrote tales of Mrs. Tittlemouse and Squirrel Nutkin to please herself "because I never grew up." The secret diary she kept till age thirty goes on about mice and especially rabbits — Benjamin Bunny, whom she took walking on a leash and fed gooseberries and hot buttered toast. Her own Peter Rabbit was Benjamin's cousin. She never went to school ("thank goodness my education was neglected"). She made railway journeys accompanied by a rabbit hutch, a mouse Hunca Munca, a pet frog Punch, a hedgehog Mrs. Tiggy-Winkle who enjoyed travel resting on her knee.

Her animals were copied from life though they stood upright in her drawings, wearing mufflers, poke bonnets, and shoes. (Birds, she found, didn't look well in clothes.) At thirty-five she published the first Peter Rabbit with twenty-six to follow. Each was a child's size, five-by-four inches, and cost a shilling because "all my little friends are shilling people." At forty, a spinster who believed in fairies, she bought Hill Top Farm in the Lake Country, grew sick of rabbits as shallow creatures and gave her love to Tom Kitten, Jemima Puddle-Duck, and Pig-wig who followed at her heels and slept in a basket beside her bed.

Then surprisingly in 1913, aged forty-seven, Miss Potter married a North Country man, William Heelis of Sawrey, and became a sheep farmer. Her character changed: "It does not do to be sentimental on a farm." From a shameless dealer in Victorian whimsy she turned into a prickly, obstinate, no-nonsense woman who hated rats, who for the next thirty years till her death in 1943 raised sheep and ate mutton, a sharp dealer at sheep fairs. She became stout, wore tweeds, and wrote no more of "those damned little books," having in fact grown up. On the last Christmas of her life, she and William had a stewed rabbit for dinner.

I am in favor of growing up, as I had done before reading Beatrix Potter. One summer night during a terrific thunderstorm in the country, I read aloud the story of Peter Rabbit to three small children huddled together whimpering in my lap: " 'Now, my dears,' said old Mrs. Rabbit, 'you may go into the fields or down the lane, but don't go into Mr. McGregor's garden.' " And I thought, as the thunder crashed and the wind howled around us, "My God, Mr. McGregor, what's going on here?"

Rabbit By Owllight

My rabbit dares not eat the crocuses,
Engrossed as he must be in appetite
Far greedier than his own,
Listening, like me, to hungry shadows,
Hearing above his head the famished owl
Whose craving to devour shivers the owllight.
Run, rabbit, run. Your rabbit fears are rabbit,
Mine are me.

("All thoughts of a turtle are turtle and of a rabbit, rabbits." — Emerson)

Lucy Stone. I kept my maiden name after I was married, and for this show of independence was teased, sometimes rebuked, as a Lucy Stoner. Finally I gave up the role of Miss Smith because it was a nuisance, people doubted that I was married, the mailman was permanently confused. Most of all I refused to saddle a child with a hyphenated name or link him with only one parent.

Lucy Stone was far more dedicated. When she was born in 1818 on a Massachusetts farm, the eighth of nine children, her mother who had milked eight cows the night before said, "Oh dear! I am sorry it is a girl. A woman's life is so hard!" Lucy grew up indignant at the way her harsh father ruled the household. When she read in the Bible "Thy desire shall be to thy husband, and he shall rule over thee," she made up her mind not to marry.

While a student at Oberlin she conceived the idea that a woman should keep her own name and identity. At twenty-five she paid her way through college, doing housework at three cents an hour in the Ladies' Hall. During the four years, she had one good dress and, with no help from her father, no money to return home. After graduation she began lecturing over the country on slavery and women's rights, twin problems in her mind since marriage was itself a form of slavery. In her day women didn't appear on public platforms; for her views she was expelled from her church in Massachusetts. Hostile audiences threw pepper or doused her with a hose. Once she was hit in the head by a prayerbook.

The man Lucy married at thirty-seven was Henry Blackwell, owner of a hardware store in Cincinnati. Henry courted her for two years before she reluctantly consented. Attracted as she was to this man, himself an advocate of women's right to equality, she found the idea of marriage intolerable, a suffocating form of death. Before saying yes Lucy consulted lawyers who assured her there was no law requiring her to take her husband's name. At the wedding the two read aloud and signed the Protest, written by Henry. It declared that no obedience was implied, that the wife was an independent, rational being with absolute equality before God and the law. Lucy was now Mrs. Stone, said to be the first woman to refuse her husband's name. Harriet Beecher Stowe expressed pained amazement. Many thought the marriage illegal, objected to it as immoral, and addressed her as Mrs. Blackwell.

The marriage lasted thirty-eight companionable years. Lucy made an excellent loving wife, an admirable homemaker, for which she was re-proved by Susan B. Anthony, who called her a little dunce for being do-mesticated. She started a newspaper, *The Woman's Journal,* advocating women's suffrage. When their child Alice was born, she was given both their names, though Henry said she should be called Stone if his wife wished.

Lucy died of cancer in 1893 at seventy-five, and Henry went on without her, still introduced as Lucy's husband. Alice never married but dedicated her life to the cause of women. More than twenty years after Lucy's death, the Lucy Stone League was formed (and disappeared, like the Ladies' Aid Society), whose sole purpose was to persuade married women to keep their maiden name. And though I never joined, I was glad to be recognized as a Lucy Stoner.

In Philip Larkin's poem "Maiden Name" he sadly deplores (to one he knew as a girl) the fact that "marrying left your maiden name disused." Since the wedding ceremony, when you were "confused by law with some-one else," your own name has no longer meant you, your face, your voice, your grace. *Who are you, anyway?*

Augusta Leigh. Byron and Augusta Leigh had the same father, "Mad Jack," who had eloped with the wife of Lord Carmarthen and, after her divorce, married her shortly before the birth of their daughter Augusta in 1783. In 1785, now a widower, Mad Jack married Catherine Gordon, a Scottish girl with a small fortune and terrible temper who be-came Byron's mother.

Augusta, four years older than Byron, grew up an orphan after their father died. She and Byron met when he was about sixteen and corre-sponded affectionately ("a Friend in whom I can confide," he wrote). Augusta married her first cousin, George Leigh, while Byron was at Trinity College, Cambridge. "She married a fool," he said, one who mis-treated and neglected her, with whom she lived in dire financial straits at Six-Mile Bottom, a hamlet not far from Cambridge.

When Augusta paid an unexpected visit to Byron in London in June

1813, she had three small children at home and a bankrupt husband. She was twenty-nine, amiable, "soft and voluptuous," with dark hair and large soulful eyes, adoring of her brother, full of chatter and laughter at his wit. During the three weeks she stayed with him, they went about to the theater and to balls, inseparable, delighted with each other's company. On Augusta's return home, Byron visited her twice and after the second visit took her back with him to London. They were together in July when she found she was pregnant.

Though Augusta clearly assented in their love affair, Byron, obsessed by her, took the blame himself. Ridden by guilt, he confessed his folly to his dear friend Lady Melbourne who, tolerant of his other scandalous affairs (most recently with her daughter-in-law, Lady Caroline Lamb), was horrified at incest and greatly alarmed. Byron considered eloping with his sister to the Continent but delayed any action till, in December, Augusta came again to London and he carried her off to Newstead Abbey where they stayed snowbound, in seclusion till nearly February. The woman he loved was, says Byron's biographer, Leslie Marchand, "amoral as a rabbit and silly as a goose."

On April 15, 1814, at Six-Mile Bottom, Augusta gave birth to a daughter, Elizabeth Medora Leigh, and called her Medora (the name of the Corsair's beloved in Byron's poem of the preceding year). That Byron was the father is all but certain, though he never acknowledged her or provided for her as he did Allegra, his child by Claire Clairmont. It may well be that he was loath to admit proof of incest. In any case, he and Augusta agreed he should take a wife, whom she attempted to find for him. Over her objection that Annabella Milbanke was not rich enough and too straitlaced, Byron proposed to Annabella and married her. Their miserable union ended in separation a year later after the birth of Byron's only legitimate child, named for his sister Augusta Ada. On January 14, 1816, having ordered Annabella to return to her parents and take the baby with her, Byron saw his wife and daughter for the last time, in the London house where he sat with Augusta. Three months later, while talk of the scandal raged about him, he left England for exile in Italy, never to return. Three years later he was writing to Augusta from Venice: "We may have been wrong — but I repent of nothing except that accursed marriage — and your refusing to continue to love me as you had loved me." He swore he was incapable of real love for any other human being.

Augusta lived on at Six-Mile Bottom with her husband and, eventually, seven children. She died at sixty-eight.

Much of Medora's short life was catastrophic. As she revealed in her autobiography, published twenty years after her death, both her older sister Georgiana and Annabella had discovered and disclosed to her the fact that Byron was her father. He died on her tenth birthday — a man she never knew. Before she was fifteen, Medora was raped by Georgiana's husband, Henry Trevanion, who, after Georgiana hastily moved out and left them in France together, forced Medora to live with him. In poverty and ill-health, completely in his power and abandoned by her family, she submitted to him for a period of ten years till she escaped. By him she had three pregnancies and one surviving child, Marie.

For most of those years all communication ceased between Augusta and her young daughter. Medora wrote that her mother disliked her, in anger blamed her alone for Henry's brutal treatment. Always bitter and accusing, Augusta coldly rejected her, even persecuted her. In 1848 Medora, still in France, married a young French soldier, Jean-Louis Taillefer, and the next year, aged thirty-four, she died, forgiving her uncaring mother and believing to the end, for what it was worth, that she was Byron's child.

Before he died, Byron wrote to his estranged wife, Lady Byron, concerning his unpublished memoirs (the 400-page manuscript that his friend Hobhouse burned at Byron's death): "It is no great pleasure to have lived — and less to live over again the details of existence."

To his publisher John Murray he wrote, "I have left out all my *loves*."

Claire Clairmont. Byron admitted to his friend Hobhouse "the carnal knowledge of Miss C." To another friend, Douglas Kinnaird, he wrote, "I never loved nor pretended to love her, but a man is a man, and if a girl of eighteen comes prancing to you at all hours, there is but one way." He called her "that odd-headed girl" who offered herself to him shortly before he left England for good, beset by his own failures in living and loving.

Claire was the stepdaughter of William Godwin. Her widowed mother was a London neighbor of Godwin's who married him after his first wife, Mary Wollstonecraft, died in childbirth, leaving a daughter Mary nearly the same age as Claire.

When Mary suddenly eloped with Shelley to France in 1814, Claire, at fifteen, went along and, nearly two years later, returned with them penniless to England. She wasn't a pretty girl but a lively one, with black hair and rather heavy features, inclined to be bold and theatrical, tenacious in getting her way. At seventeen, having written in her journal, "When will something happen to me?" she sent a flood of letters to Byron beginning, "An utter stranger takes the liberty of addressing you." Soon she proposed that he spend a night with her and, for no better reason, he obliged her and did. During his final week in England, at seven o'clock on a night early in April 1816, they met somewhere outside London in a sexual encounter that, according to Claire, lasted ten minutes. The following Monday Byron left for Switzerland with no intention of continuing the affair or ever seeing her again.

But Claire was not only determined, she was probably pregnant. She set herself to follow after Byron and, on May 8, induced Mary and Shelley, who had never met Byron, to go with her to Switzerland to be near him. They arrived in Geneva ten days before Byron did and spent the summer in a villa not far from his Villa Diodati. There he saw them often and carelessly resumed relations with Claire till August when in disgust he broke off completely with her and wrote Augusta, "Now, dearest, I have put an end to it." Claire was persuaded by Shelley and Mary to go with them to England to bear the child that Byron believed was his, though "whether this impregnation took place before I left England or since I do not know." Allegra was born in Bath on January 12, 1817, Byron's third daughter. But when Shelley and Mary returned to Italy a year later with the mother and child in tow, Byron refused point-blank to see Claire. Allegra was taken by a nurse to his palazzo in Venice where he said he would bring her up himself. His first proposal was that his sister Augusta care for her at Six-Mile Bottom.

Allegra was a beautiful little girl who resembled her father, with blue eyes and a dimple in her chin like his. In time he grew fond of her. Yet after he met and fell in love with Teresa, Countess Guiccioli, and moved to Ravenna to live with her and her husband, Allegra became a problem. She was four when he found it convenient to put her in a convent near Ravenna to be brought up a Roman Catholic. From that day neither Byron nor Claire saw her again, though Claire—denied access to the convent—frantically begged Shelley to help her kidnap the child from the nuns. Allegra died in the convent of typhus fever on April 20, 1822. She was five years old. Claire blamed Byron for her death.

That year Shelley was drowned, Byron died two years later in Greece. Claire, at twenty-four, desperately unhappy, left Italy for Vienna and a lonely life abroad as a governess. Those ten minutes of passion, she wrote her friend Jane Williams, "have discomposed the rest of my life."

Lady Blessington. A long time ago I copied out a remark of Lady Blessington's (in a letter to Bulwer-Lytton) and never forgot it: "There are so few before whom one would condescend to appear otherwise than happy." I didn't know then who Lady Blessington was, other than a friend of Byron's. But the words stayed in my head as sensible advice, not arrogant as perhaps they really were (you hear the lofty tone in *condescend*), but rather a reflection on the kindest way to spare people a recital of one's woes.

Without doubt Marguerite, Countess of Blessington, had unhappiness to hide. Born in Tipperary in 1789 to a life of wretched poverty, she was the child of a savage, drunken father, sold by him into marriage at fifteen with a brute named Farmer who beat and misused her. From him she escaped to live for five years with a Captain Jenkins before, in a drunken stupor, Farmer fell from a window in London and was killed.

A few months later she married a friend of Jenkins, the Earl of Blessington, a rich, indulgent, affectionate husband, though it appears that from the sexual abuse she received as a girl, Lady Blessington was incapable of passionate love for any man.

She was very beautiful, known as the loveliest woman in England, "the most gorgeous Lady B," with shining dark hair, white forehead, lustrous eyes. She was intelligent and amusing. At first London society shunned her as a harlot, till through wealth, extravagance, good nature she made her house in St. James's Square a gathering place of the elite, a rival of Holland House. On an evening in 1821, a young Frenchman, Count Alfred d'Orsay, came to a Blessington party. He was twenty, slim, athletic, handsome, exquisitely dressed, and with a disastrous charm. While it seems likely that Lady Blessington, at thirty-one, never took d'Orsay for a lover, she kept him at her side in a lasting intimacy, and he became a permanent member of the household. There he stayed for the next twenty-eight years till she died in his arms.

Soon after they met, d'Orsay persuaded the Blessingtons to go with him to the Continent. During the nine weeks they spent in Genoa, where Byron had settled for a few months in the Casa Saluzzo with his mistress Countess Guiccioli, Lady Blessington and Byron became close companions, riding, dining together — though she wrote in her diary of their first meeting, "I have seen Lord Byron; and am disappointed." He didn't look like a romantic poet. He was short instead of tall and commanding, frail, emaciated, his coat too large, his hair streaked with gray. She found him vain, vulgar, gossipy, and irresistible, and was pleased to take down and publish after his death her *Conversations* with the poet, a book that, in four hundred pages, gave her impressions of his personality and opinions. Byron wrote Thomas Moore that he thought Lady B very literary, very pretty (but told Augusta she was vain and affected). When he left for Greece in June 1823, "I have a presentment I shall die there," he said, and tears ran down his face at parting with her. Guiccioli was furiously jealous, but she needn't have been. She was, said Byron, "my last love, my last passion."

In 1829 Lord Blessington died abroad, and his widow returned to a hostile London accompanied by d'Orsay. The world of gossip buzzed with talk of the "Blessington Circus." Men of consequence—like the young Disraeli—frequented her salon but the ladies kept aloof (though one of her guests was Countess Guiccioli). While in Genoa, Blessington had added a codicil to his will giving his estate to d'Orsay, of whom he was genuinely fond, provided d'Orsay marry one or the other of Blessington's two daughters by a former marriage. When d'Orsay obediently married Harriet, a schoolgirl of fifteen, after promising Lady Blessington that there would be no consummation of the marriage for the next four years, then society assumed that Lady Blessington, as jealous mistress, had made this demand. The truth was that, remembering her own youth, she wanted to spare the child bride. By 1831, when d'Orsay's marriage to the unhappy Harriet collapsed and she fled from the ménage, it was Lady Blessington who was blamed. Greville's *Diary* repeats the common gossip that, besides d'Orsay, she had been "very intimate" with Byron as well as Walter Savage Landor, whose *Conversations* were imaginary and who had a vile temper and a wife and four children.

For the next twenty heartbreak years, Lady Blessington wrote novels feverishly to keep her home at Gore House and pay the debts incurred by d'Orsay, childlike in his irresponsibility, a glass of fashion, a reckless gambler. Jane Carlyle said he looked as resplendent as a diamond beetle. When he fled to France from his creditors in 1849, Lady Blessington, stout and old and exhausted, sold at a twelve-day auction all her possessions and followed him to Paris, where shortly she died. The once glittering dandy was left shattered by the loss.

Lady Holland. The best thing to be said of Lady Holland's famous dinner parties was that Sydney Smith was a frequent guest who brought down the house in uproarious laughter, the most amusing diner-out in London (to Byron "the loudest wit I was ever deafened with"). "Some of the best and happiest days of my life I have spent under your roof," he wrote his dear Lady Holland, who during the first forty years of the nineteenth century ruled at Holland House over the most brilliant and distinguished collection of Whigs of the time and, as their imperious hostess, put them soundly in their place.

As Elizabeth Lady Webster, married at sixteen to an elderly baronet whose dullness she found unendurable, she had eloped with young Lord Holland and borne him a son before a divorce was granted by the House of Lords and they could be married. Now the proud wife of an extremely wealthy baron who adored her, she returned with him to Holland House in Kensington and set to work making it a gathering place for the leading statesmen, writers, and artists, the rich and the prestigious, provided they were not Tories. Macaulay, Dickens, Thackeray, Jeremy Bentham, Byron, Walter Scott, Prime Minister Melbourne (who was said to laugh more and at less than anyone there), each and all were received nightly and sometimes left the house in a fury. She treated them with arrogance, snubbed and ordered them about with a royal air that outdid Napoleon (for whom she developed a passion) — she was dictatorial, short-tempered, on occasion rude and insolent. The experience of dining with her could be terrifying. She would irritably rearrange the seating of her guests in the middle of a meal or turn them out of the house for wearing scent. At her overcrowded dinner parties, all male (where once she squeezed sixteen into a table for nine), she was quick to silence even Macaulay, a man never known to stop talking: "Now, Macaulay, we have had enough of this." She subdued Samuel Rogers by saying, "Your poetry is bad enough, so pray be sparing of your prose." One night she dropped her fan so many times that Count d'Orsay, seated next to her, after obediently picking it up suggested he just sit on the floor and wait for it to fall. When she commanded Sydney Smith — the wittiest man present, whom she always placed at her side, the only one allowed to tease her — "Ring the bell, Sydney," he answered, "Oh yes, and shall I sweep the floor?"

Smith laughed at her high-handedness and rebuked her for her wayward manners as London's hostess. A London shop, he said, sold pills especially for those guests suffering from wounded pride. Yet with affection lifelong he declared his love of the lady and her gracious husband: "She is very handsome, very clever, and I think very agreeable. Lord Holland is quite delightful. I really never saw such a man. In addition to this, think of him possessing Holland House and that he reposes every evening on that beautiful structure of flesh and blood Lady H."

Lady Ottoline Morrell. She too was a London hostess, known for her hospitality in the 1920s toward the clannish Bloomsbury group, though never a member of it (much as she longed to be). Born an aristocrat, half-sister of the Duke of Portland, married to the Liberal MP Philip Morrell, Lady Ottoline yearned to be a writer and cultivated writers, particularly poets. These she lured to her Venetian red drawing room at 44 Bedford Square and showered with attention and gifts of chocolate, tobacco, and silk cushions. Each morning she wrote notes in sepia ink to invite talented, artistic, famous people to her Thursday evenings and Thursday afternoon teas. At Garsington Manor, her country home in Oxfordshire, she welcomed them with open arms and lavish devotion.

And for her pains D. H. Lawrence caricatured her in *Women in Love* as Hermione Roddice, a domineering, repulsive woman with "a terrible void, a lack, a deficiency of being within her." Aldous Huxley mocked her in *Crome Yellow* as Priscilla Wimbush, with "a massive projecting nose and little greenish eyes." Lytton Strachey and Virginia Woolf attended her parties and openly ridiculed her, finding her absurd, a silly noodle. In Bloomsbury she was known as "the Ott." Virginia Woolf confided to her diary concerning her book *Mrs. Dalloway,* "I want to bring in the despicableness of people like Ott."

David Cecil said she was both handsome and grotesque. She was very tall, "like a giraffe!" Nijinsky exclaimed when he met her. She towered over people and suffocated them. Her nose was too long, her jaw jutted out, she had orange-colored hair. Her barking voice sounded at times a queer nasal moan with what Stephen Spender called "horn-like blasts." She wore brightly colored, spectacular attire that made her look, said Virginia Woolf, "as garish as a strumpet," or "decorative as an Austrian baroque church," or "like a Spanish galleon hung with golden coins, & lovely silken sails." She dressed like a cossack or a shepherdess with crook or wore huge ostrich-feathered hats, billowing dresses, shawls and tassels, and went, said Lytton Strachey, "thickly encrusted with pearls and diamonds."

Bizarre as Lady Ottoline was, men were fascinated by her. And she acquired many friends—Herbert Asquith, Ramsay MacDonald, Henry James, Max Beerbohm, Yeats—and many lovers, from Axel Munthe to Augustus John to Bertrand Russell, the most ardent, who over the years from 1910 to 1916 wrote her more than two thousand letters. In them, as many as five a day, he declared his passion to be beyond passion and more than he could live with, "almost overmastering," and himself driven out of his mind. "I love you," said Russell, "and everything else is dross," offended though he was by her startling taste, her excessive use of scent and powder, her long thin face that looked to him "something like a horse," her hair the color of marmalade. She was twice his height.

As for Ottoline in this consuming love affair, she found Russell's intensity intemperate and alarming, the passion flattering but too turbulent, "a scorching flame," he wrote, "lighting up all the splendours and terrors of the world." Yet there was something strongly appealing about her that made him without conscience or remorse abandon his wife Alys, threaten suicide, and urge Ottoline to leave her devoted husband—something lovable, warm and enveloping and always kind. With her, said Russell, "life seemed all that it might be, but hardly ever is."

In his autobiography Russell claims that he was ninety-four before he finally learned what ecstasy really is. In a dedicatory verse "To Edith," his fourth wife whom he married in old age, he says that with her he found it at last. And he knew to his amazement "what life and love may be."

Ecstasy, at ninety-four?

Joanna Southcott. She was a woman who rocks the mind. In her time she gained a good deal of public notice in England by announcing, at the age of sixty-four, that she was pregnant by the Holy Ghost and would be delivered on October 19, 1814, of a son to be named Shiloh, the Prince of Peace. Joanna identified herself as "the woman clothed with the sun" referred to in Revelation 12:

And there appeared a great wonder in heaven, a woman clothed with the sun, and the moon under her feet, and upon her head a crown of twelve stars:

And she being with child cried, travailing in birth, and pained to be delivered . . .

And she brought forth a man child, who was to rule all nations with a rod of iron.

Joanna Southcott was born in 1750, a Devonshire farmer's daughter, a Methodist, for many years of her life a domestic servant. From the time she was forty-two, she heard heavenly voices telling her that God had called her to be his prophet of the Second Coming and his "true and faithful Bride." When she reached sixty-four a voice said, "Order twelve gowns for thy wedding." By her doggerel prophecies and claims that filled sixty-five books and pamphlets, and by her seals (slips of paper signed with her name, and charged for, that "sealed in" the believers with the promise of eternal life), she had attracted a following of 100,000 South-cottians that lasted throughout the century, who awaited the coming of the new Messiah in stunned belief. Her son would conquer Satan, with whom Joanna had personal battles. She revealed the story of her divine conception in her ungrammatical and incoherent book, *Prophecies announcing the Birth of the Prince of Peace.*

In October 1813 she said she experienced "a powerful visitation" upon her body, and by Christmas, while she meditated the role of the Virgin Mary, she felt a movement in her womb. As her body swelled to huge proportions, her followers showered gifts upon the expected child, including lace caps, embroidered bibs, silver cups, and a handsome satinwood crib ornamented with gold and lined with blue satin.

Ballads about Joanna and the blessed event were sung in the streets. Byron noted her attempt to establish herself as Mrs. Trinity. Seventeen of the twenty-one doctors who examined her agreed she was pregnant, though she refused to allow an internal examination. On the date set, exactly a year later, October 19, Shiloh failed to appear after she suffered labor pains. What the public had greeted with mocking laughter as the "divine afflatus" turned out to be dropsy. Instead of giving birth, on October 29 Joanna Southcott slipped into death.

Madame Blavatsky. She was less lovable a fraud than Joanna Southcott. And I would never have tried to read her incoherent memoirs or the murky *Isis Unveiled* if Yeats hadn't joined the Theosophical Society, which Madame Blavatsky founded, and if I hadn't been teaching Yeats.

Helena Blavatsky, a Russian occultist born in 1831, was at seventeen married to an elderly man named Blavatsky whom she left after a few months. Thereafter, though she had a second husband, an unknown number of lovers, and a son named Yuri, she declared she was a virgin and wore what her followers called her halo of virginity. An imposing woman, large and grossly fat, untidy and bad-tempered, she claimed to have spent seven years in Tibet where she was initiated into the occult. She became a medium, prominent among spiritualists in America — her home for six years — and in her séances produced, in swirls of ecto-plasm, two Tibetan emanations named Koot-Hoomi and Morya as her controls. When eventually she came to London after a stay in India, she was exposed as a fraud and accomplished impostor by the Theosophical Society for Psychical Research. Ten years earlier, in 1875, Madame Blavatsky had founded the Theosophical Society (theosophy meaning the wisdom of God) which charged a five-dollar initiation fee to join the as-piring brotherhood of man. By that time she considered herself messianic with insight into the nature of the divine, and had gained so many willing believers over the world that at her death she had a following of 100,000 (the same number as Joanna Southcott) which persists to this day.

Yeats met Madame Blavatsky at her house on Lansdowne Road in South London just after the Society for Psychical Research had reported her trickery. He found an old woman in a loose, dark dress chain-smoking cigarettes and playing solitaire. Yeats at twenty-one, pale and dreamy, was not to be deterred. He was already able to see ghosts and astral manifestations, such as six little green elephants tagging along be-hind him on a London street. Mystical phenomena obsessed him, and theosophy was, he thought, the place to look. Unfortunately his zeal for magic, astrology, the taking of horoscopes, the telling of fortunes by Tarot cards, reincarnation, Rosicrucianism, spiritualism, the Spiritus Mundi, and various lunatic approaches to the supernatural, tried Madame Blavatsky's nerves and made her fearful of further investigation. One night in a secret ceremony Yeats, with a group of followers, burned a flower to ashes and tried by spells to bring it back to life. After two years of bearing with his erratic behavior, Madame had her assistant ask him to resign from the society. Yeats did so reluctantly, for he admired her as "a sort of female Dr. Johnson" and found her psychic powers impressive. But it wasn't a total loss; he had already been initiated into the Hermetic Order of the Golden Dawn.

Madame Blavatsky died in her bed in 1891. She was cremated and her ashes were divided into three parts: one portion went to India, one to New York, while the third stayed inactive in London until it was dropped into the Ganges by her devoted pupil, Mrs. Annie Besant, on a visit to India. So what good to theosophy is she now, like all Gaul divided into three parts?

The Mountainous Me. Margaret Fuller, the American writer and feminist, was ever a talker, who for years conducted in a trumpeting voice conversation classes for Boston ladies ($20 for ten lessons). At Elizabeth Peabody's house she taught them to read Kant, asserting their right to equality with men while maintaining their superiority as women. "Men disappoint me so," said Margaret Fuller. "I find no intellect comparable to my own."

Her lofty sense of womanhood was too much for Horace Greeley, who in 1844 invited Miss Fuller to write literary criticism for the *New York Tribune.* When she visited in his home, Greeley would bow and repeat a ringing phrase from her feminist tract *Woman in the Nineteenth Century:* "Let them be sea captains if they will!" as he politely held the door open for her to sweep past him into the room.

Born in Massachusetts, Margaret was educated by her father who had her reading Ovid before she was eight. Over the years she developed into a leading intellectual with a strict air of mind over matter. As editor of

The Dial she was known as the Priestess of Transcendentalism. Except for Carlyle, she generally impressed men; Carlyle, whom she visited in Chelsea, snubbed and cowed her. She complained that he allowed no one a chance to talk but rushed at his opponent with an onset of words, a torment of sound. Whitman admired her militant feminism. Thoreau thought her a woman worth listening to. James Russell Lowell found formidable her relentless self-esteem, her capital *I* and infinite *me*. She challenged Longfellow's claim to be a poet. Hawthorne caricatured her as the queenly Zenobia in *The Blithedale Romance*. But it was Emerson who called her "The Mountainous Me" and after meeting her in 1836 when she was twenty-six wrote in his journal: "Her extreme plainness, a trick of incessantly opening and shutting her eyelids, the nasal tone of her voice, all repelled; and I said to myself we shall never get far."

They got far. Soon he was writing of "strange, cold-warm, attractive-repelling conversations with Margaret," whom he now respected, revered, loved. She reminded him of godlike figures — Ceres, Proserpine, most of all Minerva, goddess of wisdom — as she reminded herself. James Russell Lowell wrote, "She always keeps asking if I don't observe a / Particular likeness 'twixt her and Minerva."

"I myself am more divine than any I see," she told Emerson, who was inclined to believe her. She had a purifying mind, he said, and great powers of speech.

Margaret Fuller in Chelsea

I can accept the world, the plan
Allotted to the race of man.
But Margaret Fuller's brag was worse.
She could accept the universe.
Carlyle said, "By God, she'd better!"
And so did everyone who met her.

Fanny Brawne. It was a brief romance; they were very young. Keats met Fanny in November 1818, just before his brother Tom died of tuberculosis. He first mentions her in a letter of December 16 to his brother George in America: she was eighteen, "beautiful and elegant, graceful, silly, fashionable and strange." He was twenty-three, haunted by her, fearful of being rebuffed. On Christmas day Keats had dinner at Elm Cottage in Hampstead with Fanny, her widowed mother, brother and sister. Three years after his death, Fanny wrote his sister Fanny Keats that it had been the happiest day of her life.

In April the Brawnes moved into the other half of the house in Wentworth Place where Keats now lived with his friend Charles Brown. Brown disliked Fanny, a feeling he didn't hide, calling her "an artful bad-hearted girl." She had a reputation of being a giddy flirt, frivolous, quick-tongued, a stylish girl who loved clothes. Keats told her to her face she was a minx.

In that miraculous spring of his greatest poetry, 1819, by May he and Fanny walked daily on the Heath; by midsummer his health was failing with symptoms in his lungs. He lived in poverty and despair, consumed by love and growing jealousy. In the "Ode to Fanny" he asks, "Who now, with greedy looks, eats up my feast?" The famous love letters begin in July, the "flint-worded" letters, hysterical in their passion ("Yourself—your soul—in pity give me all") though he was never to become her lover. "Ask yourself, my love," he wrote, "whether you are not very cruel to have so entrammelled me, so destroyed my freedom." The thought of her was torture: "I have two luxuries to brood over in my walks, your loveliness and the hour of my death." "I cannot exist without you," he wrote. "I cannot breathe without you."

By December they were secretly engaged. Sometime in December Keats addressed to her the agonized lines without a title:

This living hand, now warm and capable
Of earnest grasping, would, if it were cold
And in the icy silence of the tomb,
So haunt thy days and chill thy dreaming nights
That thou wouldst wish thine own heart dry of blood
So in my veins red life might stream again,

And thou be conscience-calm'd — see here it is —
I hold it towards you.

A few weeks later, February 3, 1820, while sitting on top of a coach from London to Hampstead, he had the severe hemorrhage that spelled his fate. In his bed he said to Brown, "I know the colour of that blood — it is arterial blood — I cannot be deceived in that colour — that drop of blood is my death-warrant — I must die." His one concern was for Fanny, who refused to break the engagement when he offered to release her. He sent her a note daily as he lay ill indoors, catching sight of her lingering outside his window, refusing to allow her near him. Soon came violent palpitations, more hemorrhages. In one of his last letters to Fanny he said, "I am tormented day and night. They talk of my going to Italy," then attacked her in frantic protests, "You do not know what it is to love. . . . How have you passed this month? Who have you smiled with?"

On September 13 Keats sailed for Italy with his friend Joseph Severn. From Rome he wrote, "I can bear to die. I cannot bear to leave her. O God! God! Everything reminds me of her." He wouldn't write her now or open her letters, none of which have survived. Five months later he died in Severn's arms. He was twenty-five.

After his death Fanny wrote to Fanny Keats, "I have not got over it and never shall." She wore mourning for him for years. "Had only he returned from Italy," she said, "I should have been his wife." Twelve years later she married Louis Lindo, went to live on the Continent, and had three children. She died in 1865.

Jane Austen. Lord David Cecil has written a *Portrait of Jane Austen* without attempting a new way of depicting her — no revelation, no fresh insight into her character, no painting her portrait anew. His excuse for still another book is that he loves her, not as cultist or Janeite but as one at home in her world of three or four families in a Hampshire village (which was obviously not *his* world as a Cecil and an Oxford don). My portrait of her, if I could make one, would be of a wit, a playful, feminine wit. There was fun in her ("I dearly love a laugh"). She laughed and teased and gossiped—"I am still a cat when I see a mouse"—without the cutting malice Virginia Woolf betrayed (who said of David Cecil, a man she knew socially, that he had no juice in him). In her letters to her sister, written in a neat hand but abominably spelled (cloathes, veiw, greive), Jane loved to make Cassandra laugh. "Mr. Robert Mascall eats a great deal of butter," she wrote. "I respect Mrs. Chamberlayne for doing her hair well, but cannot feel a more tender sentiment." "Miss Langley is like any other short girl, with a broad nose and wide mouth, fashionable dress and exposed bosom."

Hers was an uneventful life in a provincial setting. Of a quiet visit to Ashe Park she wrote, "You express so little anxiety about my being murdered under Ashe Park copse by Mrs. Hubert's servant that I have a great mind not to tell you whether I was or not." On a dull evening there, spent unhappily tête-à-tête with an egregious Mr. Holder, "I said two or three amusing things," she reported, "and Mr. Holder made a few infamous puns."

At a ball in Bath, May 12, 1801—a more stylish affair than she was used to—Jane spotted a Miss Twistleton, "and I am proud to say that I have a very good eye at an Adultress, for though repeatedly assured that another in the same party was the *She,* I fixed upon the right one from the first. She was highly rouged, and looked rather quietly and contentedly silly than anything else."

Well aware of her feminine nature and quick to admit her weakness for balls, visits, paying calls, chatter, shopping, needlework, a velvet bonnet or a muslin gown, Jane never took herself seriously or undertook to discuss public events. "You know," she ran on to Cassandra, "how interesting the purchase of a sponge cake is to me." "I long to know whether you are buying stockings or what you are doing." "My black cap was openly admired by Mrs. Lefroy, and secretly I imagine by everybody else in the room."

To the one with whom she shared her life, she could laugh at her own failings, particularly a youthful habit of scribbling novels, of which her sister showed no jealousy or had reason to. "I think," Jane wrote, "I can boast myself with all possible vanity the most unlearned and uninformed being that ever dared to be an authoress." And Cassandra at her embroidery or fine satin stitch only smiled, not tempted in the least to be another one herself.

Modest as she was, Jane would no doubt be impatient at the number of biographies forever written about her and her simple life. When Southey's *Life of Nelson* appeared in 1813 she complained to Cassandra, "I am tired of lives of Nelson, being as I never read any."

The Duchess of Marlborough. She was a duchess but she was no lady. For the last time, God willing, I've read a life of the divine and terrible Sarah (Virginia Cowles, *The Great Marlborough and His Duchess*), who stays immortal partly because she behaved so abominably, partly because in spite of it she was truly loved. Sarah Jennings was a girl of fifteen, a maid of honor to Princess Anne at St. James's Palace, when John Churchill fell in love with her. She had flashing blue eyes, honey-colored hair, the temper of a devil, and he should have stayed clear of her. John was exceptionally handsome; his mistress, Lady Castlemaine by whom he had a child, was also the King's mistress. He should have looked higher for a wife, everyone said. Stricken with love of this quarrelsome girl—a born fighter who taunted and scorned him—for several years he wooed Sarah Jennings till she came to love him utterly in return.

They were happy, though Marlborough, a disciplined, courteous, silent man, had to endure Sarah's intemperance, her sound and fury. She threw things. In her most celebrated rage she seized scissors and spitefully cut off her hair of which he was so proud. Though John said not a word, after his death she found the hair locked in his strongbox, kept those many years.

She was implacable, a dangerous friend, an unforgiving enemy. Princess Anne adored her as her closest companion, required her presence as Lady of the Bedchamber, wrote her notes twice a day: "If I writt whole volumes I could never express how well I love you." When Anne became Queen of England in 1702, Sarah boasted in her memoirs, "From this time I began to be looked upon as a person of consequence." Her sense of power went to her head and with bullying she dominated the queen, once ordering her to be quiet, till the constant bickering and unbearable rudeness alienated even shy, sickly Anne, who grew to hate the sight of her. After Abigail Hill had taken her place in the queen's affections, Sarah furiously accused them of a lesbian relationship. The bitter estrangement that followed led to Sarah and her husband, one of England's greatest generals, the magnificent hero of Ramillies and Blenheim, being dismissed from the court, a final fall from grace.

Sarah was a bad mother, cold, nagging, hostile to her daughters as she had been to her own mother. Of the seven children she bore, two boys and five girls, only two daughters, Henrietta and Mary, were alive when Marlborough—a pitiable wreck, broken in body and mind—died in 1722. Sarah, who survived him by twenty-five years, never saw her daughters again but lived aggrieved and grieving, in animosity toward them that they cordially returned. She wrote *An Account of the Cruell Usage of My Children* and, full of venom, kept a list of the "detestables" whom she most hated. When she died at Blenheim Palace, bored with living, in her eighty-fifth year, no member of her family was with her. The richest woman in Europe, she had revised her will twenty-six times. In lonely old age she said, "If I could have walked out of this world I would have departed long ago."

She was a terror, outrageous yet capable of the loyalty and love she peremptorily demanded of others, that her beloved Lord Marl never ceased to give. The worst enemy she had was herself.

Nell Gwyn. "Let not poor Nelly starve," said Charles II on his deathbed, caring with his last breath for her above his many mistresses. She was the English actress Nell Gwyn, born in 1650 in an alley off Drury Lane and brought up in a bawdy house kept by her mother, where as a child she served drinks to the customers. At fifteen she was a poor but pretty girl of the streets, selling oranges in the pit of the king's theater when a leading actor, Charles Hart, noticed her, made her his mistress, and helped her to become a member of the Drury Lane Company. (With the Restoration, two theaters were now open, and women for the first

time were permitted on the stage.) Before long Nell Gwyn was delight-
ing London as a comedienne, singer and dancer, whom Pepys, a constant playgoer, loudly applauded in all but serious roles. Of her acting in
Dryden's *Secret Love, or the Maiden Queen* (which Pepys saw three times)
he wrote, "The truth is there is a comical part done by Nell, which is
Florimel, that I never can hope ever to see the like done again, by man
or woman." After seeing her in Beaumont and Fletcher's *The Humorous
Lieutenant,* to him a silly play, he was glad of the chance to meet and kiss
her, "and a mighty pretty soul she is." By October 5, 1667, Pepys knew this
seventeen-year-old well enough to go "to the women's shift room where
Nell was dressing herself, and was all unready, and is very pretty, prettier
than I thought." Witty, too, though at times no more than "a bold merry
slut" who cursed and painted her face, whose base companions and lewd
talk made him mad.

For four years Nell acted steadily in the king's playhouse, the Drury
Lane, except for a brief absence when she went to live in the fashionable
resort of Epsom as mistress of Charles Sackville, Earl of Dorset, a man of
pleasure and dissipation, crony of the king, composer of the popular bal-
lad "To all you ladies now at land / We men at sea indite." Before she was
nineteen she had caught the fancy of King Charles himself, whose pursuit was so successful that her last appearance on the London stage — in
Dryden's *Conquest of Granada* — was delayed some months till after the
birth of his child in 1670.

Nell Gwyn was a small slender girl with a good figure and reddish
brown hair. Sir Peter Lely painted her as a reclining naked Venus with
Cupid at her side. She was said to be full of wild fun and loud laughter, reckless, impudent, on occasion riotous, but always good-humored.
Being illiterate, she could barely sign her initials to letters written for
her. Charles, the merry monarch, whose passions they said stayed in the
lower regions, loved her for her high spirits and unspoiled, undemand-
ing nature. She never pretended to be more than she was. She never
made scenes as Lady Castlemaine did, or put on airs like the Duchess
of Portsmouth, nor was she unfaithful to him like the Duchess of Maza-
rin. Nell behaved generously except to her Catholic rival the Duchess of

Portsmouth, whom she disliked and ridiculed. One day when Nell was riding in her gilded coach and was insulted by a mob that mistook her for the Duchess, she leaned out the window and said pleasantly, "Pray, good people, be civil. I am the *Protestant* whore!"

She had two sons by the king: the first, named for him, was made Duke of St. Albans; the second, James, died at the age of nine. Charles freely gave her his amiable company and a fine house in the town of Windsor to live in extravagantly; and their easy affection lasted for seventeen years till his death. Amply provided for by his final wish, Nell died still mourning him two years later at the age of thirty-seven.

Ninon de Lenclos. She was the *grande cocotte* of the seventeenth century, famed for her beauty and wit, neither of which she possessed to any marked degree. Her pictures show her rather plain and insipid, though they lie about her charms. She was superb in bed, with such capacity to please, such perfect good humor that her career grew lengthy enough as to seem preposterous. She was, for example, the mistress of Madame de Sévigné's husband, of Madame de Sévigné's son, eventually (it was said) of Madame de Sévigné's grandson — she seemed to run in the family. Ninon's ability to stay young was her secret; it helped that she suffered no remorse. Her prolonged youthfulness became the talk of Paris, arousing endless conjecture, not to say envy. They called her evergreen. What were her beauty secrets, her creams and concoctions, her magic formula? Rumor spread that when she was eighteen a mysterious Man in Black brought her a phial of rose-colored liquid, of which she used one drop in her bath to keep fresh and vigorous to old age. The real answer didn't satisfy the gossips — that she was provident of her life, exercised, ate sparingly, drank only water except for the soup she made with champagne, got lots of sleep, and, an unusual habit in her time, bathed daily. She was fastidious and elegant; she wore black satin corsets, and her bedroom was yellow and gold. "I keep young," she once said, "because I love neither gambling, nor wine, nor women."

Ninon was born in Paris in 1620 and named Anne. Her mother intended her for a nunnery, but her father gave her books of philosophy, urged her to read Montaigne. She lost her virginity at fifteen to a rascal. At nineteen, with her mother dead and her father in exile after killing a man, left completely alone she sought solace briefly in the spiritual life, which through lack of conviction she was unable to find. A Jesuit told her, "Then, mademoiselle, until you find conviction, offer heaven your incredulity." Instead, she learned to speak several languages, to sing, dance, play the lute, converse, shun lamentation and self-pity, to amuse and be amused.

Just as she avoided becoming a nun, Ninon escaped being a bride. She made it clear she had no wish to marry, lacking the vocation. She lost her heart often, loved deeply but never long, at most three months. In friendship she was constant. Out of wedlock she had a son whom she seldom saw.

Her succession of lovers and valued friends, of whose number she evidently kept count, ranged among the most illustrious men of the Grand Siècle: from wits to poets, from the Great Condé (with whom she spoke Latin in bed), La Rochefoucauld, the crippled poet Scarron, to Saint-Évremond, who loved her through most of the seventeenth century and into the eighteenth. To Saint-Évremond, who wrote that Nature, benevolent and wise, had shaped Ninon's soul, she wrote in old age, "I learn with pleasure that my soul is dearer to you than my body. . . . As a matter of fact, my body is no longer worthy of attention." Molière frequented her salon and discussed his ideas for plays with her (she suggested the plot of *Tartuffe*). She may have turned down Cardinal Richelieu. At thirty-five she opened a School for Gallantry in her fashionable Paris salon in the Rue de Tournelles to teach young aristocrats the art of love and perhaps practice her theories with some of them ("It needs a hundred times more skill to make love than to command any army"). As soon as she could afford to, she accepted no money for her favors but gave freely her true affection.

Ninon wrote one book, *La coquette vengée* (in which she defended her own conduct). She met old age with spirit and intelligence, accepting her wrinkles when they came, though she wished God had put them on the soles of her feet. At eighty she is said to have inspired a young abbé with passion; when she told him her age he replied that it did nothing to lessen his desire. On the night of her death she composed these lines: "Since I am old enough to die, / Why should I longer wish to live?" She died in Paris at near ninety and was praised for her chastity, having renounced by this time the practice of love.

As was the custom of the day, the French queen kept a skull in her boudoir to pray to, lighting it with tapers and adorning it with ribbons and pearls. The skull before which she prayed was said to be that of Ninon de Lenclos.

The Incomparable Aphra. In her lifetime they called Aphra Behn incomparable to revile her as a disgrace to her sex. There was nobody to compare her to.

She was approaching thirty when she found her true vocation as the first Englishwoman to earn her living as a professional writer. Most recently she had been a spy in Antwerp, employed by Charles II at the outbreak of the Dutch War to ferret out traitors to the English cause. As a secret agent she was a disaster. In January 1667 she returned to England a penniless widow, in total misery and despair. They threw her into Newgate debtors' prison.

It was then, taking stock, that Aphra Behn resolved to dedicate her life to Pleasure and Poetry. Having made the choice, she lost no time in emerging as a woman of pleasure and a writer of frailty and wit. As the author of fifteen more or less indecent plays and several novels, she shocked even Restoration London by her bawdy comedies that harped on sex, such as *The Forced Marriage* that made her famous; *The Amorous Prince; The Rover; Sir Patient Fancy* (whose prologue begins, "Oh, the great blessing of a little wit!"). Pope later remarked she put all her characters to bed. By trying to write like the men, Dryden said, she scandalized the modesty of the female sex. V. Sackville-West wrote in admiration, "She never made any bones about her conviction that love was the pleasantest thing in the world."

Her volume of poems, *Love Letters to a Gentleman,* was addressed to John Hoyle, described in a contemporary record as "an atheist, a sodomite professed, a corrupter of youth, and a blasphemer of Christ." He was killed in a tavern brawl in 1692. While she claimed to be desperately in love with him, her mocking poem "The Disappointment" concerns a lover's impotence:

> He saw how at her length she lay:
> He saw her rising bosom bare;
> Her loose thin robes, through which appear
> A shape designed for love and play:
> Abandoned by her pride and shame
> She does her softest joys dispense,
> Off'ring her virgin innocence
> A victim to love's sacred flame;
> While the o'er-ravished shepherd lies
> Unable to perform the sacrifice.

They called her a lewd harlot. Yet when she died in 1689 she was buried in Westminster Abbey under a black marble slab engraved with John Hoyle's couplet: "Here lies a proof that wit can never be / Defence enough against mortality." I say in mild reproach that Aphra Behn's comedies are bawdy but unreadable. If she saw in London, as seems likely, Wycherley's *The Country Wife,* she must have envied its brilliant indecency, the wit of the lustful Mr. Horner only pretending to be impotent in order to seduce the ladies.

The Calling of Aphra Behn

She was a lady in mid-career.
Half was over. Her thirtieth year
Beckoned. Discreetly she scanned the view
And seeing nothing but wanting to,
Like a gold sunrise, piqued by the lack

Of rosy vistas forward or back,
She paid the matter exalted thought,
Possibly longer than women ought,
And said, "Henceforth, my life shall be
Given to Pleasure and Poetry."
Then the days grew merrier than they were,
Although her verses were singular
And certain folly engaged her leisure,
But I can't deny it gave her pleasure.
She proved her mettle, she found her calling,
The wind was chill, a sere leaf falling,
Half was over. Half would remain
To crown the talents of Aphra Behn.
For Pleasure and Poetry half was ample,
And I am smitten by her example.

Sappho. It's a pity the lesbians have claimed Sappho, when like other Greek poets she accepted love simply as love and was credited with being enamored of men as well as women.

From her nine books of lyric verse, a few scraps and fragments remain. She is said to have married a wealthy man named Cercolas and to have had at least one child, a daughter named Cleis ("I have a little daughter, like a golden flower." "My own, my Cleis, darling child").

An ode of twenty-eight lines — an invocation to Aphrodite not to break her heart — and four stanzas of a second ode survive, enough with the fragments of papyrus, some found lining Egyptian tombs, to prove that Sappho was an immortal love poet. She frequently wrote songs to celebrate marriage; no wedding was complete unless Sappho praised it ("To what, dear bridegroom, may I rightly liken thee? — To a slender sapling"). Her songs are never coarse or indelicate.

Sappho was born on the island of Lesbos in the Aegean in the sixth century before Christ. She was small and dark, attractive less in body than in grace. She became a teacher of young schoolgirls in the arts of poetry, music, dancing, and with some of them she fell in love. Anactoria, about whom she wrote, married and moved to Lydia: "So, Anactoria, you go away with what calm carelessness of sorrow." Another was Atthis, though to Atthis she said, "You seemed to me a small, ungainly child." A lament was for darling Timas, another for Dica, both of whom died young before they could be wed. Sappho sounds too maternal to be a corrupter of maidenhood. She insists that her love for these girls is pure and enduring.

The legend persists through the centuries that she died for love by throwing herself off a cliff into the Ionian Sea because she was rejected by a young man named Phaon. (Ovid in the *Heroides* wrote of her abandoned by her lover Phaon.) Without further proof, the story is dismissed by scholars as romantic invention. Yet she did write, "With love of a slender youth I am overwhelmed by Aphrodite."

She was called unmatchable, the only woman given a place among the immortals. In her time her fame equaled Homer's; she was regarded as both poet and philosopher. Aristotle lauded her wisdom, Plato named her the tenth Muse. She exists in quotations by writers inspired by her language. Her contemporary in Lesbos, the lyric poet Alcaeus, praised Sappho as holy and pure. Catullus copied her in his love poems to Lesbia. Ben Jonson, Lyly in his play *Sappho and Phao,* Madame de Staël in *Sapho,* Herrick, Wordsworth paid her homage. Byron cried, "The isles of Greece! where burning Sappho loved and sung."

Centuries after her death the accusations were made that condemned Sappho as immoral. Pope was one who took her name in vain, "As who knows Sappho laughs at other whores." Since the late nineteenth century the kind of love attributed to her has been called lesbian. The word *sapphism* dates from 1890, *homosexual* from 1892. Daudet's novel *Sapho* (of a young man's passion for a prostitute) helped to degrade her name, as did Pierre Louÿs's glorification of Sapphic love, erotic and licentious. Swinburne's distortions harmed her by making her guilty of perversion. When he wrote "Anactoria" and the "Sapphics" it was in praise and extravagant imitation. He has "the Lesbians kissing across their smitten lutes . . . mouth to mouth." He has Sappho say, "I could eat thy breasts like honey." He called her his sister.

It seems unfair to identify her with lesbianism, a word used without regard for Sappho the poet or her home in Mitylene on Lesbos, the island of mosques and monasteries. She loved roses. She understood solitude and the need for love. She wrote, "It is midnight, the hours are passing, passing. Time is on his way; and yet I lie alone."

4 🪶

The Way with Words

Samuel Beckett was asked late in life what he was working on. "Senilities," he replied. What else would Beckett say? It was a word natural to him (and welcome to it) in his last-ditch humor, an undoing word that fitted his way of blasting life and declaring to the end his low opinion of its worth.

So one proceeds, as Richard Wilbur says, "by words and the defeat of words," thankful for any word in the book that sounds undefeated. Philip Larkin took a dim view of anybody's being able to use them honestly and fairly, to put the world into words, so to speak. Even in bed with a loved one, he said, it becomes more and more difficult to find the right words that are "at once true and kind, / Or not untrue and not unkind." Yet, however they falter and deceive or fill us with high-sounding hope (so many words to say a simple thing), they're all we've got to point the way, to tell us

> . . . this is what it is like,
> or what it is like in words. — Carol Ann Duffy

Two Lives. I've been reading the letters, never before published, that John Middleton Murry wrote to Katherine Mansfield during the eleven years he was her lover and then husband. Though he wrote every day during their long separations, this collection contains no more than half the letters because his words were at times so distressing that Katherine destroyed the evidence. After her death in 1923, Murry published her letters, from which he removed some too painful to print. He wrote a confessional autobiography, *Between Two Worlds,* to perfect her image and improve his own, gave public lectures about her, and bared his soul till he was accused of exploiting his dead wife. Everybody took a poke at him. He came to be known as "the best-hated man of letters in the country," mocked by Bertrand Russell who found Murry beastly; by D. H. Lawrence who called him a coward, an obscene bug, a mud-worm; by Virginia Woolf to whom he was a cheat, a posturing Byronic little man bleating his confessions to absolve himself of blame.

These letters, appearing sixty years after Katherine Mansfield's death, help to alter the concept of Murry as the villain of the piece. They even things up a little between two miserable people, badly mated, destined to hurt each other through a profound difference in their natures — she fighting for her life, making a frantic cry for all he couldn't give. Their love stayed as constant as their helplessness. Five months before she died, Katherine wrote in a letter to be read after her death, "In spite of everything — how happy we have been! I feel no other lovers have walked the earth together more joyfully — in spite of all."

When they first met in December 1911, Murry was a nervous, shy Oxford undergraduate of twenty-two, editor of a short-lived periodical *Rhythm* for which he had accepted one of her stories. Katherine, ten months older, filled Murry with awe at her sophistication, beauty, and caustic wit. She was already married to George Borden (whom she had left the morning following their wedding night), and she had had several love affairs, a miscarriage, a stillborn child. By his fifth respectful letter, Murry had begun the apologies typical of him: "Sorry I was so boring — can't be helped." At her urging he moved to London to share her flat at 69 Clovelly Mansions, where after a few weeks she — always the aggressor — asked, "Why don't you make me your mistress?" to which, lying on the bed and waving his legs in the air, Murry replied, "I feel it would spoil — everything." When he did become her lover, inept in his timidity, and the landlord discovering they weren't married evicted them, they moved from one squalid flat to another, to Buckinghamshire, to Paris.

It was an odd, insecure, teetering affair from which neither could withdraw. In February 1915 Katherine decided to leave Murry to join a new lover, Murry's poet friend Francis Carco, in the war zone in France, and without demur Murry saw her off at the boat train. "I'm not sad, or miserable, darling — only just vaguely uncomfortable," he wrote that night, adding he was coming down with a cold. When she returned ten days later, disillusioned by the adventure, Murry was busy buying furniture for another flat for them and putting up shelves in the kitchen. "O Tiggle," he wrote, "we are the lovers of the world. We are the lovers that were dreamed by God."

Katherine's fatal illness, not diagnosed till December 1917, marked the start of the nightmare. It lasted with little respite for the next five years, separated them while she sought a cure away from England and grew steadily worse, more lonely, more terrified, more demanding of his love. The few happy times were spent when he could join her briefly in the south of France, in Italy, in Switzerland.

After George Borden divorced her in 1918, Katherine returned to London seriously ill. On May 3 she and Murry were married at the registry office though, as she wrote from Cornwall to which six weeks later she had fled, it was but part of the nightmare: "You never once held me in your arms and called me your wife." Murry replied, "My soul was struck dumb with terror at your illness." In her devouring need of him, she bitterly resented his ability to live without her, his passivity, his unwillingness to touch her. She accused him of wanting to be rid of her. He could only protest, "When I see you sick & ailing, I die." Close to nervous collapse himself, he wrote, "I'm a mean little sneak, but it can't be helped."

Early in 1919 Murry became editor of the *Athenaeum* and prospered, while Katherine went to stay on the Italian Riviera, this time accompanied by her faithful friend Ida Baker. His unfeeling letters enraged her by their hurried tone, obtuseness, self-absorption, self-pity. She wrote of spitting blood and he wrote of being constipated, "no figs that's what it is." He called her "old girl" and issued daily bulletins on their cats. Yet at the same time he was hunting a dream house to buy for her, where he promised they might settle down in peace and love and have babies.

Worn by reunions and separations, as her new husband death beckoned (and Murry's anguish mounted with a sense of guilt at having failed her), in October 1922 Katherine left suddenly for Fontainebleau and wired her farewell. She had lost faith in Murry and her doctors. She sought the spiritual cure offered by the mystic healer and occultist Gurdjieff, a step Murry couldn't understand or condone. Communication all but ceased between them. When on January 5, 1923, Katherine sent for him ("I hope you will decide to come, my dearest"), Murry, overjoyed to be asked, arrived four days later at the colony in Fontainebleau, Gurdjieff's Institute for the Harmonious Development of Man. They spent a happy afternoon about which Murry revealed, "She told me she had felt that her love for me had had to die . . . but now at last, she said, 'My love for you has all come back to me, greater than ever.' " At ten o'clock that night, while climbing the stairs with him to her room, she had a violent hemorrhage and died. Murry was thirty-three with half his life over. He was to have three more wives.

His letters, placed beside Katherine's, become eloquent of his side of the story. By their admissions they portray a weak man, indecisive and afraid, who might have given more of himself, might have prolonged Katherine's life by staying at her side. But he wasn't like that. In his inadequate way he was loyal and persistently loving, with an unfailing belief in her as a writer, encouraging till she cried, "Do not overpraise me." After the often tormented years as her lover, he chose to marry her when, had he been the coward he was called, he might have refused. Katherine, for her part, chose him again and again, always for love.

I met Middleton Murry one night in the 1930s at Brown House on the uptown campus of New York University, when the English Department that occupied President Brown's former mansion invited him to come to the small front parlor and tell us about Katherine Mansfield. She had been dead ten years, and Murry was on an extended lecture tour in America. We considered him no great shakes as a visiting celebrity except as the husband of a writer everyone knew and liked.

Murry was a little man in a dark suit, black-haired and spectacled, whose voice, I remember, was small and nonassertive. He spoke for an hour in praise of her writing. But of Katherine the person, her life with him and without him, her struggle to stay alive so poignantly revealed in her letters and journals, he had no words. It was impossible to think of this small, reserved Englishman as a stormy lover or a stricken one. "I'm a very dull dog," he had told her. It was hard to believe he had known her intimately or at all.

Afterward, when I stood beside him in the crowded room and tried to thank him, he shrugged and turned away, saying, "It's what you asked for." My impression of Middleton Murry that night was to wish for her sake she had been luckier.

Janet 'Frame's Story. In her autobiography *To the Is-Land,* the New Zealand writer Janet Frame makes a map of her childhood to discover where it went. It went from Dunedin, where she was born in 1924, to the small town of Oamaru on South Island. Her strict father, George, was a railway engineer who played the bagpipes. Her mother, Lottie, a former housemaid in Katherine Mansfield's home in Wellington, wrote poems and sold them from door to door. Janet's red hair rose in a tangle from her head; she had freckles, shabby clothes that affirmed her poverty, and she had "tics and terrors." In spite of quarrels and Dad's thrashings, the family was a closely knit one from which Janet grew apart, angered by her mother's unfathomable serenity. Her brother Bruddie, an epileptic, suffered violent rages brought on by his father's mockery. When Janet was thirteen, her sister Myrtle, a strong swimmer, was found drowned in the Oamaru Public Baths. "At first I was glad, thinking there'd be no more quarrels, cryings, thrashings, with Dad trying to control her and us listening frightened, pitying, and crying, too." The years ahead in high school were cruel. Clad in her patched school tunic, without friends, she felt a desolation that she had no words for.

Volume two, *An Angel at My Table,* begins with a lonely troubled girl traveling to the city of Dunedin, where at nineteen she was to enter the Teachers' Training College. As the train approached the town of Seacliff, she caught a glimpse of the "loony" asylum, like a dark castle between two hills. "We had no loonies in our family," she reflected, unaware how soon she would be committed to that stark community of the insane.

At Dunedin she stayed in a tiny cottage with Aunty Isy and her husband, Uncle George, who lay upstairs dying of cancer. So timid Janet was, too shy to sit with her aunt at the table, she ate alone in the scullery.

Matters grew worse when her younger sister Isabel arrived to enter the college and share a room with Janet at Aunty Isy's. Made of sterner stuff, Isabel rebelled, complained of being starved and frozen, acquired a boyfriend, went generally wild till, in the final explosion, Aunty Isy ordered them both to move. Separated from Isabel, ashamed and rejected, Janet was more than ever alone.

After two unhappy years she was to spend a probationary year teaching the second grade at Arthur Street School, Dunedin. All went well till the day the inspector entered her class unannounced to pass on her qualification. Murmuring an excuse, Janet fled in panic from the room out of the school, never to return. Her despair at another failure of courage led her to attempt suicide by swallowing a packet of aspirin, sure she would die. Instead, she found a job washing dishes in the cafeteria at the University. To a psychology professor, whose course she enrolled in, she confided in writing, "Perhaps I should mention a recent attempt at suicide," and found herself whisked off to the Dunedin hospital, confined to a psychiatric ward. When her mother came to take her home, Janet screamed at her to go away and her mother left saying, "But she's such a happy person." They sent her to Seacliff, the "loony" asylum, where, without tests, she was diagnosed as schizophrenic and declared officially insane.

For eight years she was in and out of mental hospitals, given some two hundred shock treatments that were like executions, put on probation for brief periods during which she worked in hotels as maid or waitress. From them she would escape by committing herself to another hospital, at Christchurch, at Auckland, where "the squalor and inhumanity were almost indescribable." The tragedy of Isabel's death by drowning, repeating Myrtle's death ten years earlier, led Janet to the edge of madness. Nothing was left but the obsessive need to write; and writing saved her life. Just as she was to undergo a lobotomy, the superintendent of the hospital, impressed by a newspaper account of an award Janet had won, had her discharged and sent home. But she had become a nonperson.

This was 1954, Janet was thirty. When the New Zealand writer Frank Sargeson, who seemed to her an old man in old clothes, offered her an army hut in his Auckland garden, she stayed with him for eighteen months and wrote the novel *Owls Do Cry,* whose narrator is a patient in a mental hospital. It brought her a grant to travel, but before she could leave the country her sanity was investigated; the conclusion was reached that eight years of her life had been senselessly lost. From there she had to find her way alone.

About angels. A question to ask Janet Frame is the meaning of her title taken from Rilke, *An Angel at My Table:* how to interpret Rilke's symbol. Angels appear and vanish throughout his poetry—from the early songs to the late French poems to the "Duino Elegies"—as either a guardian angel, a creative spirit of the imagination, or a terrible apparition of a higher reality, close to God. "Who are the angels?" the second elegy begins. "Every angel is terrible" (which seems to be her meaning), since in our ordinary mortal world we are aware of our need of these beings from a world beyond our reach. The angel at our table appears but momently, leaving behind his presence. As Rilke says,

> This imperceptible exchange
> that makes us tremble
> becomes the inheritance of an angel
> without belonging to us.

Are angels visible only to poets?

Blake saw a tree full of angels in Peckham Rye. Emily Dickinson said, "Angels rent the house next ours." Wallace Stevens knew one who paid visits (though in "Evening without Angels" he asks why you and I need seraphim when "bare night is best. Bare earth is best. Bare, bare"). In his "Angel Surrounded by Paysans," we peasants welcome the angel at our door, not easily recognized since he wears no white wings, gold crown, or lukewarm halo. A figure half seen, he is the necessary angel of this earth in whose sight we see the earth freed of its dreary "man-locked" appearance. For a moment he is there, and instantly vanishing leaves behind his radiance.

I'm still waiting for a visit. Only demons so far, though in 1989 Pope John Paul II announced that angels do exist. ("Now I will believe that there are unicorns" — *The Tempest*)

Two Accounts. Two autobiographies that include each other in their story are Ingmar Bergman's recent narrative of his life, *The Magic Lantern,* and Liv Ullmann's tale of her life with him, titled *Changing.* Together they show how useful it is to write about yourself, if only to give someone else your version of what happened.

When Bergman read Liv Ullmann's account of their consuming love affair, they had been separated for years. Now he learned for the first time her view of the relationship. They had met and fallen in love in 1966 when Bergman was filming his twenty-sixth picture, *Persona* (in which Liv Ullmann was cast with Bibi Andersson), a tale of two women and their withdrawal to a distant shore and identification with each other. Bergman made the film one summer the three of them spent on location at Fårö, a bleak, rocky island off Sweden in the Baltic Sea. The look of it so greatly appealed to him as his own choice of landscape that he hastened to buy land there and build a house for Liv and him, and for their child born the following spring.

In her autobiography Liv says she wanted to write of this "encounter on an island. A man who changed my life." She describes the island of Fårö that, except for a brief flowering in the summer, was nothing but stunted trees, sheep, rocks, wind, and bitter cold. For Bergman, Fårö was a safe retreat. For Liv it was a prison, more barren and lonely than any place she had known. After five years of it, the day came when she gathered up her daughter and fled.

In his autobiography Bergman writes of their love affair in words less emotional than hers, terse and matter-of-fact: "During the filming of *Persona,* Liv and I were overwhelmed by passion. With monumental lack of judgment, I built the house with the idea of a mutual existence on the island. I forgot to ask Liv what she thought. I managed to find out later from her book *Changing.* On the whole her testimony is, I think, affectionately correct. She stayed for a few years. We fought our demons as best we could."

Elsewhere he lists his demons: desire, torment, guilt, anxiety, fear, and rage. Liv calls hers bitterness, hate, loneliness, despair. She writes, "No one could be as angry as Ingmar. Possibly I."

Only when the affair was over did they become friends. In 1975, after playing Nora in a New York production of *A Doll's House,* Liv went back to Sweden to work with him on the film *Face to Face,* a searing tale of dream and reality in which she has a complete breakdown and tries to commit suicide. To be with Ingmar brought her stretches of happiness, and though they clashed and quarreled he told her, "I could never have made this film without you." In her diary she wrote, "I knew that I could never leave him, and in a way I never have."

By now Liv must have read his book, the autobiography that accords her so small a space, so brief a period of his life. It reveals a difficult abrasive man, who from an unhappy childhood in a Lutheran parsonage has lived in the midst of commotion, self-conflict, and pain. His first love was always the theater ("a powerfully erotic business") and the making of films that were the signature of himself, often wounding pictures from his life—*Scenes from a Marriage, Fanny and Alexander* of the boy that is Ingmar. As a man of strong sexuality, he was almost as wholly involved with women, from one tortured marriage or relationship to another till he acquired many wives, many children, many problems. At one period in his impoverished thirties, he was trying to support three families at once: his first wife, Else, and their daughter; his wife at the time, Ellen, and their four children; his mistress, Gun, who was already pregnant. After he married and divorced Gun, whose son was Ingmar; after an affair with Harriet and one with Bibi Andersson, Liv's friend; after marriage to Kabi, a concert pianist, whose son was Daniel—then came Liv and their daughter Linn, Bergman's eighth and last child.

His fifth and last wife, Ingrid, lives with him on the island of Fårö, where Liv visited them one summer when Linn was to spend a holiday with her father and his new wife. Liv writes of the moment of arrival:

"Ingrid, the wife, stands in the doorway. She is tan and happy." Liv notes that nothing is changed, Ingrid hasn't even rearranged the furniture. She adds, "I like her for that. She has not tried to remove me from this place. Ingmar is here."

Writers at Work. Diane Ackerman has an interesting essay in the *New York Times Book Review* on the work habits of writers—how Amy Lowell and George Sand smoked cigars to make them creative, how Colette began the day by picking fleas from her cat. I too like to know the facts about writers and their habits, whether Virginia Woolf wrote standing up, Victor Hugo wrote naked, or Benjamin Franklin wrote while soaking in a bathtub. Like Miss Ackerman I've spent hours of my life in such research and can help her out as to the number of cups of tea Dr. Johnson drank at a sitting. She says twenty-five. Robert Louis Stevenson in "Aes Triplex" said he "didn't recoil before twenty-seven individual cups of tea." Johnson wasn't being literary at teatime but sociable with an unquenchable thirst and staying power. He described himself as "a hardened and shameless tea-drinker . . . who with tea amuses the evening, with tea solaces the midnight, and with tea welcomes the morning." Mrs. Thrale, as his hostess, had a teapot that held three quarts.

Miss Ackerman writes of Wordsworth as a walker who got his inspiration from walking, but she omits the statistics. DeQuincy calculated that by middle age Wordsworth had walked 180,000 miles and concluded he must have lived a life of unclouded happiness. With Dorothy at his side he composed aloud while walking, once muttering the whole of "Tintern Abbey." The neighbors called it his booing about.

A while ago, I reviewed a book by Phyllis Bartlett, *Poems in Process,* in which she asks, "How do poets get their thoughts on paper?" She had gone through diaries, letters, biographies to track down their work habits, seeking to pinpoint the seasons, the weather, the time of day, the place, the conditions, and the state of mind that affected poets most. What I learned, if I didn't know already, was that getting down to work was the worst part. Rilke said, "I feel that to work is to live without dying," then delayed the moment to begin. It was a life, he said, full of abysses.

Wine or gin often helped. And prayer. A seasonal urge led Milton to write in winter, Keats in spring, Burns autumn, Shelley the summer months. Schiller needed the smell of rotten apples to get him going. Coleridge told Southey, "When a man is unhappy, he writes damned bad poetry, I find."

As for the prose writers, they're notional too. Jane Austen wrote in the family parlor, Montaigne in a tower, Cervantes in prison. Proust built a cork-lined room to escape distraction. Willa Cather read the Bible. Colette would write only on blue paper, by artificial light, and in her bare feet. She refused to take an aspirin lest it dim her mind. So far as I know such dithering about makes little difference—whether a person writes in a gazebo or cupola, lying on a sofa or standing on his head. Yet my choice of work habits would be to avoid at all cost writing like George Sand, a great scribbler of 109 volumes, who kept at it ten hours at a stretch without pause, erasure, or nourishment, and sent the manuscript off to the printer without reading it over. She would finish one novel and, damn the torpedoes, start another in the same hour, though she said, "I write as others might do gardening." Flaubert, on the contrary, sat all day with his head in his hands, waiting for the right word.

The real problem, of course, is how to account for the need to write at all, especially when nobody asked you to.

Being a Writer. Gertrude Stein tried to rid herself of nouns, as she explained in "How Writing Is Written," which at showing how not to she was better than anybody. Years ago I vowed never to try prose, finding verse risk enough. Prose would spill out horizontally and multiply, and it does. Words are tricksters and contrivances I spend my life removing (Jules Renard: "I am afflicted with prose the way I was once afflicted with verse. When this is over, in what shall I write?").

Somehow a writer is always out of luck, an easy target if not a victim. Max Frisch, the Swiss novelist, knew the self-exposure involved in writing anything, the price a writer pays:

> Yesterday morning in the Odeon [a Berlin café] I heard someone at a neighboring table mention my name. I was aware that the man, who does

not know me, spoke my name in a tone of real hatred — not just contempt but hatred. Should I have introduced myself? I did not do that, but paid my bill, took up my coat and left. Often enough one hates oneself. All the same, I have to admit that I am upset when I see this hatred in someone else, a stranger. . . . There is no argument against hatred. — *Sketchbook, 1946–49*

In Frisch's later *Sketchbook, 1966–71,* that painful incident was still heavy on his mind — the memory of finding himself hated without apparent reason. "If I had now to draw up a balance," he wrote, "there is nobody at the moment whom I hate." "But do you *love* anybody?" he asked himself. "Only when one loves can one bear it." And he quoted Brecht's poem "To Posterity": "Alas, we who wished to lay the foundation of kindness / Could not ourselves be kind."

He made a list of twenty-six things he loved and was thankful for, among them:

his mother
having children of his own
his meeting with Bertolt Brecht
all women, "yes, on the whole, all of them"
a bad memory for his errors and omissions
the fact that ambition declines
his passport

(My own list is the same if you substitute Bertrand Russell for Brecht, and all men, of course, for women.)

To Frisch there was no difference between living and writing about it, concerned as he became with determining the kind of man he was — certainly not the man people took him for. In his most searching novel, *I'm Not Stiller,* he considers the character of Stiller, who denies he is the self he's said to be, is accused of being.

To Frisch writing was the same as breathing, neither one an "undiluted pleasure." But in the summer of 1990 when he learned that he had a terminal illness, he stopped short because now there was nothing to say.

Death is not lived through, no way has been found to describe it, "and I don't want to do it either."

Writing Charley Smith's Girl. When my book *Charley Smith's Girl* was published in 1965, my editor Henry Simon thought it would make a good movie. To him Charley was a purely fictional character, Goodtime Charley, a card, a man larger than life and sometimes funnier. Without telling me, Henry sent the book to a film producer he knew in Hollywood and almost got it accepted. The answer came back they were interested—Charley was a character full of moxie, but the story needed elaborating to show him off, the wilder the better. If the author would consider giving him more to do, there was a chance Charley might be developed into, say, another W. C. Fields.

The idea was alarming. "No way," I wrote Henry. "No way!" I had told the truth about Charley, the little I knew of him. I wouldn't want him laughed at (though in a way he was like W. C. Fields or Pagliacci, part funny man, part incurably depressed by the world and everybody in it). I couldn't have invented him, I wouldn't make up lies about him now. Besides, I was Charley's girl; it was of my father and me I had written— Charley who left my mother when I was two and never came back. I grew up without him, though by the time I had to write about it, I knew how greatly I resembled him, how much I belonged to him. By then Charley was dead. I wanted to state the facts. And the thing I remembered and loved most about him was his laughter.

Had I written a novel instead, same cast of characters, it would have been fiction, invented, imagined, untrue. It wouldn't have been Charley. Like any autobiographical novel it would have a shape of its own. (One such novelist said recently in an interview, "I needed a sibling. So I invented Freddie.") God only knows what liberties one takes in creating one's life.

I remember Nancy Hale's mother reading Nancy's autobiography, *A New England Girlhood,* and asking in bewilderment, "Damask napkins? Why ever did you write about damask napkins?"

"Because I like damask napkins," Nancy said.

"But we never had such a thing in our house."

I remember hearing Peter Taylor read his short story "Demons" that had to do with the voices he heard as a child of seven. One voice was their black cook saying, as he sat on the toilet, "Are you going to sit on that Christmas tree all day?" One said, "Ruins. Ruins." Another said, "There is no one god. And there was no beginning and there will be no end." Peter claimed that the voices he heard are heard by all children. I asked him about it afterward, if he meant these memories to be true, or if it was the story that mattered. He said instantly, "It's always the story that matters." He was a storyteller.

Henry Simon assumed *Charley Smith's Girl* was a story. But in writing about myself, though I found, like Montaigne, the subject barren and thin, I didn't make it up, for one thing lacking the imagination. Even as a bookish child I was not fanciful. I never lived in a dream world or believed in hell or Santa Claus (who couldn't in any case have squeezed down our stovepipe). I never gave my dolls names; my mother had to name my cat, Moses Dudley (for a black man she knew in the South). I never told myself stories. I never heard voices.

"Let's pretend," my playmate Alice used to say.

"Pretend like we're girls," I would agree.

From the start I was looking for one thing: the reality, the way things are, or as Wallace Stevens said, "Nothing beyond reality. Within it everything." I was writing for the reason Robert Lowell gave in his next to last poem "Epilogue." All that he wrote, Lowell said, was paralyzed by fact. All was misalliance, all was mistaken, "yet why not say what happened?" He prayed for the grace of accuracy.

Since it was fact I was after, to his words I added, "and nothing to be gained by never saying."

Three Poets. My students used to say after poetry class, "But how can you possibly believe them *all?*" I wondered myself.

One poet was Gerard Manley Hopkins, a Jesuit priest who wrote with an overwhelming sense of God manifest in all things. He looked at the visible proof: the dappled skies, the azure-hung hills, the shining earth, and everywhere he saw a God-lit, God-centered world. "Look at the stars!" he cried, "look, look up at the skies!" On an autumn day he lifted his eyes to the silk-sack clouds and the wind-walks, half hurled off his feet by the glory of it. In the light of the world that was God, the answer was always the same: "He fathers-forth whose beauty is past change: Praise him."

But near the end of Hopkins's life, in the last five years, he who had known the ecstasy knew the terror. He had lost God. And the light went out, there was only the pitch dark. He had failed, he was forsaken, given a taste of damnation; God had turned his back and abandoned him. With this judgment upon him Hopkins wrote the six terrible sonnets, poems of desolation, panic at God's wrath and the loss of the light: "I wake and feel the fell of dark, not day, / What hours, O what black hours we have spent / This night!" A night that was eternity.

"No worst," he said, "there is none."

Wallace Stevens, too, saw the light of the world lit by the sun and graciously apparent. But the sun was not God. ("To my way of thinking, the idea of God is an instance of benign illusion.") In his poem of an unbeliever, "Sunday Morning," this was the sun's day, the source of light and life. His faith was the faith of men who are mortal and perish: "We live in an old chaos of the sun, / Or old dependency of day and night, / Or island solitude, unsponsored, free." Divinity, he said, must live within oneself, in an awareness of the changing seasons, "passions of rain, or moods in falling snow," in the transient grievings and elations of existence.

For to be free was to live unaided, without superstition or myth in a devotion to the sun that was "not as a god but as a god might be." Begin, he said, by perceiving "the inconceivable idea of the sun."

"Of course," Stevens said, "Eliot and I are dead opposites." Stevens was no wasteland poet. Eliot said, "I will show you fear in a handful of dust." He called the world a sunless place, a desert made up of Prufrocks and Sweeneys who exist in a hell of boredom and loneliness where love has failed. Like them you and I live our empty, defeated lives, and the only answer we hear is Sweeney's: "Birth, and copulation, and death, that's all, that's all, that's all, that's all."

To escape the wasteland, the cactus land, Eliot showed the way, or his way—one of suffering, penitence, ordeal—that led through the dark night of the soul out of the hell of *The Waste Land* through the purgatory of *Ash Wednesday* to the end of the journey, the *Four Quartets,* and the light of the garden where love is, "and the fire and the rose are one."

It was Eliot's *Divine Comedy.* It was the way Dante took in 1300, early one morning on the Thursday before Easter, when (he began) "Midway in the journey of my life, I found me in a dark wood where the right way was lost." It was the start of Dante's struggling climb from hell, the *Inferno,* up the penitential mountain of the *Purgatorio* to reach the *Paradiso* where "all my will was moved by love" in the garden of the multifoliate rose and the light of God.

But the worlds of Hopkins, Eliot, Stevens—these three—only prove that a real poet defines a world entirely his own, each different from the rest. He makes a region for his words to inhabit, a country of the mind, a climate, a scene visible to him and to me. And the greater the poet, the braver is that world: Chaucer's world, Dante's hell, Milton's paradise. Unless he creates one for himself (as Auden did not, as Ezra Pound did not), his signature lacks a clear identity.

After class the students would ask, "Which do you really believe?"—as if you had to choose one and only one, either of faith or unfaith. "I believe them all three," I said. "Each man described the world *as it looked to him.*"

What more can a poet say?

Anecdote of the Jar

I placed a jar in Tennessee,
And round it was, upon a hill.
It made the slovenly wilderness
Surround that hill.

The wilderness rose up to it,
And sprawled around, no longer wild.
The jar was round upon the ground
And tall and of a port in air.

It took dominion everywhere.
The jar was gray and bare.
It did not give of bird or bush,
Like nothing else in Tennessee. — Wallace Stevens

This simple anecdote tells what man can do to create order in the world. In it, "I," the artificer, has placed a small, ordinary jar on a hill in Tennessee, and the jar has imposed a necessary order on a chaotic landscape. It has tamed the sprawling wilderness and, by being round, made it surround the hill. Stevens's jar is plain and gray and bare but possesses authority, an air of command. Like Keats's Grecian urn, it is still but speaks; like Eliot's Chinese jar, it is still but moves. It has pattern and shape, a symmetry made by human hands that, by its presence, holds in check the wild disorder of nature. It alone defines the scene as no bird or bush belonging to the natural world can do.

Stevens, a man with a rage for order, a connoisseur of chaos, might well have said, "I placed a poem in Tennessee" — this plain, gray, bare poem. And it did the same thing. It took dominion everywhere.

Self-Portraits. To leaf through a volume of *Five Hundred Self-Portraits* is like reading autobiography — the artist narrated by himself. With mirror in hand to do himself justice, he appears in fancy dress: Dürer as Christ, Whistler astrut, Dante Gabriel Rossetti the perfect Pre-Raphaelite, Modigliani an elogante Pierrot. Inquiring, "Who am I?" he is Sir Joshua Reynolds shading his eyes to look; he is Chardin with glasses perched on the end of his nose; Hogarth posed with pug dog Trump and the volumes of Shakespeare, Milton, and Swift; Ingres in youth and age; Monet behind a white beard; van Gogh with one ear. Each gives a powerful sense of the artist alive before his canvas.

Rembrandt painted ninety-seven portraits of himself, the first at twenty-two with tousled curly hair and round inquiring eyes; the last in 1669, the year he died at sixty-three. They are full face, grave, unsmiling (how tiresome to pose with a perpetual grin on one's face). He wears large dashing hats or small cushiony caps, is adorned with gold chains or a single earring. Only once is he joyous, a cavalier in a plumed hat with Saskia on his knee.

Misfortune aged him. Saskia died in 1642 after bearing four children, three of whom died in infancy, his son Titus as a youth. Rembrandt had a child by his servant Hendrickje that caused public scandal. In the evil days that followed he found himself a ruined man, stripped of possessions including friends. Still he painted self-portraits, defining who he was. The face has grown battered, the wrinkles deepen round his tired eyes and bulbous nose. The look is stolid, not confessing his faults or denying them, though twice he portrayed himself in scenes from the death of Christ as one sharing the guilt. In the *Elevation* he is a soldier struggling to erect the cross. In *Descent from the Cross* he stands on a ladder next to the hand of the dead Christ.

The obsession with recording themselves—Rembrandt, van Gogh, Goya, Picasso, Cezanne—reminds me of Montaigne, whose endless study was himself. Montaigne said he would gladly paint his portrait full-length "entire and wholly naked." Yeats found more enterprise in walking naked; Robert Lowell exposed himself "naked in a raincoat"; Theodore Roethke cried, "I'm naked to the bone," though few painters go that far baring all. Mondrian in shame shot his portrait full of holes. Suzanne Valedon painted herself in a bitter likeness, one of self-hatred. Georgia O'Keeffe said, "I find that I have painted my life without knowing"—but does she mean this is O'Keeffe in pictures of clam shells and jimsonweed that resemble a vulva? In her *Pelvis with Moon*?

A writer is naturally a self-portrait painter. Unlike the artist he can start at the outset, with birth and mewling infancy—as his beginnings were drawn by Richard Steele: "I was bred by hand, and ate nothing but milk till I was a twelvemonth old; from which time I was observed to delight in pudding and potatoes." Steele grew in size to become "all width and no length." The painter at his easel could take the portrait from there.

"The mirror above all," said Leonardo, "the mirror is our teacher." Some critics think the *Mona Lisa* is a self-portrait, resembling the one he painted as a wrinkled, white-haired old man—a mirror image of Leonardo's enigmatic Gioconda smile.

How Would You Paint This Portrait?

By nature concupiscible but mild,
He was safe and sound, a square with rounded corners,
A brow not high, not low, of middling size—
The tenor of whose ways was always even,
Whose soul was naked while his well-dressed mind
And well-shod foot moved confidently forward,
Whose best was level and whose edge unfrayed,
A vapor of a man, an ablative person,
Though not, I think, an ablative absolute.

Self-portrait by Henry James: "I look as if I had swallowed a wasp." Whitman: "I go bathe and admire myself." John Ashbery, "Self-Portrait in a Convex Mirror": "the face / Riding at anchor."

My own portrait: "Je suis un pot cassé" (Psalms 31:12).

The Face Painter. It must be his name—Gainsborough—that seems to fit a painter of imposing dignity and elegance. He was said to be tall, fair, and handsome. But a new biography by Jack Lindsay shows him up as a good-natured rebel and carouser, a pursuer as he admitted of "fool's pleasures," a hard drinker and womanizer, fond of whores, actors, and tavern keepers. Literary men were his aversion. He detested reading books.

Gainsborough called himself a "face painter" and cursed the drudgery of the "face business" by which he made a living. The need to paint the rich and famous in their finery angered him; he had no taste for the fashionable society of Bath and London, though among his sitters were the Duchess of Devonshire and the exquisite Mrs. Perdita Robinson who was adored by the Prince of Wales. He was a master of portraiture. And the ladies he scorned were, in eight hundred portraits, delicate, fragile creatures in silks and satins to whom he gave grace and felicity; the men tall, well-bred, distinguished aristocrats. They said he produced strikingly exact likenesses that were character studies as well, yet to very few did he trouble to add his signature. Among them were the most famous figures of his time: Richardson, Sterne, Garrick, Sheridan, Mrs. Siddons, Burke, Dr. Johnson.

Above all he wanted to paint landscapes, for which there was no market. His own were stacked in his studio, unsold, though like Turner and Constable he was a great landscape painter, a watcher of the skies. The English countryside represented a way of life he loved. Sick of fine portraits and their sitters, even the immortal *Blue Boy* (who was an ironmonger's son), he yearned to "walk off to some sweet village where I can paint landscapes," and people them with simple country figures—shepherd boys, the *Peasant Girl Gathering Sticks,* the *Cottage Girl with a Bowl of Milk.* His skies to match, said one critic, were "rich with fervid clouds."

Both Gainsborough and Constable were from Suffolk, a half-century apart. While sketching in Suffolk Constable wrote, "I fancy I see Gainsborough in every hedge and hollow tree."

Light Verse. Bill Harmon gave me a volume he has edited, *The Oxford Book of American Light Verse,* without saying what light verse really is beyond a collection of nonsense verse, parodies, flytings, limericks, vers de société, burlesques, nursery rhymes, ditties, doggerel, puns, jingles, graffiti, and tin-eared poems.

In *A Bowl of Bishop,* Morris Bishop, practitioner, provided a definition of light verse as a mid-form between sober and comic, between playful and sublime. John Donne wrote light verse in "Go and Catch a Falling Star" and poetry in "The Ecstasy." You find it in the Greek Anthology, in Horace, Chaucer, Skelton, Shakespeare, Herrick, Marvell, Byron, Burns, Yeats, Auden, Frost. When real poets write it you say it's poetry, except when T. S. Eliot makes up rhymes about cats.

Light verse is deft, aiming at lightwit. It is a way of looking and a way of saying, its concern less with trivia than with love and taxes. It observes people irreverently with laughter oftener than tears, witty about woe, as in Frances Cornford's

> O why do you walk through the fields in gloves,
> Missing so much and so much?
> O fat white woman whom nobody loves,

though Sylvia Plath defined her terrifying poem "Daddy" in childish singsong as light verse, and Dorothy Parker neatly listed the ways to commit suicide: "Guns aren't lawful, / Nooses give, / Gas smells awful, / You might as well live." Robert Lowell was contemptuous of it, scorning to contribute to the *New Yorker* because "some of their poetry is light verse." John Updike says coolly, "I write no light verse now . . . light verse died," and purges his own of rhyme and meter, settling for very flat prose, as in "Living with a Wife,"

> it [life] stays as unaccountable
> as the underpants set to soak
> in the bowl where I brush my teeth.

Light verse is Robert Herrick saying

> Tumble me down, and I will sit
> Upon my ruins (smiling yet).

It is John Donne making love "To his mistress going to bed,"

> License my roving hands, and let them go,
> Before, behind, between, above, below,
> O my America! my newfoundland,
> My kingdome, safeliest when with one man man'd,
> My myne of precious stones, my emperie,
> How blest am I in this discovering thee!

To enter in these bonds is to be free;
Then where my hand is set, my seal shall be.

In our time it is E. B. White (the last of the light versifiers) on the mystery of love:

Animal love is the marvelous force
Marsupials take as a matter of course;
You find it in Aryan, Mongol, Norse,
In beetle, tarantula, ostrich, horse;
It creeps in the grasses and blows in the gorse,
It's something all sponges were bound to endorse —
And only in humans it causes remorse.

"I like the poetic gait," Montaigne said, "by leaps and gambols" — the light fantastic, *à sauts et à gambades.*

Saint Cecilia and Alexander the Great. Dryden's famous "Ode to St. Cecilia's Day" seems to me splendid, boisterous light verse, comic too. In David Daiches's opinion, "It is fine verbal fireworks, but in the last analysis rather cheap stuff." Mark Van Doren called it "immortal ragtime." Dryden himself was greatly relieved when all the town declared it the best of his poetry, written, Dryden said, when he was an old man of sixty-six and thought it the best but, being old, "mistrusted my own judgment."

His odd choice was to bring St. Cecilia into it. She was a Christian martyr put to death in Rome in the second century and venerated for a thousand years. According to legend, she vowed her virginity to God and inspired the love of an angel. In Dryden's time on St. Cecilia's day, November 22, a festival was held during which an original ode set to music was performed in her honor. Dryden wrote two odes to St. Cecilia to praise her purity and the power of music. In the second more famous one, 1697, better known as "Alexander's Feast," he was stirred by an event that scarcely added luster to her memory.

The tale of Alexander the Great celebrates his conquest of Persia at a royal banquet—a godlike hero "aloft in awful state" seated on his new throne with Thaïs at his side, the Athenian courtesan who had accompanied him to Asia. Alexander, far gone in wine, drunken and riotous, was decked out in a garland of roses and myrtle round his head, leering at his mistress with Dryden's full approval,

> Happy, happy, happy pair!
> > None but the brave,
> > None but the brave,
> None but the brave deserves the fair.

As the orgy increased in tempo, Alexander grew vain in his pride and fought his battles over again, weeping maudlin tears as "thrice he slew the slain." And greater his passion grew each time he looked upon Thaïs, who sat like a blooming Eastern bride beside him, till vanquished by love and wine he sank upon her breast and "stamped an image of himself," then fell into a drunken slumber. Jarred suddenly awake by cries of "Revenge, revenge!" from his followers, Alexander sprang up, seized a flaming torch and, led by Thaïs eager for her own revenge against the Persians, staggered off to set fire to Persepolis.

Unaware, of course, of these secular antics—such rage and such lust— "at last divine Cecilia came" (that would be four centuries later from Rome), and unlike old Timotheus, Alexander's musician who had sung to the lyre and roused him to these excesses, she sat quietly down to play a little organ music.

In the *Canterbury Tales,* Chaucer told the tale of Saint Cecilia more soberly, giving it to the Second Nun to relate the Christian legend: how this "maide and martyr" beseeched God "to kepe hir maydenhede," and was tortured and put to death by a Roman magistrate.

Married against her will to Valerian, a pagan, on her wedding night Cecilia cried out, "O sweet and beloved spouse, I have an angel that loves me and if you touch me he will slay you," to which Valerian replied, "Let me see that angel. If he is a real angel I will do as you ask." But first he had to be baptized a Christian by Pope Urban I himself, after which the angel came to stand beside Cecilia, holding crowns for them both of roses and lilies from heaven. Valerian not only promised to leave his wife a virgin but persuaded his brother to become a Christian too and be baptized by the pope.

When shortly the brothers were arrested and beheaded for their crime, the Roman prefect Almachius said to Cecilia, "What manner of woman are you?" and ordered her put into a bath where she sat over red flames a night and a day, sweating not a drop. Such defiance provoked Almachius into sending for a torturer, who hit her with an ax three times and all but beheaded her. For three days Cecilia lived in agony and died without once having heard of Alexander the Great.

Persepolis was burned twenty-three centuries ago. Plutarch says Alexander soon repented setting fire to what was now his palace and Persia his kingdom, the mightiest empire on earth. Seven years after that famous feast, having married a Persian princess, in 323 B.C. he died at not yet thirty-three and was buried in a gold coffin. He had sought glory in conquest and never lost a battle. What he wanted was the world.

Thaïs prospered also as the mistress of the king of Egypt, the first Ptolemy, who had been one of Alexander's generals. As his faithful wife, she bore him seven children.

Nice Poets. Anthony Hecht reminds me to be on the lookout for nice poets. In an essay in the *New York Times Book Review,* he says that contemporary poets are an unpleasant lot, with bad manners and nothing to say, naming a few exceptions all dead: Elizabeth Bishop, Marianne Moore, Conrad Aiken. "I believe there are a few nice poets still alive and writing, but they are in the distinct minority." That's a new criterion: never ask if a poet is any good, only if he's nice or not nice.

Back in the 1970s, when I used to complain to my students about the fallen state of poetry, it still passed as indispensable, having to do,

Wallace Stevens said, with self-preservation. It still was distinguishable from prose. A dozen years later a reviewer in the *Times Literary Supplement* was saying favorably of D. J. Enright's poems, "Enright is anxious to keep poetry out of his poetry." The critic Geoffrey Grigson was counting on his fingers how many poets were left since the deaths of Yeats and Eliot: "no major poets, no good poets at all, perhaps only six middling poets worth attending to, and forty or fifty bad poets who must be called inept, tedious, silly, pretentious, unintelligible." In spite of his outcry, the *TLS* went right on printing bad poems, some of which reminded me of Brecht's *Baal* where the poet compares life to a privy, as in these opening lines: "Groping back to bed after a piss," by Philip Larkin; James Simmons's "One night I strode from you to ease my bowels"; William Empson's "And now she cleans her teeth into the lake."

Eileen Simpson's memoir, *Poets in Their Youth,* found modern poets anything but nice in the way they lived and the way they bowed out. As the former wife of John Berryman she knew them well, some of the likeliest, when they flourished in ferocious competition, quarrels, discord—Berryman, Robert Lowell, Randall Jarrell, Theodore Roethke, Delmore Schwartz—a generation of poets now dead, all casualties, whose lives ended tragically in alcoholism, madness, despair, suicide. Lowell thought there was a curse on his generation. Berryman found "something evil stalking us poets."

This is an old complaint. In 1606 the Elizabethan Barnabe Rich got after the poets in a book titled *Faultes, Faultes, and Nothing Else but Faultes.* "We have such a number of Bastard Poets in these days," he said. "Some will write a whole volume neither in rime nor reason." He called it a lame halting age of rude limping lines—the age of Shakespeare, Spenser, Sir Philip Sidney, Marlowe, Ben Jonson, Campion, the young John Donne.

Possibly Barnabe Rich had the poet Barnabe Barnes on his mind, who published in 1593, as was the fashion, a collection of love sonnets. In one sonnet Barnes is so carried away that he wishes he could be dissolved in his mistress's drinking glass, travel to her heart, and emerge once more "through pleasure's part." In a Latin epigram, Campion wrote, "Perhaps you'll reach her heart; but Barnes what a fine lover you'll be when they fish you out of a chamber pot."

These days, Anthony Hecht doesn't see any solution to poetry, just finds himself in the same racket. He sounds nice.

Evelyn Waugh in *Brideshead Revisited* shows that the novelists can be unpleasant too, with the rudeness of a schoolboy. His opening chapters are brilliantly puerile, with Sebastian Flyte and his friend Charles Ryder as snobbish undergraduates at Oxford in the golden 1920s. But for me the story descends to concern with Sebastian's failure as a son in a wealthy Roman Catholic family and as a man, the breakdown of his character in alcoholism, decay, ultimate damnation.

It is the same problem that so greatly disturbed E. M. Forster—the inability of England's sons to grow up. Forster called it "the undeveloped heart." The *Times Literary Supplement* calls it "a traditional English malady." Cyril Connolly called it a Theory of Permanent Adolescence. In America we call it the Peter Pan "I won't grow up, I won't grow up" or Little Boy Blue syndrome, of those who remain schoolboys for life.

Sebastian clings to his nanny and his teddy bear, a lost child disposed of by Waugh.

In *A Doll's House,* likewise, Nora makes problematic her ever growing up into womanhood. Ibsen was writing about "the new woman" in 1879 when she had far to go. Nora's husband tells her fondly what she is: a "typical woman," a spendthrift, featherbrain, butterfly, his sweet little songbird, a child with childish ways. That's how she has behaved in the eight years of their marriage while bearing his three children. Lighthearted, full of capers, she wears her hair in a braid down her back, giggles and pouts, romps and teases, clapping her hands, performing tricks playful as a squirrel, assuring him she wants only to please and obey him. "I'll be an elf and dance in the moonlight for you, Torvald!"

Secretly Nora is beset by terror that Torvald will find out she has borrowed money from a moneylender and forged her father's name. On Christmas Eve she fibs, dances the tarantella, dresses for a masquerade party, and considers suicide. When Torvald hears of her crime, he flies into a rage, branding her a liar and hypocrite—till realizing he is safe from discovery he grandly forgives his foolish child.

It is then Nora faces the truth about her marriage and her littlegirl-hood: that she who was her father's doll has for eight years been living in a doll's house with doll children. "That's why I'm leaving you," she tells Torvald, blaming him. "I am a human being. My duty is to myself." That very night she does leave him—saying no word to her three children whom she may never see again—and walks out the door free, a woman, grown up at last.

Or is she running away, still a child?

Dickens: "No children for me" (he had ten). "Give me grown-ups." William Steig: "I don't think anybody's grown up."

Bad Poets. Martin Tupper is forgot. Yet his rise and fall as a bad poet was phenomenal, nothing like it in the history of English literature. As late as 1933 the *Oxford English Dictionary* carried the entries Tupperian, Tupperish, Tupperism, Tupperize. Then they were summarily removed since nobody would be expected to know their meaning, and the *Oxford English Dictionary of Quotations* reduced its thirty-five quotations of Tupper to one platitude: "A good book is the best of friends, the same today and forever." His rise to fame, when he became a household word, was as sensational as his fall through heartless laughter was complete.

In 1838 Martin Tupper produced *Proverbial Philosophy,* "A Book of Thoughts and Arguments" that dealt in jogging verse with moralizing about Christian love, marriage, friendship, hearth and home, all in high-sounding inanities. He called it "My soul's own son, dear image of my mind." The astonishing success it had led to more excesses, such as continuing Coleridge's unfinished "Christabel," which Tupper titled "Geraldine":

Her mouth grows wide, and her face falls in,
And her beautiful brow becomes flat and thin . . .
A serpent monster, scaly and green,
Horrors! — can this be Geraldine?

As versifier for public occasions like the Crimean War, Tupper had a genuine admirer in Queen Victoria, who invited him to Windsor Castle to read his works. He became a celebrity whom millions read, the author of what grew to thirty-nine volumes. His pious lines were carved on tombstones. In 1851 he made a triumphant visit to America, where Nathaniel P. Willis told him, "Your name is a classic amongst us." Longfellow regarded him "pure as the driven snow" and wasn't fooling. Tupper had dinner at the White House with President Millard Fillmore and called on P. T. Barnum.

But the tremendous popularity waned and sank when people tired of his preachiness. He was made the butt of ridicule, becoming "the most parodied author in English or any other language," a national joke that *Punch* took pains to expose and revile. Hawthorne visited him in England and declared him "the vainest little man of all little men, the ass of asses." Victoria's admiration cooled. Yet blinded by vanity Tupper applied to be knighted. He prepared to be made the next poet laureate at the death of Wordsworth. He wrote his autobiography, *My Life As An Author,* which contained the prediction that his name would never die.

So let Tupper live, at least as an amateur inventor who was the creator of the glass bottle top, the kind that screws on:

He left a bottle top for us.
In that was Tupper glorious.

During his tenure as England's poet laureate from 1972 to 1984, John Betjeman aroused a certain amount of righteous indignation. Maybe so brilliant a light-verse writer was never meant to be a laureate. Betjeman carried about a teddy bear named Archie, and the London *Times* dubbed him "a teddy bear to the nation." He showed you can't turn light verse into solemn music. In his "Ode to Westminster Abbey," the speaker addresses God:

Now I feel a little better
    What a treat to hear Thy Word,
Where the bones of leading statesmen
    Have so often been interr'd.
And now, dear Lord, I cannot wait
Because I have a luncheon date.

Recognition. Five English professors had lunch together in the faculty dining room on East Campus. We talked about recognition, a subject I brought up because it worries me. Were I still teaching, faced with students demanding to know what's the good of studying English literature compared with learning computer techniques, I would have to answer "recognition."

I said that a professor had stopped me in the hall after reading a piece of mine in the *Atlantic* titled "Three Nice People" (Sir Thomas More, Ben Jonson, Sydney Smith) to ask, "Your maiden name was Smith, wasn't it? Was Sydney Smith your grandfather?" My colleagues shook their heads: "Who is Sydney Smith?" Unrecognized by the illuminati? This was different, I thought, from what Calvin Trillin calls selective ignorance, different too from Virginia Woolf's possessive awareness in her diary: "I'm reading Sydney Smith—his life—with only one wish in the world: that I'd married him. Isn't it odd when the rumble tumble of time turns up some entirely lovable man?" Macaulay called him "the Smith of Smiths."

Leonard Bacon, a college professor who died in 1954, wrote, in *Semi-Centennial,* "It is necessary to read Chaucer, whereas civilized intercourse is possible between reasonable persons without a special knowledge of Walter Pater or Oscar Wilde." I would call this selective ignorance, choosing whom to be ignorant of, though it needn't be *that* selective. What about not knowing the Hermit of Hampole?

How much recognition does it take? What acquaintance with language itself? Lewis Lapham, editor of *Harper's*, says, "Literature has become a regional dialect spoken only in the universities." But if a student limits his pursuit to offbeat excursions in Science Fiction, how can he know such regional poets as Chaucer, Shakespeare, Milton, or the author of "Go, Lovely Rose"? He's impoverished in the midst of plenty.

No doubt the Symbolists asked too much recognition. When *The Waste Land* appeared in 1922, Eliot was accused of expecting an alarming degree of comprehension from his readers. In a poem of 433 lines were quotations from and allusions to thirty-five writers, with passages in six languages to describe our world as a wasteland and our plight in living in it. Eliot tried to give a sense of human history and human failure, of wastelands found in all tongues, all literatures, all times. A poem that borrowed from Dante, the Bible, Shakespeare, Virgil, Saint Augustine, Spenser, Wagner, Baudelaire, Goldsmith, the Jacobean dramatists proved so dense that Eliot was persuaded to add footnotes. But the fifty notes he tacked on were more obscure than the poem, with quotations in Latin from Ovid, in French from Baudelaire, in German from Hermann Hesse, in Italian from Dante, in Sanskrit from a *Upanishad*. Eliot himself deplored the notes as "bogus scholarship."

It's a modern Symbolist epic enormous in scope, written in a shorthand that, when it came to light, many thought a spoof or hoax ("a grunt would serve equally well"). Amy Lowell said "I think it is a piece of tripe." William Carlos Williams called it "the great catastrophe to our letters." Arnold Bennett asked Eliot if the notes were a lark or serious. "Serious," said Eliot.

To my students, *The Waste Land* gave recognition that some were sure had changed their lives, though one student admitted ruefully, "I was happier not knowing what it has to say."

> It is difficult
> to get the news from poems
> yet men die miserably every day
> for lack
> of what is found there. — William Carlos Williams

A Talent for Looking. What one needs of course is a talent for looking. When I saw a copy of John Pope-Hennessy's recent book, *Learning to Look,* I snatched it up, thinking here it is! the place to look and learn how to.

Pope-Hennessy's credentials are good. He has good eyesight. Like Bernard Berenson and Kenneth Clark, he is one of the primary art historians of the century. He has devoted his life to studying works of art, especially Italian Renaissance painting and sculpture, most of all Donatello. In the art world he is known as the Pope.

To look at art or anything else, he says, "Nothing makes one feel so unclean as simulating enthusiasm" (unlike Sir Joshua Reynolds, whose advice was "to feign a relish till we find a relish come"). In all honesty he allows himself certain prejudices and blind spots, such as Rubens who makes him uneasy, van Gogh whom he dislikes (my own prejudices are art nouveau and Hieronymus Bosch). He used to find contemporary art a source of pleasure when it consisted of Picasso, Matisse, and Gertrude Stein. But these days the avant-garde is to him stale and dull (Gore Vidal: "What garde were they avant to?") He is devoted to Siena and Florence, where he now lives, as repositories of Italian art; and as a boy was happy looking at butterflies.

Objects, Pope-Hennessy says, mean more to him than people. With an object your relationship may be kept whole and last forever, more satisfying than with a person, more constant. As this book (which is mostly a catalogue of paintings that delight him) conclusively shows, there is only one way to look at what you see, and that is the Pope-Hennessy way. It is a simple imperative: Look! closely, steadily, and long. Make passionate your sense of looking till at last you see them plain — Memling, Vermeer, Monet, the world and the bo tree.

But why not apply the same formula to people (with an eye like Aunt Mary Emerson's that went through and through you like a needle)?

Rasselas and Candide. Dr. Johnson wasn't much of a storyteller, but in his little tale of Rasselas he sounds like Voltaire on the subject of happiness in the best of all possible worlds. The two books, published in the same year, 1759, agree in their view of that world—as a place of pure evil and the cruelty of man. Voltaire, at least, managed to be witty about it.

Rasselas was a young prince of Abyssinia, who lived in an earthly paradise in Happy Valley where no sorrows existed. There he knew the riches of a palace that stood, in Dr. Johnson's lapidary language, "from century to century deriding the solstitial rains and equinoctial hurricanes, without need of reparation." But Rasselas was unhappy in paradise, so weary of its "soft vicissitudes of pleasure and repose" that he decided to run away and look for the real thing. Together with his sister and the philosopher Imlac, he escaped through a tunnel and came to Egypt, to the everyday world of discord and utter misery. Here he found no sign of happiness, only the human condition in a calamitous state—empty, ridiculous, wretchedly unhappy—as wise old Imlac could have told him in the first place.

Like Voltaire's Candide and his philosopher Pangloss (who was an optimist and so a fool), Rasselas went forth on a quest for what every man wants without catching even a whiff of it. The search failed for them both; happiness was unobtainable. Candide, after being beaten and enslaved in a world of evil, disillusioned by malice, greed, and stupidity, sensibly returned home to cultivate his garden. Rasselas also resolved to give up the search, though what he did next is untold since the story breaks off with, in Johnson's words, a "conclusion in which nothing is concluded." Perhaps there was no more to say. Whether Rasselas found his way back to the Happy Valley—or whether there ever was on this earth a Happy Valley—I seriously doubt. So, presumably, did Dr. Johnson.

Poor Goldy

"Goldsmith is a fool, the more wearing for having some sense."
　　—from a letter of Horace Walpole

He was a little man, with bulging forehead,
Face marked by smallpox, dressed in gaudy fashion,
Decked out in great wig, peach-bloom coat and breeches—

A strutter when he walked, his cane gold-headed,
Full of himself and pleading to be noticed.
For, risen at last to fame and intimacy
With men of wit—Burke, Johnson, Garrick, Reynolds—
As one who had been nameless among beggars
He prattled and spoke foolishly, indifferent
To truth, with an impassioned tendency
To say the wrong thing, pert and ludicrous.
("A Man extremely odd," said Mrs. Thrale.)
Taking him for a dunce, his wit for vanity,
His ways for childishness, they called him fool,
Dolt, simpleton, a laughingstock, a blunderer.
("Sir, he knows nothing," thundered Dr. Johnson.)
Yet at his death they gathered on his stair,
Weeping for one who wrote so like an angel,
As if an angel possibly could write
Like Oliver Goldsmith.

What Are People For? A London doctor on television recently defined an eccentric as one who tries to make people happy and wants the world to be a better place. By this measure Wendell Berry is an eccentric who, faced with an ailing world, offers his services to make people happy in it. In a collection of essays, *What Are People For?* he gives some disquieting facts leading to a cautious answer. Certainly people are good for something.

Wendell Berry is, he says, a country person, who some years ago turned from academic life to his native Henry County, Kentucky, on the Kentucky River beside which his grandfather once had a farm. There as a farmer bent on humanizing the world, he writes of the early influences on him in that place—of Thoreau, who wanted his own world kept free; of *Huckleberry Finn*, a regional tale "about a world I know, or knew" as a boy on the Kentucky, part of the river system of the Mississippi. His countryside was at one time good farming country, with farms diversified yet small enough to be owned by those tending such farms. Now it is not. His conclusion is, "We have nearly destroyed American farming, and in the process have nearly destroyed our country." We are living, he says, among punishments and ruins.

Since World War II, the popular view has been that there are too many people on the farm, a consensus that has driven too many to the city to become the unemployed. Some say these people deserve to fail because they don't produce enough. The economy prescribes rationalized plunder and abuse of the land, which "had never been more exploitive than it is now." The soil erodes, the air is poisoned, woodlands are wasted, industrial farming brings exhaustion to the land. If you live in the country as Berry does, you think about these failures. What people are for is to live not as predators but as stewards to cherish and preserve the planet.

The extent of his concern appears in his alarm over the computer, in his rejection of machines as a pestilence. Each time he sees a television set he resolves not to own anything so stupefying. He regrets having to use a car and travel by plane. He pictures himself as a writer who never touches a typewriter, a farmer who works with horses and hates a chainsaw, a lover of nature who laments having damaged his land when he hired a man with a bulldozer to dig a small pond halfway up his hillside. The woods floor slipped into the pond and left a lasting scar.

He lives on a river polluted by the eastern Kentucky coal mines and by the cities. Walking sadly round his county, he sees the piles of imperishable trash, the landfill that receives daily fifty to sixty truckloads of garbage from Pennsylvania, New Jersey, New York. He sees the fallen barns and empty houses, and he thinks of the country people who "connive in their own ruin," not only victims but perpetrators—people who once were good neighbors attached to the soil. So a place loses its memory of itself.

In an economy that corrupts and rejects the land, where everyone is a loser and catastrophe a logical end, Berry's voice is loud in anger. What are people for? People on this earth are here to save each other, to replace a destructive way of life with a return to nature, "the supreme farmer." For that is where the trouble lies.

II

The Only Way

The date is April 1991. More than ten years have passed since Philip's death. Between that day and this, through these pages among these books, writing it as I lived it, where has the search for a third way taken me? Sometimes it seems only in the direction of the sharpest pointed stick. And yet, random though the search, the issue itself remains the same. By staying alive, what have I learned? What way have I still to go? Thoreau said it for me, "If we are alive, let us go about our business."

The thing is, I have this lifelong habit of writing, as people do, to see what I have to say. (Jane Austen: "If I say all that I have to say, I hope I have no reason to hang myself.") By now I must have said it all before. Yet at eighty-five, with another book in print that should in simple futurity be my last, I must try again. The reason isn't hard to find: my age baffles me.

Lear, for instance, at fourscore and upwards, had grown old and frail, too old to be of sound judgment: " 'Tis the infirmity of his age," Regan said. "Yet he hath ever but slenderly known himself." Too late the proud king realized the poor unaccommodated man he was, lacking the wisdom one would like to associate with old men, lacking the humility. And for this he was made to suffer and die of heartbreak, while Kent asked sorrowfully, "Is this the promised end?" Goethe once said, "An aged man is always a King Lear," a hanger-on, rejected by his children, toppled in his pride, taught the one thing he can't demand or expect in this world, which is love.

"Do not let me hear of the wisdom of old men," wrote Eliot in the *Four Quartets,* "but rather of their folly." Inexorably, he found, the years fail to bring what one had anticipated, "the long hoped for calm, the autumnal serenity, and the wisdom of age." Instead the way is in a dark bramble wood, where allowance for the blind must be made. In his poem "Gerontion," Eliot described a little old man, neither wise nor heroic, who has given nothing and got nothing in return, an old man stiffening in a decayed house, saying to himself, "I have lost my passion. I have lost my sight, smell, hearing, taste and touch" — an old man driven by the winds to a sleepy corner.

Still, there is always the trying ("for us there is only the trying," Eliot said), followed by the end of trying that Lear knew. My contemporaries appear to know, as they totter down the pike to a nursing or retirement home, the truth that "men must endure their going hence," that whatever else they had hoped for, whatever road they took, this is where it ends. The question that puzzles me is, do *I* know?

Maybe it's resignation still to be learned. Maybe, since poets tend to disagree, there's another way of looking. "Grant me an old man's frenzy," wrote Yeats. "Myself I must remake." Twenty years earlier he had concluded, "An aged man is but a paltry thing," a scarecrow on a stick for whom the world has no place. Now in his last poems he saw himself as a wild old wicked man, a warty old guy mad about women, ready to relive his youth upon a woman's breast. "Who can know the year, my dear, / When an old man's blood grows cold?"

Being an old woman isn't that easy. Whether one approves the flesh and its clamor as Yeats did depends on one's ability to please; on whether, say, one more closely resembles a sylph or a tea cosy. Robert Louis Stevenson's advice in "Crabbed Age and Youth" was to be seasonable, to act one's age — whatever performance that is supposed to be — fulfilling the role of Grandma Moses or Whistler's mother. Or a senior citizen in her golden years.

In any case I can pass myself off as an authority on the twentieth century, having been born about the time of the coming of the ice cream cone and the teddy bear, the airplane, the Model T, Elinor Glyn on a tiger skin, and Mother's Day. There were forty-five states then; nobody walked on the moon or split the atom. The universe consisted of the Milky Way. It was the Age of Optimism and Innocence, the dear old Golden Rule days of Teddy Roosevelt's Square Deal. At my birth the twentieth century was six years old, some forty years after the Civil War. In my childhood I knew the white-haired, blue-coated veterans of the Grand Army of the Republic and joined them at the yearly beanbake in the Grange Hall, where we ate cold beans and hardtack on tin plates, and the old soldiers squatted round an artificial campfire to sing war songs, "Tenting tonight, tenting on the old camp ground."

So if I boast of having begun life in the first decade and survived to the last, who can deny me a panoramic view? As recording secretary, one really ought to hang on till the end of a thousand-year cycle and the close of a fabulous century, about which Bertrand Russell predicted that, following the certainty of nuclear war and the holocaust, the world wouldn't even exist.

I'd hate to take on the twenty-first.

Or suppose in the time left I'm content to laugh and tell old tales and write epiphanies to mockingbirds. (My yard man says, "Write about your man with the lawnmower.") Or turn into a dotty old character in a rocking chair, sitting out the performance. Or join God's Remnant Group that meets Sundays. Or even fall for a slippered pantaloon. The person I once was is still me, the customary self for whom nothing's changed, as Rilke said, "neither the sugar bowl, nor the glass of wine" — though it's harder now to climb trees, less tempting to chase wild geese. "My great ambition is not to grow cross," wrote Horace Walpole, and died at eighty plagued with gout, as cranky and difficult as he ever was. Well along in years, May Sarton woke one day to find herself abandoned, devalued and dwindled, "less accepted and acceptable." Whereupon she promptly wrote a book about it, a journal of solitude, herself *At Seventy*, to count over and claim her possessions — the flowers, the friends, Bramble the cat and Tamas the dog who slept with her — and to relive the dailiness of life (with notations like "It being Sunday, I changed the bed").

I too am rich in everydays.

How rich that may be is a matter of opinion. Testimonials abound that old age is not the cool of the evening but more like an incurable malady. Some say a shipwreck. The artist Suzanne Valadon looked in a mirror and made a bitter portrait of herself at sixty-three as a bleak old woman, full of wrinkles and weariness and self-hatred. I wish she might have said, "My glass shall not persuade me I am old."

Samuel Beckett dealt with the declining years by simply putting his old folks into garbage cans.

After she died at eighty-one, Colette's husband, Maurice Goudeket, wrote a silly book, *The Delights of Growing Old*. "Say to yourself," he wrote, "I am breathing, so I am happy." Jules Renard said yes, that's all it takes: "Every morning upon waking you should say: I see, I hear, I move. I am not in pain. Thank you. Life is lovely."

Such ready answers from the yea-sayers discourage me so much I went to consult my friend Dr. Brown, who diagnosed the problem: depression (a hole in the soul). Ah, I said, but there are the stratagems, the snatched and intermittent moments, though I had to admit that anyone who winces this spring at the white flowering dogwood is depressed. "Don't apologize," he said. I asked him to prescribe what Rosa (who used to work for me) swore by, a little *jolt* medicine.

Better, I thought, to heed a melancholic like Dr. Johnson, who in old age sensibly took time by the forelock. "I fancy that I grow light and airy," he said to Mrs. Thrale. "A man that does not begin to grow light and airy at seventy is certainly losing time if he intends ever to be light and airy."

Always the contradictions: this self saying "I won't give in," that self saying "You already have." Yeats, aware of his quarrel with himself, wrote a poem "Vacillation" to account for the way life is lived between extremities, in unresolved conflict between youth and age, sex and love, self and soul, remorse and blazing happiness, between being blessed and being cursed. In the end he called it the human way and took care to show how human he was. For all to hear, he claimed there was more enterprise in walking naked, yet advised Lady Gregory, "Be secret and take defeat." He found he had not only a self but multiple selves: an anti-self, an inner self, a double self and a triple self, none of them in accord, and so wore masks and gave himself three separate names and identities: Michael Robartes, Owen Aherne, Red Hanrahan.

Yeats discarded his religion yet clamored to believe in God, pursuing the occult, inventing in *A Vision* a whole cosmology to take the place of a Christian heaven. He personally communed with ghosts yet doubted their existence. He loved Maud Gonne yet hated her shrill ways as a political agitator who preached violence, just as he loved and hated Ireland, my "fool-driven land." He sailed to Byzantium yet never went. He sought his soul yet to the last sided with the flesh, even though "You think it horrible that lust and rage / Should dance attention upon my old age." Let me die, he prayed, "a foolish, passionate man." And he called it vacillation—a state so well adapted to the contradictions and conflicts of this world, and of his own nature, that he first titled the poem "Wisdom." The quarrel with oneself, he said, is poetry. It is a definition of life.

While writing recently *The World and the Bo Tree,* I came upon a consistency in myself, a pattern formed back in graduate school when I spent most of an innocent year reading the fourteen volumes of Thoreau's journal. Though concerned with nature (wildflowers, winter birds, bullfrogs), Thoreau's subject was himself. It was about a way to live. While alive, he was thought provokingly shiftless and queer: Oliver Wendell Holmes said he nibbled his asparagus at the wrong end. But his provident way of seeking peace of mind up there in Concord seemed to me reasonable. "Simplify, simplify," he cried, an answer similar to Einstein's, who said that everything should be made as simple as possible (as simple as $E = mc^2$). Thoreau's housing needs were few. His way was nonattachment to possessions, clearing the mind of clutter in an untidy world, living at ease with oneself, "no more lonely than the loon in the pond." It's the answer that prompts me as a minimalist to murmur "Peace" over the morning news, my solution to world confusion and riot.

I found it defined in Eliot's poetry as in Yeats's poetry, in their symbol of the ceaselessly turning wheel (night and day, the seasons, the cycles of birth and death), the frantic wheel of being from which, Eliot wrote, if you care enough you seek a way to the still center, to "a condition of complete simplicity (costing not less than everything)." Escape from the same circling wheel Buddha offered to the five disciples in the Deer Park—the ever turning, suffering world from which he found the way to the still center.

"There, perhaps," wrote Christopher Fry, "by a serene elimination of three-quarters of the earth, you can exist beside the still waters."

Is the cry always in the air? Just now when I switched on the radio, a lusty voice was belting out a rock number popular on the charts, pleading for clearer directions and an even break. "Show me the way," it went, "show me the way and take my confusion away. Give me the courage and strength to believe I'll get there some day."

To sit and write, I said. To stand alone. To keep the forked end down. To travel light, carrying the body along (in Fry's words) because of its sentimental value. Needless to say there were other ways to go (Billy Graham: "I really believe I am going to a literal heaven"), each in his own direction —including headlong in the wrong direction. As Shaw said "The wrong road always goes somewhere." Once while driving over strange roads, a friend of mine stopped at a fork, uncertain which road to take. She took the right-hand one, then called out to a man at work on construction:

"Am I going the right way?"

He thought a while. "That depends, lady," he said, "on where the hell it is you want to get to."

(Yogi Berra: "When you come to a fork in the road, take it.")

Hemingway said he would go his way or not at all. He demanded as his due three things from life: good food, good work, good time in bed. When he lost these, not to be found again, he shot himself. Faulkner said of this death, "I don't like a man that takes the short way home."

Someone asked John Cheever why he chose to write. He replied without hesitation, "to try to make sense of my life." But the journals he kept for thirty years made no sense of the catapulting way he took—of alcohol, sex, drugs—that went blindly, unswervingly nowhere. Too late he cried, "Oh, to be so much better a man than I happen to be."

Yet the search goes on, because it has to. Jeremy Bentham helpfully listed fourteen kinds of pleasure the whole world feels and fourteen kinds of pain. And he came out even.

Eventually Thoreau told why he went to Walden for his sojourn in the woods: to find a way (which Whittier called "wicked and heathenish") because "I did not wish to live what was not life, living is so dear." After two years of the solitude more companionable than the world outside, he wrote, "I left the woods for as good a reason as I went there." When he had found what he went for and had several more lives to live, he moved the two miles back to Concord to his mother's cooking and Mr. Emerson's talk (a friend of his who liked to say, "Let us be men instead of woodchucks"). But he hadn't much time or many lives left. After *Walden* was published in 1854, Thoreau lived eight more years, kept busy observing meanwhile how seeds are dispersed by the chickadees. When he died he was planning further travel in Concord, studying the seasons and "learning the language of these fields."

This morning, picking up *Walden,* I wondered if Thoreau still told me what I wanted to do in my own numbered days. "Do what you love," he said. "Pursue your life." He didn't say how to exactly, only how he did so himself. I counted the things I'd be giving up if I left this countryside — the pine woods and meadow, the five white-tailed deer wandering over my dooryard, the peepers in the pond, the scarlet azaleas at the door and scarlet cardinals perched on the clothesline. I counted the roominess, with space to pursue my life, out here on Guess Road (wherever it may be going).

And I thought of the time B. and the boys and I paid a visit to Walden Pond, went swimming in it, then stood at the edge where his one-room cabin had been that Thoreau borrowed an axe to build. It reminded me of Sadō's haiku: "My poor hut in spring / True, there is nothing in it— / There is everything!" I wondered how often Thoreau returned to this spot to look at his contentment again.

So far I'd sooner live under a lone pine tree than in a retirement home. Not so my friends who chose to move this year into The Forest at Duke, a massive 42-acre retirement community just opened on Pickett Road. Many are retired professors seeking permanent retirement, aware the time has come to say, like Paulina at the end of *The Winter's Tale,* "I, an old turtle, will wing me to some withered bough."

As a dovecote to fly to for refuge, it's a costly haven if it means not to be on your own again. You may in years past have traveled to the ends of the earth, but this is the end of the road. Whether your house is the House of Atreus or a Sabine farm, you rid yourself of it (except for the framed family pictures) in exchange for a resting place where everyone is old, no children play, no birds sing. The signs beckon, "This is the way the world ends," in good hands, secure in the shelter that is there, in comfortable quarters till you die, one meal a day on the house, croquet for exercise, long-term nursing care as needed. No one works at a retirement home.

At least one of my friends is optimistic the arrangement will prove idyllic. "It will be like going away to college," she said.

It's hard to catch on. There is, I think, little use in reliving the past and no point in calculating the future, since neither exists. The time is always now, but now doesn't exist either, being of zero duration. Who can claim that time stands still? Or delays its operations? I marveled at first why the movie *Driving Miss Daisy* was so entertaining when it concerned progressive old age, ending futureless with Miss Daisy institutionalized in a home, deprived of most of her wits, being fed by her chauffeur a piece of pumpkin pie. As Jessica Tandy, herself in her eighties, played the part, Miss Daisy was a bossy old girl, willful and intolerant, who learned from the black man the values of courtesy, loyalty, true affection. Not a sentimental tale, often funny (provided you don't identify with Daisy), it viewed lightly the spectacle of deterioration, a sorry sight unless looked at with an easy mind. For if one can look and laugh, what does the answer matter? The laughter must be kept. It must be kept.

But what laughter? More and more the absurdity seems to mock us, you and me, for trying so hard. Such recent hellgazers as Camus, Sartre, Samuel Beckett have brought the matter closer to our attention after calling human existence absurd and receiving the Nobel Prize for it. In his essay *The Myth of Sisyphus,* Camus considered the absurdity—heroic man surrounded by the unknown in a godless universe wholly indifferent to him. The more he is deprived of certainty, the more he continues to believe in his salvation and a life everlasting, in himself as the center of creation, in the efficacy of prayer, in the stars absorbed in his destiny and daily offering their guidance. Sartre stated in *Being and Nothingness* his view of man's plight in a world where "nothing, absolutely nothing, justifies his existence." Accepting the fact, Sartre believed, is a necessary condition of being alive—the ultimate reality.

Beckett found man not only absurd but trivial, a loser. In *Waiting for Godot,* two sad sacks unable to save themselves wait for—what? for meaning, help, deliverance. But the waiting is pointless since whoever they wait for will not come and presumably doesn't exist. Their best solution is suicide. Beckett made an absurdity of being born when we must die, thrown into existence without asking for it, ending in senility and the inane futility of living—as in *Endgame,* with Hamm, a blind old man dying in a collapsed world. Nothingness has a dull plot.

If the laughter is there, it sounds like a cry for help. When the Theatre of the Absurd, influenced by Camus, Sartre, Beckett, sprang up in the 50's and 60's, it presented the absurdity with ridicule and derision, in black humor, "comedies of dread," "comedies of menace." Life is laughable, Harold Pinter declared, because it makes no sense, filled with the isolation that his plays, *The Caretaker, The Homecoming,* convey in a terrifying world without purpose or meaning. Eugene Ionesco, who dramatized the same world, said, "Personally, I regard existence as a misfortune." In his *Rhinoceros* men turn into rhinos. In *The Chairs* two old people on an island await the arrival of important guests, and the stage fills with empty chairs.

This is humorless stuff that overplays the tragedy, a way of looking whose novelty has rather worn off. Which is the better way, Sydney Smith's amused laughter or Kafka's loss of the castle, Kierkegaard's fear and trembling? With either choice, the joke is obviously on us. We are the "quick comedians" who are guilty of inventing paradise, and should be able to laugh at ourselves and at our cheek. For if this is a tale told by idiot or shaggy dog, not to see the joke is to be the butt of it. The only remedy is laughter that is an admission and an acceptance.

Democritus found the condition of man absurd and laughed.

Heraclitus found it absurd and his eyes filled with tears.

Montaigne saw the absurdity and agreed with Democritus: man is the fool of the farce. His solution was a scandalous serenity: "I do nothing without gaiety." Careless of salvation, he put his faith in being alive among the available pleasures, which he enumerated. Order was one, I remember, and cleanliness and kisses and good conversation.

Lightly was the way Sydney Smith regarded his state, notably the plight of being old—"a bore, I admit, for you are left for execution, and are daily expecting the death warrant." To him the world was still an entertaining place. Though at the time he could neither walk nor breathe, "in other particulars," he said, "am well." Though he had retired from business as a diner-out and was eating nothing he liked and doing nothing he wished, "I am careless and good-humoured," he wrote Lady Holland, "at least good-humoured for me."

It was Sir Thomas More's way to "die merrily," taking leave as he went to the scaffold to be beheaded: "I pray you, see me safe up, and for my coming down let me shift for myself." Others have been nearly as imperturbed. Montaigne said, "Let death find me planting my cabbages." With only months to live, Dr. Johnson resolved to learn Dutch. A month before he died Yeats wrote, "I do nothing but write verse." Socrates, condemned to death, turned to a musician: "Teach me your song."

"What use, when you are going to die?"

"So as to know it before I die."

"Are you afraid to die, Spartacus?"

"No more than I was to be born."

But death is part of the inquiry. Everything I meant to do and haven't yet done, like climbing the Matterhorn, requires being veritably alive rather than face to face with extinction. Yet the question I always used to ask now answers itself: "How does the story end?" When his wife Katherine died, E. B. White told a friend, "I am just a little man in a ten-room house, with nowhere to go but on." Matisse (who had said, "L'oeuvre est paradis") in his seventies sat in a wheelchair no longer able to paint, making hundreds of paper cutouts. Harold Nicolson, called by *The Times* "a professional human being," wrote at seventy, "I always have the feeling, considering that we live in a world of chaos and transition, I ought to be more unhappy than I am," and died in ruins at eighty-two oblivious of the world that had delighted him. Clive Bell, whom I knew, Vanessa's husband, died a senile old man who talked baby talk and went around with his fly unzipped. Henry James on his deathbed traced words with his fingers on the bedsheets. May Sarton at eighty wrote *Endgame* with its mocking title to say she was undone: "So this is the beginning of a new journal of a woman who now knows she will never get well." (She died in July 1995.)

All of which must be borne in mind — not, however, forgetting the wild old wicked men like Yeats, wherever they are, with eyes "glittering and gay," who scandalously defer the day of reckoning. On *Masterpiece Theatre* last night, in the film *Summer's Lease,* John Gielgud played to the hilt the comic part (sometimes referred to as "Old Couchez Avec") of a jaunty old goat spending the summer in Italy, still crazy about women, brazen and unrepentant.

In an interview David Frost recently had with him, Gielgud at eighty-seven looked indestructible, reminiscing with an unfailing memory, sitting bald, big-nosed, and erect during Frost's probing, his face full of laughter as he reflected, "It is marvelous not to be blind or deaf or dotty." He appears in commercials for champagne. Last year at eighty-six he did his first nude scene. His exhibitionism, he says, is rampant as ever, but with no need to outwit or outlive anybody. Aware that old characters become caricatures of themselves, he has less dread of death than of becoming an old guru, treated with awe. When Frost inquired what were his favorite lines, Gielgud quoted Hamlet asking Horatio, at the end of the play: Since no man knows what the future will bring, what does an early death matter? "If it be now, 'tis not to come; if it be not to come, it will be now; if it be not now, yet it will come: the readiness is all."

George Sand set Flaubert's teeth on edge when she defined old age as "the happiest and most propitious part of life." No doubt he winced at Robert Browning, who in the same year was shouting "Grow old along with me! / The best is yet to be." As pious optimists, both were putting us on; nobody *likes* to be old, no one ages like vintage wine. George Sand's outrageous claim at sixty-two of having reached the time when old age "reveals itself in all its sweetness" was meant to impress Flaubert. A grandmother with her nights of passion behind her and fires abated, she enjoyed assuring him that the close of life was the happiest and best. He didn't have to believe her, it being a flat-out lie.

Yet the opposite view (Cyril Connolly: "Decay along with me, / The worst is yet to be") seems equally wrong. Muriel Spark was forty-one when she published her condescending satiric novel of old age, *Memento Mori*, whose infirm characters are between seventy-nine and ninety-three, twelve of them females confined to the Maud Long Medical Ward, ready for the scrap heap and all called Granny. At intervals most of Mrs. Spark's cast receive a mysterious phone call, a voice saying "Remember you must die"—a fact of life, you would think, each had got wind of by now. But they respond to this black humor by making no sense of the message, confused and vulnerable as they are, absorbed most unbecomingly in the long defeat, stricken with every known ill of old age from arthritis, cataracts, deafness, incontinence, impotence, brittle bones, tremors, stroke, to humiliation and despair, senility, loss of their faculties. (Walt Whitman also listed constipation and ungracious gloom.) They haven't even compassion for each other; love is entirely missing. In the end they die, everyone dies, which may be a record Muriel Spark has set, killing off all her characters, more than the dead in *King Lear*. A funeral with cremation is fittingly included. In this macabre novel, preoccupied with death and meant to amuse, the one remedy for the plight of ripe old age is to avoid reaching it—or to become like the single alert individual, Miss Jean Taylor, at eighty-two profoundly religious therefore peaceful and acceptant, resigned to awaiting the last things, "death, judgment, heaven and hell."

The critics agreed in calling the book comic.

I remember my mother undaunted and scrappy at eighty-five, thinking herself ageless. It was other people, the wizened old codgers and duffers, who had lived too long and become grunts (or become public monuments, like the old man in Conrad's story: "He must be eighty-five today. The calmness of advanced age gives a solemnity to his manner"). There was nothing solemn about my mother. "I have a bone in my leg," she would complain if someone inquired too solicitously about her health. Her memory had grown so conveniently flexible that she recalled what she wanted to of the past, the way it ought to have been, especially the ideal Victorian childhood and her youth as a Gibson girl with starched bosom and pompadour. Even her slang harked back: *bumbershoot,* current in 1896 when Lizzie was twenty; *skedaddle,* the whole *caboodle.* Though occasionally irate at the way the world had gone to the dogs and threatened her with the poorhouse (at the inroads too made by beer, sex, mashers, short skirts, Sunday movies, the pope, and Woodrow Wilson), she was unsinkable. There was no defeat in her, no giving in. She liked being alive, age couldn't wither her, longevity became her. More fearless than God-fearing, she met death with scorn as unworthy of notice, and died believing she would live to pay her electric bill and sweep the snow from her sidewalk. From her hospital bed with almost her last breath she said, "I'll be home by Christmas."

Like her I live alone, less eventfully than could be called a lifetime burning in every moment. I saw a program on PBS the other night about "the nighttime activities of the sea turtle," and they appeared few, strikingly similar to my own. Stay tuned. The world, of course, is judgmental, offering kind discouragement. It would assign me a lessened if not submerged role fitting to my years, would disqualify me, help me across the street; with deference, put me in my place; with patient concern advise and admonish me to fasten my seat belt. Though I still enjoy aerobic dancing to the "Salty Dog Rag"—a last try to be airborne—I'm treated with unbearable respect and occasional alarm for remaining upright. I have no defense against solicitude. Age is diminution, what more to say of it? (in Frost's words, "What to make of a diminished thing?").

"You know, Helen," people tell me, "you're remarkable *for your age.*" And I stop at the bakery for some poppy-seed rolls and wonder how lucky I am, and whether I'm getting to be like the old woman in Lafcadio Hearn's story who lost her dumplings—which, alas, appears more than likely when, on the way home, at the filling station for gas I say to Ben Crabtree, "Please fill up my carburetor."

"With what, ma'am?"

"Water, of course."

He looks under the hood without cracking a smile. "Carburetor's full, ma'am."

As for the obligation not to be unhappy, not even God manages that. We both quail a lot. For years I hated my solitude, having no talent for it, till it came to seem less a predicament than a company of one, nature's beneficent plan to set me free—free, that is, of undue hope of a new dispensation, free not to care. Most of all, not to care.

Whatever way it was I intended to go—what third way I had in mind to take and presumably am taking (there being fourteen ways to Sunday)— I must be practically there. Into the third act, so to speak. At least I know, however the performance ends, the laughter must be kept. I know that the only way—for me, I mean—is to accept the absurdity, even though I forget it all the time and leave the laughter to the gods (who, said Plato, love a joke). Now when my son David phones I say, "Fine, everything's fine," which is true enough without going so far as the actor Herbert Beerbohm Tree each time someone asked "How are you, Mr. Tree?" "I, oh, I'm radiant!" he cried.

The thing perhaps is to keep a firm grip on the devices at hand— the books, typewriter, and corner of my study where the sun streams in, plus five acres available for cross-country travel with meanders along the way. "In my room the world is beyond my understanding," wrote Wallace Stevens. "But when I walk I see that it consists of three or four trees and a cloud."

"The thing perhaps is," said Cummings, "to eat flowers and not to be afraid."

And Yet

And yet it's always so:
The way you try to outwit nemesis
And laugh at doom, mock fate, show
Disrespect for wrath, escape
Your destiny. But, look, it's only
Part of the jest, the same absurdity.
And I'm the one to know.

When I Was Born and Full of Beans

Oklahoma wasn't a state
And the Model T wasn't a flivver,
The heavens roared, the earth did shake
In San Francisco's great earthquake,
And Proust had his bedroom lined with cork,
And Ibsen died. On this glorious date,
I distinctly remember my father singing
"Come, Josephine, in my flying machine,"
Which, scared of flying, he didn't mean,
And my mother's name was Lizzie.

The Woman Whose Birthday Was Charlemagne's

Having grown lately younger than I am,
Less withered than the self I used to be
With sagging soul and wrinkled in my mind,

Now young like Yeats's wild old wicked man,
A thing of flesh, a foolish passionate crone,
All passion spent and plenty more to spend,
Negotiable before the night is done—
Say it's playacting if you will,
I am Duchess of Malfi still.

(Charlemagne will be 1,250 years old on April 2.)

One Goes Abreast

You ask me where I am going.
Quoting from *Don Quixote*
I answer honestly,
"That is as it may turn out."

I leave the matter hopeful
Like the man in Sandburg's poem
Who, asked the unfathomable question,
Answers, "Omaha."

Yet in a strait so narrow
(Quoting now from Shakespeare)
Who knows the destination
Where one but goes abreast?

5 ⬅

Reunion

While flying this June to my college reunion, I began John Updike's latest novel, *Rabbit at Rest,* which starts off with Rabbit Angstrom in a Florida airport feeling something ominous threatening him that was "his own death, shaped like an airplane." Poor scared Rabbit — staring down the sky at old age and dissolution, thinking *there is no mercy* — was giving up the rabbit chase at fifty-six. And all the while here I was staving off equally ominous thoughts at the idea of returning for my sixty-fifth reunion — as if with any sense of propriety one would want to. What possessed me to make this improbable journey?

Anne met me at the airport in Elmira, New York, bringing with her Tebe, another member of the Class of 1926, who was waiting unnerved out in the car. I hadn't seen either of them since I was eighteen. So when a little old white-haired lady stood nearby peering uncertainly about, I assumed it had to be Anne (once tall, raven-haired and beautiful), who with a start greeted me and then forgot where she had parked the car as I forgot I had to go and pick up my suitcase. The same startled reunion occurred with Tebe, murmuring her name to introduce herself. I loved them both for being alive, keeping their identity, presumably their sanity, against heavy odds in these going-on-a-hundred years. Luckily we had all three become great talkers, given our big chance now to hark back to the twenties.

I was there as an impostor, having left Elmira College at the end of sophomore year to transfer to another school, another discipline. I had gone in the first place to this upstate woman's college sixty miles from home because I had a full scholarship, but chiefly because there were the four of us who entered together — Lucy, Tebe, Dottie, and I — friends since childhood. We lived that first year in Dwight Cottage on the edge of campus, and my roommate Dottie and I (only we two) amused ourselves as if we were away at summer camp, breaking the rules, messing around, blithe and noisy. For two years we managed to have it both ways: to stay on the honor roll and to learn as little as possible from our professors except in English courses. I had rebelled at home against my mother's strict rule, and I rebelled, often at real inconvenience, at Elmira for the pleasure of it. "But you were so young," Anne said today. I was sixteen, old enough to know better. Yet this afternoon as we took a quick tour of the place and I saw Cowles Hall again beside the lake, and Dwight Cottage now somebody's private residence, I reflected that Elmira hadn't been such a bad choice. It had given me time in the midst of friends and companions to grow up a little before facing the consequences at a big school like the University of Chicago.

Instead of a fool's errand, the reunion wasn't so bad either; in a strange way it justified itself. If you can't go home again, maybe you shouldn't try until it no longer matters that you can't, until nothing remains either of sadness or regret. I went back to learn about the passing of time, if there was anything good to say about it. I went, being curious, to see how the Class of 1926 had turned out; and the result was what you'd expect, the same way everybody in Philadelphia or Upper Sandusky turns out. Inevitably I was most aware of the ones lately dead, who had also returned for their reunion—Lucy, Dottie, Louise, and the rest. Twelve of us from a class of three hundred showed up in the flesh, several escorted by their daughters who with a steadying hand kept them on track. A few were vague, frail and bewildered, staring with trembling lips and questioning eyes. "Jesus loves you," one said to me. But as the most venerable group there, we attended the functions—which meant riding around campus on mechanized carts driven by deferential students chosen to give us life support. And we accepted praise for apparent survival, in particular Betty Humeston, who flew in from California to prove she was alive: her name had been listed in the *Alumni News* in the obituary column.

Dottie and I left Elmira together, she never to attend college again, and now she was dead of leukemia. I missed her suddenly, her laughter, her joyous mockery of the passing scene. She would have loved the noon picnic on the lawn with beer and balloons, the go-cart candlelight procession to serenade the President, the President's reception where we were plied with gin and tonic, the class dinner with choice of wines where nobody knew the words to Alma Mater. She would have agreed we'd wasted time breaking the 101 rules in the Gray Book when today Elmira gave the student "the chance to be himself" with no rules to break, chock full of freedoms. Though begun as a pioneer woman's college in 1855, twenty years ago it became coeducational. And the three of us who shared a suite in Peary Hall this weekend were struck by the sight on our floor of one toilet labeled Men, the other Women, a proximity of the sexes that Dottie and I would have applauded, but what would our mothers say?

As it happenened, any lessons in conduct I meant to profit by were not being offered this year at Elmira: how not to grow too visibly geriatric, not to become through time's undoing a cliché, a lingerer — forgetful, repetitious, deaf, out of it. My two companions were widowed old ladies who hadn't yet caved in. Long ago I had escaped Elmira and gone my own way, and they had not. They had conformed, obeyed the rules. But in the end had it made any difference? Tebe, stout and spectacled, lived alone now on the family farm where she was born and grew up; Anne was a CPA in her hometown who still read the *Wall Street Journal.* We all three drove Oldsmobiles. We no longer used words like "swell" and "you said a mouthful" and "the cat's pajamas." Nor did we talk much of imponderables. They at least were churchgoing and conservative. They gave me fond salutation and farewell, offering consolation from my peers but no real remedy for being my age and single. We made no plan to meet again.

Had my roommate Dottie been alive beside me, I would have whispered the answer in her ear, "Only to gods in heaven comes no old age, nor death of anything." And we would have laughed aloud at our predicament.

6

Colette's Way

Of her seventy-three books Colette's masterpiece is surely *Chéri*, a novel I read again the other day and found wiser than ever in understanding. Trust Colette to know how it feels for an older woman to fall in love with a man half her age or younger. She was fifty-two, enough like her character Léa to play the part when *Chéri* was adapted for the stage — the story of a love affair between the aging courtesan Léa and the twenty-year-old son of her friend Charlotte Peloux. Chéri she calls him, a handsome young gigolo, spoiled, vain, childishly demanding, accustomed to taking what he wants. The difference in their ages defines the plot when what should have been a passing affair turns into a liaison of six years, finally into incurable love from which neither can be free. With Chéri's marriage, arranged by his mother to a young heiress, Edmée, who bores and wearies him, Léa struggles to release herself from the unbearable loss, to accept the end of her lovemaking, her youthfulness, her love. After months of separation, one night Chéri suddenly appears, throwing himself sobbing upon her, and for the first time they declare their love and Léa lets herself believe he has returned to her forever: "How stupid I was not to understand that you were my love, the love, the great love which only comes once." Léa is cruelly mistaken. In the morning Chéri sees her as she is, betrayed by daylight, with a double chin and wrinkled neck. At his instinctive withdrawal Léa cries, "You came here and found an old woman" and sends him out of her life: "Quick, child, quick, go hunt your youth. I love you. It's too late." The book ends with Chéri walking quickly away like a man escaping from prison.

Six years later (after meeting Maurice Goudeket, nearly twenty years younger than she), Colette wrote a sequel, *La fin de Chéri*, as if she needed to make clearer to herself a point already made, to say again what a woman's aging can do to love. Five years have passed since Chéri left

Léa's bed, and the accidental meeting between them, cleverly arranged by his conniving mother, is a fatal one. The time is 1919. Léa, now in her sixties, has deliberately allowed herself to grow into an immensely stout, wrinkled, gray-haired, elderly lady. She has accepted old age, she has embraced her fate with a terrible finality, who never before went without makeup, who said of her appearance, "Naked, if one wishes, but not half-dressed." Old and sexless, Léa is inaccessible, beyond desire, beyond reach and beyond recall. With this knowledge, Chéri, now thirty years old, leaves her for the last time. He wants to cry out, "Stop! Show me your real self." But that Léa no longer exists. In his grief, Chéri spends the final month of his life listening to the reminiscences of an old and miserable woman, La Copine, another of his mother's friends. Then he shoots himself.

The tale is tragic and is meant to be. Colette recognizes the ultimate way that love, however deep and eternal, can be denied. But she didn't let it frighten her. When she married Maurice Goudeket she was sixty-two and arthritic.

A Thousand Pardons. The only mystery in Katinka Loeser's book is its title. A thousand pardons for what? I looked it up in concordances as possibly a quotation from Shakespeare or the Bible, phoned the *New York Times Book Review* (who had asked me to review it) to see what they thought it meant, who phoned the publisher at Atheneum, who didn't know either and phoned the author, who said in some surprise, "It's just something you say."

So, a thousand pardons for what? She can't mean "Excuse me for living" when she gives unassailable proof she has found by this time a way to live in an autumnal world. Maybe it's something she says when she steps on a cat.

Katinka Loeser didn't invent the quiet days and four seasons of the later years she writes about, the azaleas at the doorstep, the two white cats winding round her feet, her husband—the writer Peter De Vries—wandering in and out of her house and her consciousness, the children grown and gone from home. Though in these pieces she may call him Gladstone and herself Betsy, it's always the same man, same woman, same cats. She begins, "What has happened here is this: there's been a lot of rain." She ought to start weeding the garden. Last year seven deer entered the yard and ate the lilies. Her friend Louise phones she has lung cancer, and Betsy listens, slowly replaces the phone.

Take care, the book says, to live it up while you can, as long as you can. They have been burglarized twice but Gladstone refuses to let her buy a gun; the cats are no good as watchdogs. After the second break-in they add an alarm system, a main alarm with alarms to alarm it, and people say "Take care." She lets a cat in, the alarm goes off, the police arrive and say "Take care." Then the phone rings. Her friend who has cancer is calling, and Betsy tells her "Take care."

She lives her days conscious of their terrible brevity and need to be counted. On a September morning, "My heart sinks as I begin to understand that this is going to be what is called a perfect day." In the mailbox will be nothing but Christmas catalogues, the soup will boil over, the roof will leak, the rain will remind her how she abjured salvation when as a child she watched baptism by submersion. Salvation was a condition that left you sopping wet. Suddenly she says, "Louise's house is empty now, what shall I do with the telephone number?"

Or it's February, a month for which she has no respect and reduces to a scornful "Feb" because nothing happens in it. Gladstone's birthday is in Feb, but since he deplores birthdays they observe the occasion by his inviting her to his weekly trip to the dump. She glances in her closet, says she hasn't a thing to wear. "We don't dress," he tells her. Or it's Sunday, when she lies in bed to work the acrostic in the Sunday paper, and Gladstone in his faded yellow pajamas looks "like a frayed stalk of last week's celery." At dusk they go to a neighborhood cocktail party that is of less consequence than the walk home, when she directs the flashlight as Gladstone collects litter along the road and drops it into a garbage bag. He has, she reflects sadly, "the hopeless ideal of an impeccable earth." But so has she, or nearly.

Is she begging our pardon for that? More likely it's for holding on fiercely with both hands to what she's got—the two of them together—taking care to keep it that way while she still can.

On September 25, 1993, Peter De Vries died of pneumonia at his home in Westport, Connecticut.

Héloïse. I'm like the old lady who loved the word Mesopotamia. I think with longing of world's ends but sit at home with a book and travel tonight to the Paris of eight centuries ago—like Colette who read her way round the world, and Emily Dickinson who read herself out of Amherst.

Héloïse was an uncommon woman whom the medieval poet of the *Roman de la Rose,* Jean de Meun, called beyond compare:

By my soul I do not believe
That another like her ever lived.

She was born about 1100 of noble family, attended a convent school near Paris where she showed exceptional gifts, and at seventeen went to live with her uncle Fulbert, a canon of Notre Dame, in a cloister of the cathedral.

Héloïse was beautiful, "a combination of everything that can rouse a man to love." The man who loved her and wrote these words, Peter Abelard, was the son of a Breton nobleman, a scholar and philosopher proficient in logic and dialectic. For years he had wandered from school to school before coming to teach at Notre Dame. At thirty-seven, a Schoolman at the height of his fame, Abelard persuaded Canon Fulbert to take him to live in his house and become the tutor of his talented young niece. Till then Abelard had led a life of continence—that is, till he saw Héloïse and, as he wrote in *Historia calamitatum,* the tale of his misfortunes, "I was consumed with the fever of arrogance and lust." She made no attempt to resist the advances of this handsome scholar, his eloquence or his passion. From the moment she saw him she loved him. Day and night they were left together, and on the pretext of studying, wrote Abelard, "we gave ourselves unreservedly to love."

His students saw the change in their teacher, who composed love poems (none have survived) that were circulated till everyone knew of the affair except simple, trusting Fulbert. Several months passed before the lovers were caught, probably by Fulbert, in the act of love, and Abelard was ordered from the house. When Héloïse realized she was pregnant, she sent word secretly to him "with transports of joy."

On a night when Canon Fulbert was away from home, Abelard entered the house and, clothing her in a nun's habit, spirited Héloïse to Brittany, where his sister Denyse gladly welcomed her. In due time she gave birth to a son whom she named Peter Astrolabe. Meanwhile, Fulbert was like a man crazed with grief and fury at her disappearance. Five or six months later, after the baby was born, Abelard sought him out to make apology and offer reparation by marrying Héloïse—on one condition, that the marriage be kept secret "so that I might suffer no loss of reputation." With Fulbert's quick consent, Abelard set out again for Brittany to tell Héloïse the joyful news and make her his wife. To his dismay she refused, crying "Of a certainty we shall both be destroyed." He must remain bound to her by love not duty. Only when he forced her did she return with him to Paris, leaving the child behind. They were married in the presence of Fulbert, who soon broke his promise to keep the fact secret. Defying him, Héloïse denied it was true, "swearing by all the gods that nothing could be more false." To escape Fulbert's wrath, Abelard sent her to Argenteuil, the convent where she had been schooled, obliging her to wear the nun's habit—an act Fulbert angrily interpreted as Abelard's attempt to be rid of his wife. One dark night the old man with some others broke into Abelard's room, and as he described explicitly in the *Historia,* "they cut off those parts of my body with which I had committed the offense of which they complained, and then they fled." Abelard's shame was worse than the agony he suffered; his carefully kept reputation was gone. It was a public catastrophe so terrible that, when two of the assailants were caught, they were savagely punished, their eyes put out, their genitals cut off.

The only course open to the disgraced lovers was to enter the monastic life, though since Héloïse at his command took her vows first, Abelard was blamed for having driven her to it. At twenty she became a nun, not for God but for him; on that day she went to the altar sobbing. Aware that "God holds eunuchs in abomination," Abelard, at forty, retired to the abbey at St. Denis, where he found life in a monastery intolerable. After rousing deep hostility and hatred, slandered and charged with heresy, he fled by night and sought a desert place near Troyes where he built a chapel of stalks and reeds and turned hermit. When his students discovered where he was, they rebuilt the oratory named by Abelard the Paraclete (the Holy Ghost). But again he found no peace. Again he fled to another refuge, St. Gildas in Brittany, where as abbot for ten years he endured the monks and their concubines, "their vile and untameable way of life." He roused further hatred by his most famous book, *Sic et non* (Yes and No), in which he listed 158 points of Christian doctrine and 158 contradictions of it. One of them was "that faith should be founded on human reason." Yes and no. There he wrote his confession and self-portrait, the *Historia.*

Héloïse as prioress was expelled by force with her nuns from the convent at Argenteuil. Abelard, accused of being still lustful for her, established her as abbess of a nunnery at the abandoned Paraclete, where she shut herself in her cell and prayed. In passionate letters wracked by desire, she declared her absolute and undying love, while Abelard advised her to accept their role of brother and sister, her role as the bride of Christ. "You alone I love," she wrote, "I am still young and full of life. I love you more than ever and suffer bitterly from living a life for which I have no vocation."

At St. Gildas the monks tried to kill Abelard with poison. He fell from his horse, breaking a bone in his neck. In 1142 he died, an old and broken man, and his body, carried in secrecy to the Paraclete, was given to Héloïse. When she died and was buried in his tomb, legend says he opened his arms to receive her. They now lie together in the cemetery of Père Lachaise in Paris.

In a foreword to the *Historia calamitatum*—which he wrote not to Héloïse (who read it in tears), but as a letter to a friend to justify God's judgment in punishing him—he says, "in comparing your sorrows with mine, you may discover that yours are in truth nought, or at the most but of small account, and so shall you come to bear them more easily."

Three hundred years later François Villon asked, where are they now?

> Where's Héloïse, the learned nun
> For whose sake Abelard, I ween,
> Lost manhood and put priesthood on? . . .
> Mother of God, where are they then?
> But where are the snows of yesteryear?

Two Deaths. In 1983 Arthur Koestler and his wife Cynthia committed suicide in their house in Montpelier Square, London. Koestler was found sitting in an armchair with a brandy in his hand. Cynthia lay near him on a sofa, a whiskey on the table beside her. Each had taken a fatal overdose of barbiturates.

Koestler, who believed in euthanasia, was seventy-seven, suffering from Parkinson's disease and leukemia, both in a terminal stage. Cynthia was twenty-two years younger, in good health. At the end of his farewell note she had typed, "I should have liked to finish my account of working for Arthur. . . . However, I cannot live without him, despite certain inner resources." A manuscript of their love story, published as *Stranger on the Square,* was found among the papers on Koestler's desk. It is their combined autobiography, written in alternate chapters by the two of them. Cynthia, a pretty girl from South Africa, then living in Paris, had answered an advertisement and become Koestler's secretary in 1949, while he was living with the beautiful Mamaine Paget. He was the celebrated author of *Darkness at Noon,* an ex-Communist who had served the party till revulsion set in. Having fallen in love with him, Cynthia stayed on for the next six years, separated from him briefly when she left to seek other jobs, even to marry unsuccessfully in an attempt to forget her love for this man. Mamaine, who married and divorced him, died in 1954. In 1955, on receiving Koestler's telegram in New York where she had fled, Cynthia gave up her job and hurried back to London, ecstatic at the thought that he needed her. Ten years later they were married and spent the rest of their lives in the house in Montpelier Square.

Koestler was an excessive drinker whose depressions were frequent, love affairs numerous, rages formidable. From the start he treated Cynthia with indifference as hired help. When she became his mistress he showed a callous lack of tenderness; she had two abortions because he refused to have children. If at last he recognized her devotion and returned her love, in their combined account the stranger of the title is Koestler, who lived with a permanent sense of exile and self-destruction. The tale is Cynthia's, her loyalty and her loss.

In his novel *The Gladiators* Koestler wrote, in the words of Spartacus, " 'Anyone can live—but dying is an art and takes some learning.' "

Jorges Luis Borges set the date of his eighty-fourth birthday, August 24, 1983, for his suicide. Six years earlier he had written a short story with this date for title in which he described taking his own life. As he explained later, "I have thought about suicide many times. I wrote the story in 1977 and selected a date I believed would most certainly be posterior to my death." In the story he swallows a bottle of pills and sits on a bed in a hotel room waiting with relief for death to escape the humiliation of being old. He had written a poem "My Suicide" to say "I will die and with me the sum / of the intolerable universe."

On the date itself when he became eighty-four, Borges decided against taking the step: "Laziness and cowardice prevent me. Why should I kill myself? Time is killing me. Besides, I am constantly falling in love."

Two years later, aware he was dying, Borges married his secretary in April 1986 and died in June of cancer of the liver.

I'm haunted by his words in "Remorse":

I have committed the worst sin of all
That a man can commit. I have not been
Happy.

A Memorandum of It

Say, Helen, are you unaware
How changed the sky is, how unbeckoning
The days are, how less bright the air? (You've noticed.)

O lady, reckoning how late,
How *late* the hour is, have you flipped the page
To where no words are? And no date? (You've done that too.)

Then add this memorandum, Helen,
Remindful of a world that ended:
Say that my love for him was true,
Say that my patch of sky was splendid. (I'll see to it tomorrow.)

7

Looking Back

"Margaret, are you grieving
Over Goldengrove unleaving?"

There was a day while Philip and I were together when he reminded me that, after the dozen years since his father's death, it wasn't B. I grieved for. "One lets go," he said. Without thinking I said aloud the last line of Hopkins's poem, one we both knew, written to a young child, Margaret, whom he discovered one autumn day weeping over a Goldengrove and the falling of its golden leaves.

Hopkins asks himself the meaning of her tears. Is it for the dying leaves in the death of the year that the child weeps? No, not that. Something else. Her grief is the grief we all share, "the blight man was born for." Young and innocent as she is, unaware of the reason for her sadness, she weeps for her own mortality:

"It is Margaret you mourn for."

A Memory of Steve. I think often of his face from out of the past. How did it happen, how could so unaccountable a thing have happened? And whatever became of Steve?

He was a graduate student at Columbia University when I was a graduate student. Since he was starting work that fall toward a Ph.D. in psychology and I was in English, we might never have met save for the fact that each of us had a job three mornings a week in the Home Study Department. This was a correspondence school offering college courses by mail that Columbia ran for a number of years before dropping it from the curriculum. I was a typist who copied the mail-order lessons in, say, Biblical Literature or the Contemporary Novel that the instructors had scribbled out for us to send their students in Waukegan, Illinois, or maybe Brooklyn. Steve handled the mailing of materials and textbooks. Our friendship began with the scorn we shared for this poor excuse for an education. We used to walk from the building together at one o'clock, storming at Home Study, the nerve of them promising to teach you child psychology or the history of art by mail. I don't recall why we thought it couldn't be done. Then Steve would ask me to lunch and I would refuse because I was on my way to meet B.

I was in love with B. and nothing, nobody else mattered. Steve was a nice guy, two years older than I. He was twenty-two, sandy-haired, blue-eyed, tall and athletic, bright, funny besides. He made me laugh even when he was serious.

"What is the most important thing in the world?" he asked one day, and when I hesitated to say love because I didn't want to bring that up, he answered for me.

"Perhaps you are."

Just graduated from Stanford, Steve was without friends in this first time east. Each Tuesday, Thursday, Saturday morning at 9:00 I would find him waiting outside the office building to walk up the stairs with me. When he passed my desk during the day, he would wait till I looked up from the typewriter.

"Will you go to a movie with me tonight?"

"Sorry, Steve, I can't."

"Why not?"

"I have a date."

One Saturday morning in November he failed to appear on the front steps, nor was he in the mailing room upstairs. "Is Steve sick?" I asked, but nobody knew. Just before noon I glanced up to find him standing in his leather jacket at my desk. He was weeping.

"Oh my God, Steve!"

"Come out in the hall a minute," he said. "Something's happened."

In the empty corridor he tried to speak. "My father — " he began and choked on the words.

"What is it? Your father, is he ill?"

"No, it's not that. My father phoned me. He called this morning from

Palo Alto. I was still asleep. He said—" Steve gasped and the tears ran down his face. "He said my mother was killed last night, my mother and my kid sister Margaret. They were driving home on the freeway, and they were hit head-on, and they were both killed instantly. They're dead! My mother is dead and my sister is dead, and, Jesus Christ, what am I going to do?"

He gripped my hands. "We'll find out about trains," I said. "We have to get you home, Steve. I'll go down to Grand Central with you."

"But I can't go! That's it, I *can't*. Dad said I wasn't to come home, it takes too long to get there, I wasn't to spend the money. He said, 'I'm counting on you, Steve. There's nothing you can do. Hold on, go to your classes, stay where you are. I'll take care of everything.' He was crying too. He's alone now, I'm his son and he won't let me come home." Suddenly Steve threw his arms around me. "Don't leave me," he said. "I can't take it alone."

"I'll get my coat."

We walked out the building and down the street, hand gripping hand, saying nothing. At Broadway and 116th Street, we went down the stairs and took the first subway train, riding pressed close together, staring in a trance at the floor. At 14th Street we got off and began an aimless wandering, following the narrow streets through the Village, through Washington Park, up Fifth Avenue, where we passed Brentano's and I remembered a book I wanted to buy for B. My God, B.! It was already three o'clock! How would I explain my disappearance this afternoon? I looked over at Steve stumbling along, and he looked into my eyes and shook his head. "I wish I could help," I said, but all he said was "Stay with me." Never letting go of hands, we went on till it began to grow dark and I said, "Steve, I've got to go now." We had walked for six hours all the way back to 116th Street, and I left him standing in front of John Jay Hall where he lived. "Will you be all right?" I asked. For answer he pulled me to him and kissed me hard on the mouth. Then I ran across campus to my room and phoned B.

That weekend I tried but failed to reach Steve in his dorm. He didn't return my messages. I imagined him walking the streets. It scared me to think of him sweating it out alone. Tuesday morning he wasn't waiting on the steps; he was already upstairs sorting the mail. When I said to him, "Steve, can we talk?" he didn't look up or answer, nor did he come near my desk that day or the next. I knew it was grief, and I grieved with him. I knew I had let him down, I had failed him. On Saturday he quit his job at Home Study. I didn't see him again.

Not till the following June. B. and I had spent the year working, studying together, being in love. During the last week of school, a graduate student we knew, Ann Lefler, gave a farewell party in her small apartment. As it happened, the first person I saw on our arrival was Steve. He was standing near the door, talking to a tall, attractive girl, very blonde and tanned, who clung to him as if she didn't mean to let go, and he was laughing in her face like the old Steve. I was genuinely glad to see him.

"Steve! It's you!"

He turned with a start, hesitated, and slowly took the hand I offered. I introduced him to B. who had never seen him before and probably didn't remember who he was. Then Steve said in a low voice, with marked restraint, "I want you to meet my date. Actually she's my sister. This is my sister Margaret."

"Margaret?" I said.

"My sister," he said.

"From California?"

"Oh yes," she broke in eagerly, glancing up at Steve. "I've never in my life been to New York before. My mother and I came just last night to take Steve back home for the summer. It's been such a long year without my big brother."

Before B. and I left the party, I managed to follow Steve into the kitchen and catch him for a moment alone.

"Why did you do it?" I asked. "That's all I want to know."

His face was stony. He moved away toward the door, then turned back with a shrug. "I don't know myself," he said. "I honestly can't talk about it. I'm sorry, God, you don't know how sorry. It was a terrible, terrible thing to do."

He stopped and stood absolutely still. I put my hand on his arm.

"Please, Steve," I said. "Why?" He stared at me and started over.

"I don't *know* why. I was lonely, I guess, sort of desperate. I was so damned unhappy I — well, I did this crazy thing. I tried to imagine what some really awful grief would be like, the worst possible thing that could happen, losing someone like that, tearing your heart out. You know I'm in psychology."

He tried to laugh and looked down, avoiding my eyes. "But that wasn't the only reason. It wasn't even the real reason."

"What was it, Steve?"

"I wanted you to love me."

The Ten Childhoods. It was a strange journey I took with B. back to the scene of his childhoods. He had ten childhoods. To none of them had he returned till a notion to revisit struck him in the middle of a heat wave one scorching July. (Hemingway called it "chasing yesterdays.") On the trip in the Chrysler from North Carolina to southeastern Ohio, where the ten childhoods occurred within an area of three or four inches on the Ohio map, B. considered the profit and loss of being a Methodist minister's son. "The thing is, you move on every year or so to a new parsonage and start over," he said. "Without a hometown you have nowhere to grow up. You're free, the cat who walks by himself."

I was a Methodist minister's daughter, born in a parsonage like B., and well I knew my father's restless habit of changing pulpits. It puzzled me that the Episcopalian, Presbyterian, and Baptist preachers stayed put into mumbling old age. Only Methodists kept on the go. After his fourth or fifth move, my father resigned from his church and the Methodist Conference. He gave up and left for good to become a traveling salesman. My mother turned Episcopalian.

We had another thing in common, B. and I. He was born on the Ohio River at Powhatan Point that in his day flourished as a river hamlet and steamboat landing. I was born on the banks of the Susquehanna. Since neither of us stayed long enough to acquire a memory of our birthplace — my parents left town when I was two weeks old, B. left with his at two months — we spent that first day river-minded, walking beside the Ohio in the companionable present and sweltering heat. He hadn't abandoned me yet to return to his beginnings.

For the next week we lingered in nine more Ohio towns — Centerville, Beverly, Bethesda, Kimbolton, Newport (pop. 450), Senecaville (pop. 586), and so on — each village so like the last in Ohio's countryside that I forgot on arrival where we were. Each looked denominational, strictly Protestant. Beside the white frame M. E. Church pointing its thin spire into the eye of the Lord would be the cramped parsonage with front porch and porch swing, window box of pink petunias. Nobody waited hand outstretched to make us welcome. Over the years Methodists had come and gone in a quick turnover. We spoke to nobody.

Yet at each stop on the tour of B.'s childhoods, he left me behind and went back alone, and I had no way of following him. It was queer how his memories and my lack of them separated us, as hadn't happened in our travels before. I was bored with the itinerant Methodists. To forget the heat I tried to cool off with a line of Yeats: "My barren thoughts have chilled me to the bone." Inside each church were the bare pews, imitation stained-glass windows, American flag, lectern with open Bible, last Sunday's tiger lilies dead in a fluted vase.

For B. the scene might be Sunday morning, the service about to start, his father entering the pulpit as he, the new preacher's son, rushed tardily down the center aisle. A foot was stuck out to trip him. Falling on his face, he jumped up and yanked a boy to the aisle where they fought, kicking and sprawling, till a vestryman pulled them apart. A preacher's kid was marked for a sissy. B. had to clarify from the start who he was, which he established weekdays when he had to wheel his baby sister down the street in her carriage. It took a lot of scrapping to defend his name.

On the fifth day — I think Lore City, Ohio — while we stood before the Methodist parsonage, B. whistled and pointed to the yard between his house and the next. "There's the spot where I tried to rape Marie," he said, "in broad daylight." He was about ten. I stared dutifully but all I saw was a patch of grass.

"You're kidding."

"Yes," he said. "But I knew what it was you had to do. Marie was the girl next door and I liked her a lot. After school we played catch or wrestled, till the day I threw her on her back and pulled up her dress. She whacked me hard and ran in her house. She yelled from the back door, 'You think you're smart, the new preacher's boy and all. You're just dumb, I hate you. So go on home!' She never spoke to me again."

"Did you mind?"

"I minded."

In Flushing, Ohio, we searched for a corner grocery where B., now in high school, had worked after school as delivery boy. It was an empty shop on Main Street, and as we peered through the dirty windowpane I glimpsed the sweat on my face. B. saw himself rushing out the store one winter afternoon with arms full of groceries, bumping head-on into a customer. "Hey, babe!" she cried, catching him in her arms. He looked up and recognized her—the one and only town whore. Everybody in Flushing knew who *she* was.

"Hold on," she cried, hugging him and the bags to her plump body. "So you're the new preacher's son. I hear your name is Merle. Well, lover boy, that happens to be my name too." She kissed the top of his head. "So we'll have to call you Little Merle and me Big Merle."

B. pulled away and ran for the door. The storekeeper and several customers hooted with laughter. "Oh, lover boy," they yelled after him. "We'll have to call you Little Merle and her Big Merle."

The name stuck. Even when people didn't say it, he knew they wanted to. He was Little Merle in that town till his father's next charge took the family to Loudonville, last of the ten childhoods. Here the presiding elder came to Sunday dinner and prayed that, like John Wesley, B. would become a Methodist preacher and toil in the Lord's vineyards. "Amen," said B.'s father.

"Are you glad we went?" I asked when the journey was over.

"The effect was sobering," B. said. "It was a mad and monstrous plan."

The History of Malden. More and more my survival on this earth amazes me. Yet guilty as I am of the role of longstayer, I've seldom thought of the survival of my ancestors, each of whom existed long enough to become my progenitor, no easy task in their own threatened times.

But recently I happened to look into *The History of Malden, 1633–1785* by D. P. Corey, a book my father sent me years ago with the admonition to prize it. Charley loved genealogy, which was odd considering his name was Smith. The fact was, he told me—though I couldn't have cared less at the time—my great-great-great-great-great-great-great-great-grandfather, William Sargent, was in the book as one of the founders of Malden, Massachusetts (now a suburb of Boston). William, born 1602 during the reign of Elizabeth, arrived from England in 1638 with his third wife, Sarah, and two daughters. He was made a freeman of the Massachusetts Bay Colony under Governor Winthrop, who eight years before had brought the company of Puritans to the new world. By 1640 William had acquired a farm of twenty acres at the brow of Sargent's Hill—a settlement of a dozen Puritan families that in 1649 became the town of Malden. That year Charles I was beheaded, Governor Winthrop died, and there was a great mortality among the children in New England.

When I belatedly examined this ponderous book, full of Sargents (with lovely names like Delight, Relief, Thankful), I opened it toward the end and came upon young Jacob Sargent, sixth generation from William. I saw how heroic he was to have become my ancestor. Jacob was a boy not sixteen when, on April 19, 1775, as one of the Minutemen of Malden he marched out of town to the beat of Cousin Winslow Sargent's drum. Early that morning a horseman had come galloping along Medford Road crying, "The regulars are out!" While the meetinghouse bell rang, the Minutemen were mustered on the green in front of Kettell's Tavern, four or five Sargents among the seventy-four in Captain Blaney's Company. The women and children followed after till they disappeared out of sight up the hill. At the juncture of Lexington and Medford roads they halted to take captive several British soldiers. Jacob survived that day of skirmishes known as the Lexington Alarm, fought in the lines at Boston, married young Lydia Paine of Malden in February 1781, and fathered nine children. His second child was my great-great-grandmother Sally Sargent.

It was a close call for me, since on the same day in 1775 John Raymond, on my mother's side, was killed in Lexington, a dozen miles from Malden. John Raymond was forty-four, a private in Captain Parker's Company of Minutemen who lined up, some sixty or seventy, the morning of April 19 on the village green to try to stop the eight hundred British regulars sent out from Boston by General Gage. The struggle lasted a few minutes, eight Americans were killed, and the British moved on to Concord, where at the bridge five hundred Minutemen confronted them and drove them in disorder back to Lexington. On the retreat they stopped at Munroe's Tavern to dress their wounded. Since the tavern keeper had fled, somehow they rounded up and compelled John Raymond, who was lame, to serve them, drank freely and became noisy and quarrelsome. As he was attempting to escape by the side door, they shot and killed him "in a brutal and cowardly manner" (Charles Hudson, *History of Lexington*). John Raymond's body was found a few yards from the tavern.

His youngest child, Isaac, was five years old. Luckily he survived to marry Rebecca Livermore, whose father Jason of nearby Weston, Massachusetts, in the same county of Middlesex, had been a Minuteman in Phineas Moore's Company. Jason also marched on April 19 and fought at Bunker Hill on June 17, having already risked his life in the French and Indian War. Like the other patriots in my family tree, he came as near as any to shaking me out of its branches.

Hooked by now, I turned back and started over with Great-something-William Sargent, whose father Roger was mayor of Northampton, England. In 1626 Roger wrote in his will, "I give my five silver spoons to my five children viz. to my sons Joseph John William and to my daughters Elizabeth and Dorothy, desiring that they live together in love and help each other." Whether or not the silver spoon crossed the Atlantic to reach William, he never saw his family again. In the new town of Malden with its meetinghouse in "uncouth wilderness," William became the lay preacher. "They had a godly Christian named W. Sarjant who did preach the Word unto them till the year 1650," wrote Edward Johnson in his history of New England, *The Wonder-Working Providence*, 1654. William was not allowed to baptize or administer the bread and wine but could exhort the flock, hearten the wavering, and visit the sick.

In 1650 the people of Malden acquired their first pastor, Marmaduke Mathews, a fiery Welshman, graduate of All Soul's Oxford, who lasted one year before he was summoned by the General Court of Massachusetts to answer twenty-two accusations of offensive and heretical remarks in his sermons. One remark was: "When the body of Christ was lifted up on his cross his soul was in hell what in hell? yea in hell, in that hell where the devil rules and reigns." Despite such "unfettered" oratory, Mathews was held by the town in high esteem; a petition in his behalf, defending the right to free speech, bore the names of thirty-six wives and mothers, Mrs. Sargent among them. Another signer was Thankslord Shepperd. Nevertheless a committee of the court, one of them Anne Bradstreet's husband Simon and another Edward Johnson, who said, "Christ cannot trash indure," censured Mathews and imposed a fine on the church of £50, which they indignantly resented and for ten years didn't pay. After Mathews's hurried departure for Wales, William Sargent again filled in in the pulpit. Since the sermons lasted two hours, he must have done a lot of exhorting.

Into this state of upheaval came young Michael Wigglesworth, age twenty-four, born in Yorkshire and brought as a child in 1638 (the year William Sargent migrated) to New England. He was a Harvard graduate and strict Puritan whose Calvinist theology was more disquieting than Mathews's so-called "miscarriages" and far less cheerful, though Wigglesworth said in his diary that one of his corruptions was frothiness. Cotton Mather introduced him, "From Cambridge the Star made his remove, till he comes to dispense his sweet influences upon thee, O Malden!" (Later Mather called him "a little feeble shadow of a man.") Malden, soon disenchanted, was less than grateful. From the day he arrived in 1656, reproving them for "lightness and mad mirth," Wigglesworth caused rebellion among his parishioners. After two years he was complaining to the Lord: "How long, Lord, wilt thou be angry with us? What? for ever? of what will you do with this poor sinful afflicted people? What meaneth the heat of this great indignation? where is thy zeal and thy strength; the sounding of thy bowels (Lord!) are they restrained?"

Though Wigglesworth remained their pastor forty-nine years till his death in 1705, the clamorings were loud and frequent that he lay down his office. He was accounted a burden, a sickly man — who fathered eight children, outlived two wives and married a third — a confirmed invalid with a weak voice and chronic sore throat (not ailing but conceited, they said), often absent from service. For years the town didn't pay him a salary. Wigglesworth replied to his congregation by writing in 224 stanzas the lurid *Day of Doom,* the day of wrath to remind those poor sinners how they will quake on Judgment Day:

> They wring their hands, their caitiff hands,
>   and gnash their teeth for terror;
> They cry, they roar for anguish sore,
>   and gnaw their tongues for horror.
> But get away without delay;
>   Christ pities not your cry.
> Depart to hell; there may you yell
>   and roar eternally.

Go to hell, he told them. (How did Grandfather Sargent like being told he was a naked sinner, one of the damned "wallowing in all kind of sin"? It must have tried his soul.) This was the great American epic of the seventeenth century. England had Milton, New England had Wigglesworth. From Malden it shook to its depths the Puritan world, and Wigglesworth was invited to become president of Harvard.

William Sargent moved to Barnstable (to get away from Wigglesworth?) and was made a freeman of the Plymouth colony. He died in 1682 after forty-four turbulent years in America. His eldest son, John, born in Malden in 1639, married Deborah Hillier of Barnstable, thus mingling Puritan and Pilgrim blood in his descendants. John returned to Malden, took part as one of twenty-three men from Malden in King Philip's war with the Narragansett Indians, became a selectman, and had fifteen children. In 1692 when he was fifty-three, the insanity of witchcraft attacked Salem, where after sensational trials 115 were accused of demonic powers and 23 witches and warlocks put to death. The madness spread over New England; forty towns were party to it. Malden among them. Elizabeth Fosdick and Elizabeth Paine (an ancestor of Lydia Paine who married Jacob Sargent) were two arrested on a charge of witchcraft, which allows me to claim descent from a witch. Just how far Michael Wigglesworth supported the witch hunt is unknown, though Samuel Sewall, a judge at the Salem trials, was his good friend, as were Cotton Mather and his father Increase, who believed in witches (and the Bible said, "Thou shalt not suffer a witch to live" Exodus 22:18). A few months before his death Wigglesworth wrote in a trembling hand to Increase Mather, "I fear that innocent blood hath been shed: & that many have had their hands defiled therewith." Whatever my forebears thought of witches, or the wrath of God and the power of Satan, they left no comment behind.

Wigglesworth was followed fifteen years later by young Joseph Emerson, who in 1721 married Mary Moody, and the happy couple occupied Wigglesworth's house that was infested with big black bugs. It was put in "good repair" by Jabez Sargent, the joiner, grandson of John. Three years later it burned to the ground, and Mr. Emerson preached a daylong sermon on Job. Unlike Wigglesworth, he was free of infirmities, missing only two Sundays in forty-six years. He prayed every night that no descendant of his might become rich. But I'm not his descendant. Ralph Waldo is.

Beholden as I am to these ancestors for persistence in living, I regret their oversight in leaving no words behind to say how it was done. It's too late for Tom Spaulding, my mother's grandfather, to testify as to how he bore his terrible sojourn in Libby Prison during the Civil War. On August 30, 1862, age forty-one, this hardy farmer from Broome County, New York, left his wife Narcissa, and four small daughters (like the four in *Little Women*) to join the 161st New York Volunteer Infantry. Two years later he was captured by the Confederates and from suffering and starvation died soon after the war ended.

As a child I was told about infamous Libby Prison by my great-aunt

Net, one of Tom Spaulding's daughters, who as a young girl had nursed her dying father. She never tired of the appalling tale. Libby, second only in horror to Andersonville, was a former warehouse beside the James River in Richmond, Virginia, a three-story building full of rats, where some thousand Union soldiers at a time were held and, covered with vermin, thousands died of untreated wounds, starvation, smallpox. On the bare floor a man was allotted just space for his body. Though Lincoln said, "Leave it as a monument," after the war the prison was sold, dismantled, moved brick by brick (600,000, carefully numbered) to Chicago, and rebuilt to become the popular Libby Prison War Museum, a house of horrors where they sold wooden napkin rings from the original flooring, bloodstains and all.

The prison diary of Lieut. Colonel F. F. Cavada (*Libby Life: Experiences of a Prisoner of War in Richmond, Va., 1863–64*) describes the loathesome, foul-smelling hell Libby was. He arrived to find men lying backed in rows in a suffocating room, "a host of shoeless, shirtless, shameless spectres," mummies recalled to live again "as if it were an unearthed cemetery." The life was inhuman — the awful tedium, the hunger — desperate men jammed together, jostling, wrangling over morsels of food. After rumors of attempted escapes, the inmates were counted and recounted at frequent intervals, forbidden to go near the windows. "The shooting of prisoners at the windows continues," wrote Cavada. "The sentinels seem to consider it very fine sport." He was aghast at the implacable hatred shown the North with the streets outside the prison crowded with sightseers come to jeer at the Yankees.

One more ancestor I never met was Elizabeth Raymond, my mother's grandmother, who in the 1850s was known and sought after as "the handsomest widow in Tioga County, N.Y." She would be as sorry as I to leave it at that. I stare at the daguerrotype of a handsome, buxom lady in a silk dress, deeply regretful that I know her face but not her fortune, how she talked, what she liked to eat, what love affairs if any. Her son was another John Raymond, my grandfather, who played the ocarina, married Tom

Spaulding's daughter Effie Ann, and was too young to go to the Civil War.

Most inscrutable of the lot are Charley and Lizzie, my parents. What wouldn't I give to read the hidden history of their young lives, all the passion and, afterward, all the grief. But in the telling they'd be bound to admit that having me was the last thing they intended—a child never meant to be born of their faltering marriage. With them as progenitors, I was at the greatest possible risk of not seeing the light of day.

Günter Grass, *From the Diary of a Snail:* "I'm an accident, who has accidentally survived."

Charley and the Model T. My father Charley was a man who owned a Model T. It was his pride and punishment, his first automobile and Henry Ford's first, one of fifteen million cars he built after 1908 "for the great multitude" and sold for five hundred dollars. The last Model T appeared in 1927, scrapped and soon obsolete, replaced by the new four-door Model A. Charley bought his headstrong beast about 1911 when the Model T, while scarcely a Pierce Arrow, was hailed as "without doubt the greatest creation in automobiles ever placed before a people." E. B. White wrote in "Farewell, My Lovely!"—his love song to the Model T he bought in 1922—that it was practically the American scene, the miracle God had wrought. Tearing along at ten miles an hour, it still frightened horses off the road. Charley loved his stylish little runabout with a passion, convinced though he was that the car had it in for him and meant to break his arm or knock him down and run over him. Machines took strong exception to Charley, and his fear of them he strongly conveyed to me. The Model T scared the living daylights out of both of us.

Before attempting to start his Tin Lizzie (not named for my mother, he said), he would pat and smooth the coat of its black erect body the way he used to quiet his race horse, summoning up courage—it took courage—to show who was master. Soon a crowd gathered to wonder and admire, while I, a child of five (on a visit to my grandparents), sat enthroned and uneasy high on the front seat with my hat on, waiting for my father to take us for a joyride. At last he would roll up his sleeves, reach over the wheel to set the spark, squat in front of the engine, groan aloud, and insert the crank. For the next minutes he cranked and sweated, while the car played dead and nothing happened, till suddenly with a roar coming alive, it would lunge forward like an angry bull—and me screaming and Charley yelling bloody murder and leaping into the ditch. As he picked himself up, cursing and feeling around for broken bones, the little car, now trembling on all four cylinders with obvious readiness for the road, quivered and shook as if about to tear off toward eternity without him. "Pull on the emergency brake!" Charley would yell at me, waving his arms, as I, not knowing what on earth to do, began to sob. Just then the flivver with a sad little explosion would give up and die, and I would jump out in a hurry and run for dear life into the house.

"Come on back, baby! Let's go!" Charley would shout as he cranked it again and it caught hold a second time, and he would race back and hurl himself headlong into the driver's seat. And it would die.

Happy Endings. I remember a night years ago when B. stood up in the middle of a movie and said aloud, "This is the damnedest most immoral piece I've ever seen in my life," and sat down. The audience didn't applaud or turn round to glare at him. They went on watching the picture and at the end filed out without asking B. what was wrong with it.

The manipulation of the plot exasperated him, the immorality of the lies it told about people. It concerned a young couple—Doris Day and Rock Hudson in *Pillow Talk*—who detested each other on sight and battled their way through reels of pure contempt, insult, and mayhem, only to fall into each other's arms in permanent bliss. It happens all the while except in real life. Recently I saw "Terms of Endearment," with Shirley MacLaine in the role of a spoiled, possessive, dyed-blonde widow whom children fear, who intimidates her daughter and fights with her next-door neighbor (Jack Nicholson), a middle-aged lecher and alcoholic. The daughter escapes into marriage and three children in Iowa, dies of cancer, and leaves her children to Mother. Mother marries the fruitcake—the lush she has loathed for fifteen years as he has avoided her like poison—and together they prepare to bring up the little ones in tender loving care. The Oscars it won proclaimed it the best picture of the year, sure to warm your heart.

Even Jane Austen had trouble creating characters who end happily in a perfect union with the right mate. Only in *Pride and Prejudice,* it seems to me, does Elizabeth Bennet come close to making sense of marrying Mr. Darcy and he of marrying her.

From one miserable evening spent at a ball where Fitzwilliam Darcy is present, Elizabeth considers him "the proudest, most disagreeable man in the world." At first sight of Elizabeth he says, loudly enough for her to overhear, "She is tolerable but not handsome enough to tempt *me.*" Offended by further examples of his icy conceit, the most she can feel for this "hateful man" is aversion and a deeply rooted dislike. When partway through the novel Darcy, having stared at her at intervals, tells her that though he has struggled against it he loves her and proposes to make her his wife, she rejects him indignantly. She calls him patronizing. He calls her uncivil. They quarrel. She says, "You could not have made me the offer of your hand in any possible way that would have tempted me to accept it."

Meant for each other, they have merely to change their attitude completely; the novel depends on it. But can they *reverse* their natures? Darcy shows undeniable improvement in manners. Elizabeth, falling in love, is ashamed of herself for having rightly questioned his character. Yet to make this marriage succeed, they must reform their ways and remodel their lives. Darcy must accept with good grace her faulty upbringing and family that he finds vulgar. Elizabeth will require training in decorum for union with a mate of superior social rank; she must learn to control her laughter to match his reserve. Jane Austen liked Elizabeth best of her heroines (though she never really objected to any of their shortcomings).

On the other hand, Emma Woodhouse will make an unmanageable wife. Charming as she is, she has a fault that increases with age, a well-meaning desire to meddle in other people's lives. She is an officious arranger of matches for people who don't match, and Mr. Knightley is annoyed with her. He reprimands her, disapproving of her blind schemes to marry Harriet Smith off to several of the wrong men. "Emma," he says, "you have been no friend to Harriet Smith!" In the end she is repentant, but is she cured or curable?

Mr. Knightley, a sensible man seventeen years older than she, will be a patient husband, like a father to Emma, but his patience will be tried. He will leave his handsome Abbey to move in with Emma and her father, a fussy old hypochondriac who says things like "Let us all take a little gruel together" and "An egg boiled very soft is not unwholesome." Imagine the three each night at dinner.

The poorest bet is little Fanny Price. I doubt if she will *survive* marriage, so timid and fragile is she, a bundle of nerves, the most agitated heroine in fiction. Fanny sinks to the ground if looked at, her cheeks flush scarlet, her mind is disordered, her heart fails. If she ventures to step outside the house she is "knocked up," Jane Austen's felicitous phrase for collapsing from exhaustion.

At Mansfield Park, where she was taken in as a poor relation, nobody notices her for nearly nine years—not the heedless young people, not her indolent aunt Lady Bertram, who treats her as a housemaid, not her cruel aunt Mrs. Norris—nobody but Cousin Edmund, who pities little Fanny and is brotherly kind. She loves Edmund, but fearful of betraying her emotions "in some unpardonable excess" suffers in silence and low spirits when, with a singular lack of tact, he urges her to marry his friend Henry Crawford while he himself plans to possess Mary Crawford, who has no wish to wed a future clergyman. In the end Fanny is left the winner, glowing with gratitude, to fill the role of Edmund's wife. She seems unequal to the nuptials.

B. totally approved of Jane Austen, and so do I. He didn't call her immoral at all. She simply liked happy endings.

Shelley on Love. Today I found on the bookshelf an old volume of Shelley—the slim green leather Oxford edition I gave B. when we were graduate students at Columbia. It looked scuffed and worn, as well it might since he carried it in his coat pocket the way Shelley carried Sophocles. Because of the green ribbon marking the place, the book in my hand fell open to "Epipsychidion."

God, I hated that poem. As I sat down to read it again, recalling its six hundred gasping lines ("I pant, I sink, I tremble, I expire!"), I wondered how it would sound to me now. Shelley wrote the poem while he and Mary were living in Pisa to an Italian girl, Emilia Viviani. Emilia's father, governor of Pisa, had placed her in the convent of St. Anna where, a "prisoner" for nearly three years, she awaited at nineteen the completion of marriage plans made against her will. Needless to say, Emilia appealed instantly to Shelley, this "poor captive bird" with her exquisite young beauty, faultless features, dark eyes, mass of black hair, and volatile romantic nature. He was in agony over her sufferings, an emotion Mary not only didn't share but thought ridiculous. Mary was a possessive wife. Her pride was hurt by his infatuation, her feelings were wounded by the poem, which never mentions her. She called it his Italian Platonics.

Shelley probably wrote "Epipyschidion"—inventing the title from the Greek *epi* (on) and *psychidion* (little soul)—during February 1821, after two months of visits to Emilia and ardent letters between them. It was published without his name, only a hundred copies, in which he pretended that the lines were by a fictional poet "wounded and weak and panting" who had died in Florence. Though the theme purports to be platonic love, one reviewer took it for a defense of marrying one's sister and attributed it to Byron. In breathless couplets Shelley addresses Emily as a seraph from heaven, an ideal of perfection beyond his reach ("Spouse! Sister! Angel! O too late Beloved! O too soon adored, by me!"), but nearly a third of the poem deals with an amorous scheme to elope with her to a far-off island ("Say, my heart's sister, wilt thou sail with me?") There they will achieve a unique union with Emily both vestal sister and bride ("Our breath shall intermix, our bosoms bound, / And our veins beat together"). The day never came. Emilia was reluctantly married on September 8 of that year, without inviting the Shelleys to the wedding. Ten months later, on July 8, Shelley drowned in the Bay of Spezia. It remained a poem of exalted desire.

All his life Shelley held the view that it's possible for a man to love more than one woman at a time, especially if one of them is the sister of his soul (as Elizabeth Hitchener had been when he was married to Harriet, as Mary was when he left Harriet to elope with her). He rejected the idea that love need be limited to a single being and described marriage, chained to one person, as "the dreariest and the longest journey." Mary the Moon of his world, Emilia the Sun were adored simultaneously for different qualities: "True love in this differs from gold and clay, / That to divide is not to take away." This he believed.

And so did B. But whether a woman can love equally two men at once never came up between us.

Life in Middlemarch. Now that a movie is made of it, readers turn to the novel, George Eliot's *Middlemarch,* many for the first time after its neglect for more than a century. It has been a keepsake in my family for years. B. and I practically started married life by disagreeing over that book, happily opposed. B. loved to tease me about his superior recognition of its worth, since he was not only a Victorian scholar but born in Victoria's reign. I claimed to look at its imperfections with a fuller awareness because I knew a lot more than he did about women. B. considered *Middlemarch* the greatest novel of the nineteenth century.

"Better than *Anna Karenina?*" I would cry. "Better than *Madame Bovary?* Come on."

"Why not? Prove me wrong."

"Better than Jane Austen? Oh no, *not* Jane Austen!"

I complained of its wordiness, its high-minded concern for propriety, its moral rectitude. "There isn't any adultery in it," I would say. And he would laugh. And so would I.

When B. became terminally ill for those many months, the one book he allowed me to read to him was *Middlemarch.* He especially liked its humor: Mrs. Cadwallader saying to the rector: "These charitable people never know vinegar from wine till they have swallowed it and got the colic." He found Dorothea Brooke adorable, even after her two recklessly bad marriages the wisest and most beautiful of heroines, comparable to Saint Theresa of Ávila as George Eliot said she was. He would lie on the sofa absorbed in the plot he knew so well while I read on day after day that long hot summer, till the day came when I looked up and he had stopped listening. He had slipped into the coma from which he never regained consciousness. Shortly after his death, B.'s graduate students held a ceremony one afternoon in the Rare Book Room of the main library, where they presented to Duke University in his name and memory a first edition of *Middlemarch*.

Thirty years later I've read it again, marveling this time at the monumental novel it is, at its abundant life, and at how much I had missed. George Eliot was a great writer, powerful in recreating a world clearly identifiable as her own. But to praise her as another Jane Austen, as the critics are set on doing, seems extravagant, since she is exactly what Jane Austen was not — heavyhanded. Lacking is the Austen wit and lightness of touch, the clarity of language, the brevity. To compare George Eliot to Henry James would be more like it.

But it's the portrait of Dorothea Brooke as a woman that concerns me still, the extraordinary lack of judgment she shows that is so contradictory to her strong moral character. The story moves at a deliberate pace through three years of Dorothea's adult life in the provincial town of Middlemarch, just before the Reform Bill of 1832. She and her sister are living in the care of their genial uncle Brooke, and Dorothea is presented at nineteen as a highly intelligent, mature, strong-willed girl who knows her own mind. She is also ardent. Yet when Mr. Casaubon comes wooing, a dried-up old bookworm more than twice her age, she is attracted by what she thinks is his intellect, and imagines that marrying him would be like marrying Pascal!

The brief courtship is timid and dreary. As for the passion he exhibits: "Mr. Casaubon found that sprinkling was the utmost approach to a plunge which his stream would afford him." Was ever a wooing so pale and loveless? asks the narrator. "Has any one ever pinched into the pilulous smallness the cobweb of pre-matrimonial acquaintanceship?"

On their disastrous honeymoon in Rome, which Casaubon spends inspecting manuscripts in the Vatican, Dorothea realizes to her dismay what she has got for a mate, a dull, sterile pedant who dreams of footnotes. Disillusioned and unhappy, she is saved from despair by Casaubon's attractive second cousin, Will Ladislaw, a romantically inclined young man whose smile should have warned her away. It was, Eliot says, "a gush of inward light illuminating the transparent skin as well as the eyes, and playing about every curve and line as if some Ariel were touching them with a new charm, and banishing forever the traces of moodiness."

The nightmare marriage spent in Casaubon's house in the village, where he shuts himself in his library "to chew a cud of erudite mistake," lasts for eighteen months till Casaubon dies—after revising his will denying Dorothea his fortune if she marries Ladislaw, whom he detests. Dorothea, widowed at twenty-one, finds herself in love with Ladislaw, by whose shallow nature she is not deterred. Another man in town, Dr. Lydgate (who also chooses the wrong mate) would have been more suitable, more her equal intellectually. But Dorothea is no good at picking husbands. She gives up Casaubon's money, marries the impoverished Ladislaw, and ends a contented housewife, her mental capacities never tested, the life she intended never fulfilled.

"We are all of us born in moral stupidity," says George Eliot, a trace of which appears to linger in Dorothea's makeup, leaving her not as bright as she might be. Even as an innocent child she believed in "the gratitude of wasps."

The Rhines and ESP. When B. and I moved to Durham, N.C., in the 1940s, we lived in a white house in Tuscaloosa Forest—a wooded section of town—that J. B. Rhine and his wife Louisa had owned. He was the founder of parapsychology, a professor at Duke who devoted most of his academic life to investigating psychic phenomena, such as telepathy, clairvoyance, precognition, communication with the dead. J. B.'s main laboratory experiments were with a deck of twenty-five playing cards with five different symbols by which he tested people, often Duke students for what he called their extrasensory perception, or the ability to name the correct symbol without seeing the card. He also visited haunted houses, interviewed mediums and once a talking horse. Unfortunately, from these inquiries he found no way, nor has one been found, to predict or control a psychic event, no way to show that the dead can speak.

In the Rhines' former house where we lived for several years, we found ESP cards under the linoleum but experienced no hauntings or other disturbances. J. B. and Louisa became our good friends who never asked us to submit to testing our psychic powers. In London one year we heard J. B. speak at the annual meeting of the Society for Psychical Research, where he explained his scientific experiments and was respectfully received, though the year before they had enjoyed a more lively talk on "Apparitions." Aldous Huxley and Arthur Koestler were two of the many followers interested at that time in parapsychology. We used to dine at the Rhine home with mediums and poets, with "sensitives" like Eileen Garrett who sought out the Rhines to reveal their personal intimations of immortality, though neither Rhine ever professed to have a psychic happening or glimpse into the unknown. Louisa was a matter-of-fact, sensible, non-mystical woman who nevertheless became tireless in her search. Sceptical at first and wary of psychics and their claims, she once told me that the mass of evidence she had collected of people possessing such powers was too overwhelming to be denied. J. B. was a warm, lovable, generous man, convinced that these frontiers of the mind exist and knowledge of them can be put to everyday use.

Then one day Louisa phoned to ask us to dinner on Saturday night and to beg a special favor of me. Their honored guest that evening was to be the wife of a newspaper man in New York who had recently died and was sending back reams of his own poems from the Other Side by means of a Ouija board. After the lady's reading of his posthumous works to the assembled group, Louisa wanted me to discuss these poems and criticize them in any way I liked, not necessarily, she said, for any message they might carry from the grave.

I couldn't do that. The Rhines said they understood and were forgiving, but we weren't invited again.

Indians on the Eno. In New Mexico where the nuclear bomb was born, I heard people say, "Let's give the country back to the Indians." They meant the Pueblos, Navajos, Zuni—the peaceful first settlers who would not in a thousand years have blown up the earth they loved, which rightly belonged to them.

My land is Indian land. I give them credit for Indian summer in this countryside. Three hundred years ago the Eno Indians lived where I live, a mighty insignificant Sioux tribe for whom the Eno River below my house is named. Like the little stream, barely negotiable in a canoe, they didn't amount to much. They hunted bear, venison, wild turkey, an occasional bison in my pine woods, fished in the Eno, and disappeared in a mist nobody knows where. I see them of a morning roaming Indian file over the dooryard, the last man scuffling the earth to hide their tracks. In 1670 John Lederer, a German explorer, came upon the tent village of Eno Indians and said they were small and thievish and slung stones. In 1701 young John Lawson, a surveyor from Charleston, found them a friendly tribe whose chief was Eno Will. Lawson invited him to become a Christian, and wrote, "Eno Will was of the best and most agreeable Temper that ever I met with in an Indian."

When the white settlers first came to North Carolina in the seventeenth century, already located east of here was a tribe of the Iroquois, the savage Tuscaroras, who lived in some fifteen settlements along the banks of the Neuse River. By 1700 the Indians had become bitterly resentful of the colonists, who, they claimed, cheated them of their tribal lands, raped their women, kidnapped their people and sold them into slavery. On September 22, 1711, five hundred Tuscarora warriors, divided into parties, descended on the unsuspecting settlers, and the bloody Tuscarora War began that lasted nearly three years, killing several hundred settlers and thousands of the Tuscaroras. Their first victim was John Lawson, whom they seized and, during an all-night dance round a huge fire, tortured to death by sticking pine splinters into his body from head to toe and lighting them one by one to turn him into a flaming torch.

Finally defeated, the Tuscaroras fled north to New York State where they joined the Iroquois. And the poor Eno Indians may have fled after them and lost their tribal unity, though in 1733 William Byrd, colonial gentleman of Virginia, who had purchased 20,000 acres of land in North Carolina and named it the Land of Eden, came one day upon Eno Will. By his reckoning seventy-eight years old, Eno Will offered to conduct Byrd to a silver mine on the Eno River. Byrd gave him a bottle of rum instead "to comfort his heart." We haven't found the silver yet.

One positive good I know about the Eno Indians (true, they say, of the Apaches and other tribes) is that they would have nothing whatever to do with their mother-in-law. She wasn't allowed near their person or permitted to live with her married daughter or even *speak* to her son-in-law — one sure way of keeping the peace.

The Three Arts Club. Fifty years ago Nan Cole, wife of the provost at Duke, started a little club with the ambitious name Three Arts. It differed from other clubs in town in that everyone invited to join was an artist, musician, or writer and was asked to bring what she had on hand to show, perform, or read at the monthly meetings.

The wonder is, the club still meets fifty years later. From the start twenty young women, many of them faculty wives, ignored the perils of talent under scrutiny and settled for sociability, unlimited approval, and unrestrained praise. Three arts at a time proved too many to argue about. Nobody claimed to be expert in all three — able to paint a watercolor, play a Byrd tune, and write a verse simultaneously — which lessened the competition. As Camus said, "Life is too short for afternoon teas." Our afternoon teas were too short for passing judgment on three arts before supper.

We settled for enjoyment of each other. Now, among the artists, Lib, Ruth, Nadine show their paintings and we brood over them, hearing about acrylics and collages, endorsing everything in sight and calling it beautiful. Joan, who works in stained glass, creates in her studio full-length figures of Mary Magdalene and St. Francis, the saints and the apostles. Eventually she'll have to build a church to hold them. Sylvia is an internationally known weaver of tapestries, whose living room is graced by an enormous loom and the walls by her huge designs. When asked how, with house, husband, children and outdoor pool, she manages to weave twelve hours a day, she replies, "I am disciplined." Sally is a well-known potter. Florence is a sculptor in marble, molding with loving hands and chisel her smooth gray abstract forms. Shirley molds out of cloth stuffed with cotton ("soft sculpture") nearly life-size figures of Leda and the Swan, a herd of buffalo heads with Buffalo Bill dead center, a group of banana trees, and, my favorite, Aphrodite emerging from the foam on a large artichoke.

The musicians are professionals who may arrange a program together — Ruth and Junita on two pianos — or Sylvia plays her violin, Nancy her cello. For a while we had a recorder group, followed by a harpist followed by a flutist. Two are composers: Lola, who sets Shakespeare's songs to modern arrangements; Barbara, who composes devotional hymns and has written a cookbook.

The writers remain the least ready to perform, for the reason, it's said, that all writers hate to write and avoid getting started. Once under way they will read of an afternoon a whole play, like Ginny, or chapters of a novel, like Betsy. Lee's musical comedy, *The Scandalous Mrs. Jack,* was given a stage production in Raleigh; Fanny's bestselling novel, *Good Morning, Miss Dove,* became a Hollywood movie. Babs is an essayist, Mena a biographer of General Julian S. Carr, Camilla publishes short stories, Julie writes paperback romances that sell in supermarkets. Two are newspaper women: Jerry, an editorial writer, makes portraits of people; Betty, who reviews books, reads us excerpts from her journal.

For a while I lamented the lack of criticism that reduces everything to a show-and-tell exercise greeted with applause. After teaching creative writing for years at Duke, I expected some comment at our sessions accompanied by free advice. But by now I'm glad to get away with undermining the arts by, say, a travelogue of Tibet or Lapland—places nobody but me could be dragged to. Only once did I disturb the peace with something I read. That time I chose two accounts of unhappy marriages, the tale of Héloïse and Abelard, and the story of Effie Gray's union with John Ruskin. Everyone was quietly attentive till I reached the part where Effie learned why her marriage had not been consummated. Well! Voices were raised, confusion and tumult descended. The plight of poor Héloïse and her unmanned husband was forgot. Instead a public debate began, followed by the airing of strong views on the delicate subject of Effie's pubic hair and Ruskin's objection to it. I don't recall what the upshot was— whether the final vote went for or against Effie, only that it took me several days to recover from the to-do and laugh about it. Up to then I was flummoxed.

According to the art historian Anne Hollander, "Pubic hair is an extremely ambiguous and illusive subject to pursue." Though in modern art the dark triangle is frequently displayed, in classical art, both painting and sculpture, it was a way of distinguishing the sexes: males had pubic hair, even under the fig leaf. Females did not.

In real life it has long been considered inelegant by ladies of quality, for example, courtesans and strippers. (A famous exception was Lady Caroline Lamb, who for love of Byron enclosed in a letter a gift of her pubic hair and requested his in exchange.)

"But from classical times onward," writes Ms. Hollander, "the harmony of the female body seemed to require the absence of hair." So John Ruskin must have thought.

Caroline Gordon at Home. I recall meeting Caroline Gordon, Allen Tate's wife, one evening in Durham. When we were introduced she gave me a scrutinizing look, frowned, turned abruptly to her hostess, and said, "May I have two aspirins, please?"

Now Caroline Gordon is dead, and left is a collection of letters to her friend Sally Wood, 1924–1937, to whom she sent hurried, dashed-off notes concerning domestic events like "Cousin Sis is quite well except for a rash on her stomach." It's clear from them that she should have written a memoir of her tumultuous days with Allen Tate, when a generation of writers invaded their household and her struggle with the literary temperament was a losing one. "When I think of all the people I've had here," she wrote Sally, "feeding them on a shoe string . . ." well, it was hectic, it was infuriating. "I've never seen anything like the way they come. I have gotten a bit bitter about it."

The letters begin the year the Tates were married and lived on Morton Street in New York, trying unsuccessfully to support themselves by writing. After they fled to an isolated farmhouse in upstate New York, Hart Crane moved in with them for several months while writing "The Bridge," and proved so exasperating a guest that they reached a pass of not speaking but of shoving notes to each other under the door. "Hart is a fine poet," Caroline wrote, "but God save me from ever having another romantic in the house." Robert Penn Warren brought his fiancée and stayed six weeks, till she nearly threw them both out the window. Her husband Allen, a dedicated Southern Agrarian, showed a respectful indifference to nature and refused to hoe the garden. In a "fiendishly" cold winter there were times when they didn't eat.

Then Allen got a Guggenheim and they spent a year in Paris, coming home in 1930 to a house overlooking the Cumberland River in Tennessee that Allen's brother Ben helped them buy. Caroline called it Benfolly in his honor. Near Nashville, it became a gathering place for young poets from Vanderbilt, besides such regular boarders as Edmund Wilson, Malcolm Cowley, Katherine Anne Porter who stayed five weeks too many. Caroline did the cooking while she worked on her fourth novel. In each room of the house someone was writing a book, pounding a typewriter with frenzied industry. Or they would sit immovable at the table arguing from lunch to dinner. Life with the Tates was no game of tiddlywinks. It was exhausting.

One hot summer in 1937 Robert Lowell arrived at the gate. Told by Caroline, "I'm sorry. There's no place to put you unless we put up a tent on the lawn," next day he set up a Sears Roebuck tent under a lotus tree and camped there for three months, loudly declaiming his poetry through the night. Ford Madox Ford, with his mistress Janice Biala and Janice's sister-in-law (to whom Ford dictated a thousand words a day) were already settled in for two months with the Tates. Ford, who was sixty-three and suffered from insomnia, indigestion, gout, and a deep loathing of Southern cooking, was so enraged by Lowell that he ignored his presence. At table Ford, refusing to eat, tore up and threw pieces of bread about. He called the Tates intellectual desperadoes. They said he flushed the toilet too much. As for his mistress, Caroline wrote, "I took Janice by the horns last night before she had time to get really obnoxious." It cost Caroline months to recover from the Ford visit. Allen told her she had a homicidal complex.

Out of her encounters with superegos, their squabbles and strife, she came to hold strong views of writers in general, in the flesh, and underfoot. Faulkner, she said, was a piece of cheese. Ellen Glasgow was a grand old girl. She regarded E. E. Cummings as one of the greatest bores that ever lived. Robert Lowell deeply offended by giving her a list of her husband's love affairs. She couldn't abide Louise Bogan. No one dared mention in her presence the author of *Gone with the Wind*. Hart Crane's suicide was, she said when she read it in the papers, an inevitable end of such a life. He left a note saying the world had no place for poets.

Had she chosen to, Caroline Gordon could have made an illuminating report of the literary life in America of which she was so consciously a part. With memories like these, too bad she didn't.

Quentin Bell. He was a shy young man when I met him at Charleston, his home in Sussex outside London. You wouldn't guess he was Vanessa's son, when she was so beautiful—strangely beautiful, even sensual in old age, with gray hair parted in the middle and drawn severely back, granny glasses down her nose, her stooped self huddled in a rocker. Quentin's mistake was to resemble his father, the art critic Clive Bell—reddish-haired, stout and round-faced—when he might have inherited his mother's looks and his father's inextinguishable desire to be amusing.

At lunch that day Quentin's silence matched Vanessa's own, while Clive entertained with scandalous gossip, gleeful at his indiscretions. Duncan Grant, who lived with Vanessa (as Clive did not, a guest like B. and me), helped with the serving of Clive's gift of pheasants, and paid polite attention while his lovely face stayed grave when he was supposed to laugh. In this household of professional artists, Quentin appeared slightly out of it. He had no formal education, never attended school, and his artistic talent lay in the making of pots. Julian, his older brother killed in the Spanish Civil War, was a promising poet adored by Vanessa and endlessly grieved for, whose poems she brought out like jewels and asked us to read. Angelica, her daughter by Duncan Grant, was married and away.

Ten years later Quentin surprised us by turning up without warning one day to visit us in North Carolina. He had grown large and impressive with a red beard. B. said he looked like Dante Gabriel Rossetti. Quentin was still a potter. More than that, he was a serene guest who laughed easily and endeared himself, who obediently downed six martinis (remaining calm) when we took him to a cocktail party, an absorbing talker with forceful views on art who admired our house and made no mention of its peculiar lack of pots. By the time we visited them in England, Quentin was married and living in Yorkshire, a Professor of Fine Art at the University of Leeds, where, in order to hire him, they had to give him an honorary degree. His wife was the exceptionally beautiful Ann Olivier, cousin of Laurence Olivier and daughter of Hugh Popham, Keeper of Prints at the British Museum. I loved being with them, loved their lively, amusing company, their niceness. They had three young children and a rumpled house that reminded me of Vanessa's careless one, with the addition of Quentin's splendid pots. He had found exactly the life he wanted. He was a happy man, a merry one in his home, a historian of Bloomsbury engaged in writing a biography of his aunt Virginia Woolf, whose large portrait painted by Vanessa hung over our bed.

Now years later, Quentin and I have lost touch. "Dear Helen," he wrote when B. died, "is it any consolation to you to know that no one who ever knew you and Bev could have failed to love you?" Only yesterday I came across an article about Quentin in the *Architectural Review* that calls him a voice from the past, "the gentle thinking potter of Sussex." A picture of him shows a dismayingly ancient fellow with white, wispy hair and a long white beard, leaning on a cane, sitting content among his pots. He and his wife live in a house only a mile from Charleston where we first met. In the article that discusses him as a successful artist, he is quoted as saying, "I put myself somewhere in between cake decorating and Raphael. And since I'm not Raphael it's best to stick to pottery." Dear Quentin.

Hildegarde and Company. On a night in the 1930s B. and I went to hear an entrancing salon singer named Hildegarde in a New York nightclub. We thought she was French by her accent, especially when she sang "The Last Time I Saw Paris," and she added a Parisian air of elegance dressed in a long white gown and full-length gloves, tossing about a large chiffon handkerchief. We had just heard Toscanini conduct the Philharmonic in the Beethoven Seventh that night at Carnegie Hall. Afterward we took a cab to the Savoy-Plaza, and it was no letdown to listen to Hildegarde, who was the Incomparable (she said so herself), like Toscanini highly professional, with absolute confidence she was the greatest.

Now I see by the papers that Hildegarde is turning up sixty years later, at eighty-five ("I'm still here"), singing at the Russian Tea Room in New York, elegant as ever tossing her handkerchief like a banner with the strange device, Excelsior! pleasing the crowd with "The Last Time I Saw Paris." They say she hails from Wisconsin.

Ginger Rogers is another such veteran from the 30's — the one who danced with Fred Astaire — whom you needn't trust to a lingering memory of. She is visible on television these nights not only in an old movie (*Top Hat*) as the young dancer she was sixty years ago, but also live on the screen to talk about her recent autobiography, *Ginger,* still the star — pink, smiling, spectacled, five times married, and fifty pounds heavier. Or Katherine Hepburn comes on full of years, trembling with palsy, as abundantly herself as if she had stepped out of *Woman of the Year* with Spencer Tracy, dead these many years. It's a kind of screen magic that makes me wish I could watch Queen Elizabeth I as she danced with the Earl of Essex four hundred years ago. We could if we had the tapes.

Hepburn at eighty-four is interviewed on *20-20* by Barbara Walters because she has completed *her* autobiography titled simply *Me* (me, she says, is all she thinks about). She lives alone in an eight-bedroom house filled with pictures of Spencer Tracy, the love of her life. Her affair with him, a married man, lasted twenty-seven years ("I don't approve of marriage"). In her late role of survivor, she told Barbara Walters, she never cries, owes her longevity to a one-track mind. In *Me* she says, "I'm like the Statue of Liberty to a lot of people."

Martha Graham, who died last April at ninety-six, dictated her autobiography, *Blood Memory*, claiming always to have been possessed with herself (is this the secret to longevity?). Her impulse from childhood was to be better than the best, a goddess, and she danced with this in mind. She never married her lovers (except for a brief union with her partner, Erick Hawkins) but kept the person of Martha Graham strictly singular. "She was really God-driven or devil-driven, whichever side you want to take," said one of her dancers. Another said, "She took our insides out," cuffing and slapping them around to get what she wanted.

When old age came, "Martha," they told her, "you are not a goddess, you are not immortal," and advised her to accept the fact.

"The hell I will," she said.

For some reason, old age has become a timely subject, the most popular concern since the Gulf War. Tonight on *Prime Time Live* with Diane Sawyer, the talk was of "Life after Ninety," as if such an eventuality were likely or even advisable. Two questions asked but left in considerable doubt were: "How old can you be and still function as a human being?" and "How does it feel to be eighty or ninety?" (The answer to that is, you have to get there first, and the feeling is one of impermanence.) On the show they produced in fair preservation a ninety-year-old man who trots round a track every day and takes multiple vitamins but revealed no further activity, and an old woman who lifts weights and looked for her years as imperishable as Monet's plump wife of a pastry cook.

Where will I get by making these respectful notes of old-timers and Aged P's? Answer: older. It just takes time.

> Time will say nothing but I told you so,
> Time only knows the price we have to pay,
> If I could tell you I would let you know.
> 　　　— W. H. Auden

Late Night Thoughts. Lewis Thomas's books used to overflow with faith in life and whatever keeps one sane. These days he seems to be going nuts. In *Late Night Thoughts on Listening to Mahler's Ninth Symphony* (which in its emotional intensity he cannot now bear to listen to), he looks at the current scene, at the world's apparent intention if not determination to self-destruct: "What I cannot imagine is what it would be like to be young. How do the young stand it? How can they keep their sanity? If I were very young, sixteen or seventeen years old, I think I would begin, perhaps very slowly and imperceptibly, to go crazy."

He might listen to Bach instead, to "Ich habe genug" or the Coffee Cantata that says, "Don't our children give us a hundred thousand headaches!"

E. B. White remarked in a letter that the feeling one is going nuts is a common sensation in this century: "I myself no longer take sanity as seriously as I used to and have felt a whole lot better since dropping it for the hot potato it is."

Later night thoughts (3:00 A.M.): the ships that pass in the night are no longer your usual run of traffic but a stormy sea of dreadnoughts, destroyers, and a few scared windjammers. Yet

> It is useless to worry,
> Wakeful while the long night goes. — Tu Fu, "One Hundred Worries"

(Tu Fu is known to have said, about 1,229 years ago, "It will certainly rain, which impels me to write this poem.")

Winds at Mt. Airy. "We just thought the Lord had raptured us all," said Rev. Winford Davis when tornadic winds and williwaws blew the roof clean off his church in Mt. Airy, N.C. as the service was about to start. The moment of rapture was upon them and glory at hand, a prelude to the Second Coming. They the Chosen any minute now would lift off and soar homeward to heaven as the sinful world beneath ended in Armageddon and everlasting hellfire. Otherwise such stormy weather had to be construed as sign of God's wrath, or the overdoing of divine intervention (if a so-called act of God is to be blamed on God). The roof-lifting tempest that exalted Rev. Davis and his flock right out of their seats came after a wasteland summer in the Bible Belt, thunder without rain. The last I heard they were still stuck in Mt. Airy, building a new roof.

It reminded me of a story told by Washington columnist George Will about a man falling from a cliff who managed to clutch at a root that saved him from plunging to certain death on the rocks far below. But there he was, hanging on, unable to climb back to safety. He shouted, "Is anyone up there?" And the voice of God answered him to have faith and pray, then he could safely let go and land unhurt. The man took another look down at the rocks and raging surf and yelled, "Is anyone *else* up there?"

The Big Bang. It was a pleasure the other Sunday to listen to Murray Gell-Mann being interviewed by Bill Moyers on PBS. It was like going to church and feeling reverential. Gell-Mann is the particle physicist who discovered the quark and gave it a name from Joyce's *Finnegans Wake*, "Three quarks for Muster Mark!" He now leads a group in Santa Fe that make bold investigations into the nature of the universe, such as what was there *before* the big bang? And why a big bang anyway?

About mid-century the cosmologist Fred Hoyle invented the term

Big Bang to mock and ridicule the childish idea of a universe spontaneously created by the explosion of a fireball. A better understanding of the theory came along in the 1960s. By 1976 Stephen Weinberg had written *The First Three Minutes* to describe the moment of creation (while reflecting, "the more the universe seems comprehensible, the more it also seems pointless"). In 1988 Stephen Hawking published *The History of Time from the Big Bang to Black Holes,* presenting his theory of the origin of our world of time and space, his belief that the big bang did happen and that bottomless black holes do exist that swallow up the stars. But if a universe was already there before the big bang occurred, as Hawking says it was, then has it always been there, a limitless universe that never began and will never end? And if it was never created yet does exist, *why* does it exist? Why do *we* exist? (Or, as Samuel Beckett said, "Why is there not nothing?") Hawking writes, "I am still trying to understand how the universe works, why it is the way it is, and why it exists at all. I think there is a reasonable chance we may succeed in the first two aims, but I am not so optimistic about finding why." (If Philip were alive, he too as a physicist would be asking the how and why of the universe.)

Yet in the *New York Times* of June 3, 1991, the big bang theory was reported to be in deep trouble. That year Eric J. Lerner published *The Big Bang Never Happened*—which excited no public lament. A sweeping revolution was said to be taking place, as great as the upheavals when Copernicus and Galileo redefined the solar system. The big bang theory appeared to be crumbling like the Ptolemaic system that lasted for 1,500 years.

A year later, April 23, 1992, the *New York Times* announced, as if the question had never come up, that the big bang *did* happen. It said a spacecraft had obtained pictures of wispy clouds that indicated an explosion had led to the formation of stars and galaxies fifteen billion years ago. Hawking called it "the discovery of the century, if not of all time." The astrophysicist George Smoot said, "If you're religious, it's like looking into the face of God." I hope he will tell us frankly if that is what he is doing.

(Einstein said: "What really interests me is whether God had any choice in the creation of the world.")

Like Carl Sagan and the astronomers, Murray Gell-Mann finds it unthinkable that, in a universe of a hundred billion galaxies where our sun is insignificant among countless suns, ours alone should have intelligent life. Yet so far there is no evidence. His words ended the Sunday morning service: "Life in such a universe is not so remarkable. It could be snuffed out on this planet and never be missed."

Gardens. Spenser wrote in his *Shepheardes Calender,* "Strew me the ground with daffadowndillies," and it was April. Four hundred years later it's April in my garden, where a pale daffodil or two struggles to strew the ground. Wordsworth said he saw ten thousand at a glance. I need him here to do the counting.

Tulips in the Duke gardens are the peacocks of spring. They wait till daffodils are gone before, blinding and vainglorious, they make their display. In eighteenth-century England tulips bore proud names like "Alexander the Great" and "The Duke of Marlborough." One of the proudest in our gardens is "Jewel of Spring." Another is "Mrs. J. T. Scheepers," which if I were a tulip I would resent. (More so if I were the Whoopi Goldberg rose.)

The New York Times recommends a blue flower garden for summer. I'd like a garden of perpetual blue, a clarity of blue where bluebirds, blue jays, and indigo buntings met their match. Colette said God was stingy when he handed out blue flowers. But there would be plenty of Delft blue larkspur, Alice blue forget-me-nots, China blue asters, wild iris, bachelor's buttons, bellflowers, bluets, morning glories, gentians, bluebonnets, cornflowers, a little periwinkle, a tub of blue hydrangeas, Monet's waterlilies, and someone on hand to say, "There is a garden in her face, where bluebells and white lilies blow."

Wallace Stevens: "God, what a thing blue is!"
Andrew Marvell: "No white nor red was ever seen

So amorous as this lovely green."
van Gogh: "I have tried to express the terrible passions of humanity by
    means of red and green and yellow."
Wallace Stevens: "All din and gobble, blasphemously pink."

Colors Like Green. Yellow. Blue

The journey began with water music.
"Never go back!" it wailed like an oboe
As we left in a woodwind up the winding sealanes.
And my dress was Paris green.

Mornings that sunflowered in the sun
By evening light were primroses.
In all Provence as van Gogh told someone,
"How lovely yellow is!"

I wore the blue gloves in the Church of the Madeleine,
My folded hands like doves,
And they were blue as lapis lazuli,
Spiritual like me.
I wore them in the Musée du Jeu de Paume,
And they were sunstruck, skylit as midday.
They had become
Blue as a Renoir, blue as a Monet.
I wore them on the Boulevard Saint-Michel
And there, as well,
They were the spit and counterpart
Of the blue gentians in a flower cart.

The blue *du pays,* the blue of the locale—
The gloves you bought me on the Rue Royale.

Subject: Trees. "Suche apple tre, suche frute."

The importance of trees began with the trees of Paradise, planted by

God ("But only God can make a tree"). Everywhere in Eden, says Milton, grew the noblest and fairest of trees laden with blossom and fruit at the same time, while in their midst rose the Tree of Life, blooming with ambrosial fruit of golden hue. And next to life,

> Our death, the Tree of Knowledge, grew fast by,
> Knowledge of good bought dear by knowing ill.

Adam stood under the apple tree beside the accommodating fig that hid his nakedness—the same Tree of Death on which Christ was crucified ("Jesus, whom ye slew and hanged on a tree" Acts 5:30).

Lucian praised a similar paradise, the Elysian Fields, a place of bliss without suffering, where the fields grew homemade bread, the trees were shining glass, and the fruit they bore were cups filled with wine. There Persephone walked under a pomegranate tree and, as Ovid told the story,

> She had been hungry wandering in the gardens,
> Poor simple child, and plucked from the leaning bough
> A pomegranate

and ate the forbidden fruit exactly as Eve did when she lost paradise.

My mind is full of trees. My cedars are the Cedars of Lebanon, my sycamore is the tree that the Persian king Xerxes fell madly in love with and halted his army to contemplate its loveliness. Confucius's tree is the mulberry, in the hollow of which he was born. Keats sat under a mulberry and heard a nightingale. Buddha was a veritable tree man, born under a sal tree, enlightened under a bo tree, dead beneath the shade of two sal trees. Plato walked under a plane tree, conceiving the meaning of Platonic love, while Sir Isaac Newton stood under an apple and was hit on the head, grasping the laws of gravitation. Judas hanged himself on an elder. Augustine flung himself under a fig tree to talk with God and repent his sins. George Herbert wrote, "I read, and sigh, and wish I were a tree," just as the nymph Daphne sighed and fled when Apollo attempted to ravish her and, wishing to stay a virgin, she cried out to the pitying gods. Suddenly her breasts turned to bark and her arms to branches, her feet were rooted to the ground, her head became a treetop. Apollo looked with love at this laurel tree and embraced and kissed it, and the laurel seemed to consent, to be saying yes oh yes. Sir Thomas Browne wished we were all propagated like trees.

Hercules climbed the trees of the Hesperides to gather golden apples. From the bough of an oak Aeneas plucked the prophetic leaves before descending into hell. Druids, who prayed to trees, went to live in oak groves where mistletoe grew to which they made human sacrifice. Zeus himself dwelt in a mighty oak and rustled its leaves with answers at the oracle of Dodona. Noah's dove carried a leaf in its mouth from an olive tree, and the rain ended.

Aristotle said trees are aware of us, in their wisdom possess reason to inspire us with noble passions. Yet the philosopher's tree doesn't exist. The yew tree, quite without reason, promises eternal life. "Stones have been known to move, and trees to speak," says Macbeth, but when they speak it is of man's murderous ways. Gods themselves once lived in trees, but where, O Lord, where are they now?

"These tears are shaken from the wrath-bearing tree."

8 🖋

Ways of Travel

You might guess offhand that a book called *The Mind of the Traveler* was written by a traveler to describe his journeys on this planet and their effect on his mind. But the subtitle, *From Gilgamesh to Global Tourism,* quickly enlarges the picture far beyond one man's experience. In his preface Eric Leed says his study of travel began with his first trip in 1942 in his mother's womb from Hawaii to Montana. The only other trip he mentions taking was to Rochester, New York. There as a graduate student he began the manifestly inward journey that taught him "how to use the books."

This is no guidebook for the tourist. It's a historian's account, rich in material, of travel through the ages, the nature of the journey and the mind transformed by what it encountered. Mr. Leed is the traveler who never went, content in the library to read the words of those who have traveled or thought about it—a voluminous report by Plato, Seneca, Pliny, the Venerable Bede, Marco Polo, Captain Cook, Darwin, Henry James, Einstein, Jack Kerouac, and Joan Didion, to name but a few. He quotes Socrates, who told Phaedrus, "For only hold up before me . . . a book, and you may lead me all around Attica, and over the wide world."

One certainty Mr. Leed has reached is that travel is no longer heroic. Everyone travels, though one's right to is a recent freedom for the common man. Times were different in *The Epic of Gilgamesh* (about 2000 B.C.) that tells of a young Sumerian king who sets forth on a heroic journey because a god has revealed that his human fate is to die. On a journey of extreme peril and suffering he learns the truth, that there is no eternal youth or life everlasting, and returns home to weep and carve his tale upon a stone. In Chrétien de Troyes' twelfth-century epic poem *Yvain*, the knight rides out on his palfrey to achieve glory and win the lady, but in the process is humbled, becomes temporarily mad, and gains some hard-won self-knowledge. In our time Mr. Leed finds a redefinition of the quest by Alexander Kinglake, a wellborn Englishman who, in the classic *Eōthen* (1844) travels on horseback through the Middle East in search of himself "free from the stale civilization of Europe," an escape that ultimately fails. By this testing of self, through penance, exile, clash with the unknown, the traveler has sought valiantly to know who he is, what world he inhabits. Goethe in Italy sought to discover "myself in the objects I see."

Montaigne said it was the journey and not the arrival anywhere that matters. In the ancient world, years of wandering were thought an appropriate, even necessary choice of philosophers, those looking for the meaning of life. They were not undertaken lightly or for pleasure, but to inform and illuminate the mind. Philosophical travel was a way of exploring the past—first in Egypt, believed to be the place from which all culture and civilization sprang; then in the Holy Land as a hallowed place of pilgrimage. There were the Crusaders, who extended the boundary of Christendom, after them the wandering scholars of the Middle Ages, who in their love of knowledge looked for enlightenment wherever it might lead. With the invention of printing, a reason existed for humanistic travel in pursuit of book learning, which led to the Renaissance. With the discovery of the New World of the Americas came new distances to explore that would expand the mind. Even the idea of the Grand Tour, in the eighteenth and nineteenth centuries, was one of self-improvement, the education of the gentleman who, fresh from Oxford or Cambridge accompanied by his tutor, was expected to copy the manners of the upper classes and keep a journal of his itinerary. William Cowper observed: "How much a dunce that has been sent to roam / Excels a dunce that has been kept at home!"

From the Grand Tourist emerged the plain tourist, whose travel became global but whose tastes, limited to mere pleasure—acquiring souvenirs and sending postcards—proved him at best idle, purposeless, and consequently despised. Meanwhile, four centuries of scientific travel, of examining nature, identifying fossils and early man, led to Darwin and his voyages on the *Beagle,* to the discovery of evolution, and to the great scientific expeditions of the twentieth century. At the size of his subject,

Mr. Leed confesses a feeling of vertigo; he omits travel to outer space or a glance moonward.

As time went on, travelers no longer brought back fabulous tales but facts no less staggering. Of course they found—wherever they went or why—no earthly paradise or utopian world of peace and accord, nor did they leave it that way. Those like the Vikings by plunder and conquest, or military invaders by war and occupation, remind us that the traveler throughout history has been not only a threat to world peace, but exclusively male. On his own dark errand, he was also bent on what Mr. Leed calls the "spermatic journey in which the male seed is broadcast" that has long served to populate other worlds.

Nowadays in an age of mass tourism, departure is more uneventful, easy and commonplace, engaged in indiscriminately by men and women become little children on their way to Disneyland. Eric Leed doesn't pause long for the history of tourism or tour groups, their identity or character, which, being less than heroic, philosophical, or scientific, leaves little to say. Nevertheless he believes travel is broadening, the journey to elsewhere a natural impulse and worth the trouble—a search for answers, a part of life. It's encouraging to see how one's own travel through his book tends to broaden the mind.

Tourist vs. Traveler. If there is a difference between a tourist and a traveler, which one am I? Tourists complain, travelers enjoy. A tourist is by custom discontent; if the trip were to Nirvana, he would object to the expense. Unwilling to be pleased, the tourist suffers from other tourists and the injustices of travel that give him a head cold or jet lag, whereas a traveler is a pleasurist who stays healthy at high altitudes and on stormy seas. He learns to say hello—"bula" in Fiji and "jambo" in Kenya—with the same broad smile and, when the times comes, "kwaheri" in Swahili, goodbye, always goodbye. He enjoys the local fare: vichyssoise Vichy, lima beams in Lima, Châteauneuf-du-Pape at Châteauneuf-du-Pape. He never loses his passport. Instead of souvenirs he takes home a piece of English landscape or the memory of a Degas; or collects a small magic stone from Merlin's cave in Tintagel, worry beads from Athens, a leaf of the bo tree from Benares, a pebble from Niagara Falls. He avoids excessive expectation and blames nobody for mishaps, not even God.

In his travel books, Paul Theroux notes that travelers are optimists and chooses the other kind, "I cultivated complainers." Americans, he says, are famous for complaining. Like him.

Travel was originally the same word as *travail,* meaning work or torture. It had stern purpose behind it and wasn't meant to amuse. Camus in his *Notebooks* reflects, "There is no pleasure in traveling and I look upon it as an occasion for spiritual testing." Yet one needn't be a Marco Polo or one of the Three Magi. One needn't *shun* pleasure. Travel these days is classed as light entertainment taken for relaxation and escape, and till lately was affordable (my travel guide of the 1960s was *Europe on Five Dollars a Day*). If it lacks a goal such as world conquest or enlightenment; if the sights (museums, monuments, McDonald's) soon fade like old snapshots and places blur till Pavia becomes Piacenza—who was looking for the Holy Grail? (The mad poet, John Clare, was looking for the horizon, and one day he found it.)

Graham Greene, in *Travels with My Aunt,* wrote of Uncle Jo who "wanted to make his life last longer. So he decided on a tour round the world." Like Uncle Jo I've traveled to extend my life—and been to paradise at least twice—partly also to escape from solitude, partly because I like to live out of a suitcase. It's one way to reduce the number of possessions you need to live by, and to avoid acquiring souvenirs that only add bulk to the store.

But people differ in their taste for travel. Once when I was about to leave for the South Seas, a friend of mine asked in genuine pity, "Why in God's name would anyone want to go to Tahiti?"

Claude Lévi-Strauss on Travel. This anthropologist begins his travel book about Brazil, *Tristes Tropiques,* "I hate travel and explorers." He sounds fed up, bent on discouraging a desire to see Brazil, which to him means hardship and fatigue, and to read travel books, which are delusory. "What do we find in travel books?" he asks, denouncing them as accounts of "trivial circumstances and insignificant happenings." So he writes this book and forbids me to read it. He thinks travelers should be made to stay put and not bore people.

Lévi-Strauss was probably bored young, like me, by travelers and their tales. As a child I sat through one too many of Burton Holmes's 8,000 travelogues with lantern slides that made the world a dull place. I leafed through too many copies of *National Geographic,* searching in vain for an instructive view of really naked South Sea natives. In college in a required course in Religion, which consisted largely of pictures projected on a screen of Egypt and the Holy Land, at first sight of a camel I would slip down from my chair and on hands and knees crawl out of the darkened room and down the hall, followed rather noisily by my roommate Dottie. In North Carolina a lady traveler I knew, home from her annual European tour, would summon us to her house and spend the evening showing her slides of what turned out to be, repeatedly and unaccountably, the battlefield of Waterloo. When she paused in her lecture, unable to identify the next slide, someone would call out "Waterloo," till we grew weak with smothered laughter.

After such encounters, a body might well, like Lévi-Strauss, come to question the advantages of travel. "I hate museums," wrote Thoreau, a reluctant traveler, adding, "How long, pray, would a man hunt giraffes if he could?"

Journey Proud

My head is in a nimbus cloud.
Who makes a journey is journey proud
And will not sleep this night in his bed,
But on strangers' linen
Lay his head,
And by small contrary winds is shaken
At this poor folly undertaken.

His hand is aspen, his mind aflutter,
He pales at the sight of bread and butter,

Yearns to be missed and sighs aloud,
Being tremulous
And journey proud
And temporarily askew —
Like me at the thought of leaving you.

The Return of Jan Morris. A world traveler for half her days, one of the wandering kind, Jan Morris has come back to Wales. As a way of life, she admits to two addictions: traveling and staying at home, each of which can be done well or badly. She is as glad to be back as her house is infatuated with her presence, purring a loud welcome accompanied by the two Abyssinian cats. Her house, she says, is her very self, like her "properly egotistical," frankly reflecting her own style and personality. "Trefan Morys is unmistakably, indeed brazenly, *me.*"

Trefan Morys is the converted stables of a former eighteenth-century manor house, built in 1774 of rough, gigantic stones. It consists of two huge living rooms, one above the other, each forty-two feet long to hold her 30,000 books. The front door is Welsh blue. Upstairs, in a corner of the room, stands her tombstone, suitably carved with her name and ready for instant use.

Much as Jan Morris loved to explore other worlds, other places, other states of mind — the Taj Mahal, Venice, Oxford, Kashmir, Indianapolis, and the fall of Queen Victoria's empire — all splendid spectacles arranged for her benefit (though as a traveler without complaint, she says the basic rule is you can't see everything) — in the end she loves her house the most. Long it has stood, beaming with expectation, marking the years like the patient tombstone awaiting her return. "And I am going to die in it, I hope." Home is the sailor, home from sea.

The Tour to the Hebrides. The only pictures on my wall worth bidding for at Sotheby's are three contemporary prints made by Thomas Rowlandson in 1786. I found them in New York one day in the 1930s in a secondhand bookshop on Fourth Avenue. They turned up in a torn folder among an assortment of oddments clearly discarded as junk, and the price marked on the outside was twenty-five cents each. I picked out the four grimiest—the Rowlandsons—and took them to the bookseller at his desk. "How much?" I said. He barely glanced up. "Four for a dollar," he said, as if I couldn't add. Call it affordable art.

Thomas Rowlandson was born in 1756, the son of a London merchant, and died in 1827 at seventy, leaving behind some ten thousand watercolors, drawings, prints of eighteenth-century life. As a serious painter, a devotee of Rubens, he made endless studies of trees, gardens, and lovely ladies, as well as a set of etchings for the *Vicar of Wakefield* and three books of drawings of the immensely popular Dr. Syntax, a character he invented. But most of all Rowlandson was a caricaturist, the cleverest of his day, one whom Goya imitated. His ridicule of high and low life, coarse and sottish as it often was—from willing wenches to blowsy beldames, from tavern scenes to dogfights—gained him a place next to Hogarth in English comic art. V. S. Pritchett once observed that to Rowlandson the human race were cattle and swine, but that was obvious hyperbole.

In 1786 E. Jackson, the bookseller, printed *Picturesque Beauties of Boswell* containing twenty plates by Rowlandson. It appeared a year after Boswell had published his *Journal of a Tour to the Hebrides,* the three-month journey he and Dr. Johnson took in 1773. Rowlandson's method as illustrator was to copy a passage from the *Journal* that amused him and place his cartoon above it. His satire was never cruel or gross. It was comic.

The first of my three prints (I gave the fourth to a friend) is of Dr. Johnson arriving in Edinburgh on Saturday evening, August 14, 1773, where Boswell met his coach at Boyd's Inn and proudly escorted the great man to his home. It was Dr. Johnson's first visit, at sixty-three, to the Scotland he disliked and the Scots he despised as barbarians. Boswell was thirty-two:

> Mr. Johnson and I walked arm in arm up the High Street to my house in James Court; it was a dusky night: I could not prevent his being assailed by the evening effluvia of Edinburgh.—As we marched along, he grumbled in my ear, "I smell you in the dark." Vide Journal P.13

Rowlandson has drawn Dr. Johnson as his lumbering self, clad in boots and a greatcoat and hat, carrying a big oak stick. He is holding his finger to his nose, grumbling in Boswell's ear "I smell you in the dark," while Boswell the showman prances along beside him, highly gratified to be in such illustrious company.

The second print takes the two of them next day inside Boswell's house with his family, where Mrs. Boswell has tea ready for the guest, which (to quote Boswell) "it was well known he delighted to drink at all hours." Boswell hovers over Dr. Johnson's chair with a copy of Ogden's *Sermons on Prayer* in his hands and a fatuous beam on his face, as the baby Veronica leans out of her nurse's arms and snatches Dr. Johnson's large bushy wig off his bald head. Johnson frowns heavily at the liberty while Mrs. Boswell and the servants titter at the child's antics. The caption says,

> Mr. Johnson was pleased with my daughter Veronica, then a child of about four months old. She had the appearance of listening to him. His motions seemed to her to be intended for her amusement, and when he stopped she fluttered and made a little infantine noise and a kind of signal for him to begin again. She would be held close to him, which was a proof from simple nature that his figure was not horrid. Her fondness for him endeared her still more to me, and I declared she should have five hundred pounds of additional fortune. Vide Journal P.17

Veronica was then Boswell's only child. But Rowlandson has imagined the wig pulling, which never happened, nor did Boswell keep his promise to reward her, since soon he had four other children to provide for. Each night Mrs. Boswell gave up her bed to Dr. Johnson, though they didn't hit it off. She disliked him on sight for his uncouth manners and objected to Boswell's traveling with him.

For the next three days Boswell led his friend on a walking tour of Edinburgh. On August 18 they set off by carriage north through Aberdeen to Inverness, and there changed to horseback. At the west coast they crossed by boat to Skye and the Hebrides and spent a month rambling over the western islands in "vigorous exertion" in cold and stormy weather, even sleeping in barns — all of which Dr. Johnson faced with extraordinary good nature, displaying both fortitude and endurance.

For some reason, perhaps embarrassment, Boswell failed to mention in his journal the most dramatic incident of the tour (a tale told by one who witnessed it) which occurred at Inverness on August 29. That night at the inn some local people dropped by to meet the great Dr. Johnson. At supper he entertained them in high spirits by describing a remarkable animal discovered only three years before in Australia called the kangaroo. While they stared in stunned amazement, he raised his huge bulk from his chair, put out his hands like paws, gathered his coattails round him to resemble a pouch, and in two or three leaps bounded across the room in imitation of a kangaroo. The pity is, Rowlandson never knew of that solo performance.

In the third drawing it's a month later, September 26, when they are in the Hebrides. The young laird of the Isle of Coll, who was conducting them in the islands, had taken them in an open boat in wind and rain to Coll. On arrival Dr. Johnson went right to bed, while Boswell stayed up drinking the Saturday night away, merrier and merrier, till at five in the morning he staggered to bed. In the caption, Boswell with a hangover confesses his shame to his journal:

> I awaked at noon with a severe headache. I was much vexed that I should have been guilty of such a riot, and afraid of a reproof from Dr. Johnson. — When I rose, I went into Dr. Johnson's room, and taking up Mrs. MacKinnon's prayerbook, I opened it at the twentieth Sunday after Trinity, in the epistle for which I read, "And be not drunk with wine, wherein there is excess." Some would have taken this as a divine interposition. Vide Journal p. 318

Rowlandson has placed Boswell at a table opposite Dr. Johnson with the open prayerbook before him, his finger pointing to the divine rebuke. He holds his aching head with a white cloth tied round it, and his expression is woeful. Above his head is a framed picture of a fat pig, while peeping from his pocket is Ogden's *Sermons on Prayer*. In the *Journal*, a penitent

Boswell told Dr. Johnson they had kept him up all hours last night. "No," said Dr. Johnson mildly, "you kept them up, you drunken dog."

In November, with the journey over, they returned to Edinburgh and Johnson took the coach back to London. It had been a success, a holiday for them both: Johnson had talked a lot, Boswell had basked in his company.

When the Rowlandson cartoons of the tour appeared in 1786, Johnson had been dead two years. He had published his version of the trip, *A Journey to the Western Islands of Scotland,* a descriptive account with moral reflections, compared with Boswell's pretty dry and uneventful. Earlier he had written, in *The Idler,* "It may, I think, be justly observed that few books disappoint their readers more than the narrations of travelers."

Yet he remembered those three months with the Scots as among the best of his life.

The Stratford Festival. We drove from their summer home in Ohio — David, his wife Peggy, and I — across the Canadian border to Stratford, Ontario, that like Stratford-upon-Avon is a quiet town with a River Avon and the Shakespeare theaters. During the four-day stay we managed to see six plays, and lusted for more.

The Stratford Festival has the largest theater company in North America. It runs from May to October with daily performances primarily of Shakespeare but other classics as well. The acting and staging are so remarkable that the University of Chicago, for one, sends study tours each summer to Stratford with a professor to discuss the plays and hold picnics beside the Avon. This tour had David, Shakespeare scholar and editor, to do the talking. Fifty playgoers came up from Chicago, and we stayed at a hotel called Twenty-Three Albert Place and frequented Bentley's Pub for the fish and chips.

The first night's play was not by Shakespeare but a younger contemporary, Thomas Middleton, whose *The Changeling,* in collaboration with William Rowley, is a bloody Jacobean revenge tragedy of unrelieved evil and horror. In it a pretty girl, Beatrice-Joanna, to escape marriage to a man she detests hires the villain De Flores to murder him. The deed done,

De Flores who is obsessed with her takes his payment in raping her, "the murderer of my honour." Now free to marry her true love Alsemero, but fearful lest he discover she's not a virgin, Beatrice substitutes her maid on the wedding night, then jealous of the maid in his arms conspires with the unspeakable De Flores to kill the girl. When their guilt is discovered, their degradation complete, De Flores kills them both. The play ends, "All we can do to comfort one another . . . is to no purpose." (Pepys said when he saw it in 1661, "It takes exceedingly.")

As a horror tale *The Changeling* can still horrify, but its real virtue is that it led, two nights later, to Shakespeare's tragic *Titus Andronicus,* the bloodiest, most terrible revenge play of all time.

Next night in *The Merchant of Venice* Shakespeare lived again, so contemporary in spirit that he must be constantly rediscovered, reinterpreted, redefined, understood anew. This deeply troubling revenge play seems more controversial than ever—a love comedy so nearly tragic, so involved with the meaning of mercy that the title might better have been *The Quality of Mercy.* As a study in revenge against not a merchant of Venice but a Jewish moneylender, Shylock is the victim. Over the centuries he has been cast (like Marlowe's Barabas, the greedy, unscrupulous Jew of Malta) as a merciless stage villain exacting his pound of flesh; as a low comic buffoon laughed at and dismissed; or most poignantly as a tragic Jew of dignity and humanity without hope of justice in a Christian society. How do we see him now? In Portia's exalted speech about mercy, there is no denying the irony of her words: the quality of mercy, "an attribute to God himself," is strained to the breaking point. No mercy is shown Shylock, no love, no tolerance, no forgiveness, no justice, only hate, only revenge. He is despised and cast out, forced against his will to become a Christian. Love and friendship triumph for the others but not for Shylock. In our world of the Holocaust, the play appears more than ever anti-Semitic.

Chekhov's *The Three Sisters* brought a change of pace, a splendid performance intentionally static, as if the three unhappy figures of the sisters were made of stone, trapped in their drab exile in rural Russia, never to escape to the Moscow they yearn for. Chekhov wrote the part of Masha for his actress-wife when he too was exiled in Yalta, denied a return to Moscow and happiness with her.

Nothing changes for the Prozorov sisters, nothing will come of their impossible dream. In this provincial town far from the world of their childhood, no one will rescue them. Colonel Vershinin, whom Masha loves, tells her as he turns away, "Happiness is not for us and never can be. All we can do is long for it."

In the end the three sisters are left standing together, entwined, helpless in the boredom of their lives. Olga, exhausted and careworn, will teach in the high school, Masha the passionate one will stay married to a dull man, Irina's suitor is killed in a duel. They can only say, as the curtain falls, "It does not matter."

T. S. Eliot called *Titus Andronicus* "one of the stupidest and most uninspired plays ever written." But he couldn't dispose of it by condescending to something so powerful. *Titus* is a bloody nightmare, an appalling and inhuman study of the nature of evil. When the Roman general Titus returns victorious to Rome after a ten-year war with the Goths, he brings with him Tamora, Queen of the Goths, her lover Aaron the Moor, and her three sons. By killing one son, Titus sets in motion the unstoppable events that destroy him and leave the stage littered with the dead. Tamora, having married Saturninus, Emperor of Rome, remorseless in her hatred of Titus, enlists the help of her two remaining sons, Demetrius and Chiron, who rape Titus's daughter Lavinia, chop off her hands, and cut out her tongue. On finding her mutilated body, feigning madness, Titus slits the throats of Tamora's sons and at a banquet feeds their flesh in a pie to Tamora before he kills her. Titus then slays his ruined Lavinia to save her from dishonor. Saturninus kills Titus, Lucius (Titus's remaining son) kills Saturninus and directs the burying alive of Aaron the Moor: "Set his breast deep in earth and famish him." Used as we are to violence in our time, we are ready witness to rape, mutilation, torture, murder, cannibalism, and death by starvation.

In this, Shakespeare's earliest tragedy, Titus is a King Lear without Lear's nobility or compassion. Like Lear, Titus is old, infirm of judgment, close to madness, Tamora, "beastlike and devoid of pity," is depraved like Goneril and Regan, Lavinia is an innocent victim like Cordelia. But Titus, debased by hate, only serves to magnify Lear's greatness of spirit and Shakespeare's ability to write a tragedy with love and pity in it.

In 1957 at the Old Vic in London, *Titus Andronicus* and *The Comedy of Errors* were performed together in a double bill—as happened at Stratford tonight. In ancient Greece a tragedy filled with terror was sometimes followed by a skit or farce, as if to let the audience laugh and catch its breath, to assure it that life is not entirely the monstrous affair it appears.

The Comedy of Errors was a lighthearted romp, made of bawdy and slapstick, monkeyshine and mistaken identity compounded by two pairs of identical twins. It was played in a whirlwind of confusion while the cast raced about Ephesus, up and down ramps and through the aisles at top speed. The noise was as great as the versatility of the acting, notably of the actress Lucy Peacock, who this afternoon was Chekhov's unhappy Masha and tonight became the suffering, mutilated, dying Lavinia and, as convincingly, moments later the lively Luciana in a comic farce, dancing about as the beloved of Antipholus of Syracuse.

On Sunday morning in Stratford we walked in the green park beside the Avon, picnicked by the river, and talked with Seana McKenna, the young and charming Portia of the *Merchant of Venice,* who told of hours spent asking herself how Portia was to be played, a role that grew less merciful the more she understood it.

Afterward we went to the Avon Theater for the last of the six plays, *A Midsummer Night's Dream,* appropriate for a midsummer's parting. How could a man as stagestruck as Pepys have called it "the most insipid, ridiculous play that ever I saw in my life"?—a play so well dreamed that it ended, for lunatic, lover, and poet, with all human problems solved in the reality of true love. Thus lightly the turmoil of these four days of blood revenge and man's inhumanity was dismissed and the heartbreak presumably forgot — save for the echo in our ears, "Lord, what fools . . . what fools!"

Much Ado at the University of Chicago. David, smiling, sits on the flattop desk in his classroom, book in hand, absorbed in teaching *Much Ado about Nothing.* It's not a lecture, it's a celebration going on of Shakespeare's comedy, especially the love affair between Beatrice and Benedick. Everyone is laughing at the bickering of the combative lovers being witty at each other's expense, taunting, and abusive: "What, my dear Lady Disdain!" Benedick asks, "are you yet living?" while Beatrice, sharp-tongued and rude, replies with every word stabbing, "Is it possible disdain should die while she hath such meet food to feed it as Signor Benedick?" Benedick swears he can't endure my Lady Tongue, Beatrice swears she had rather hear her dog bark at a crow. Much ado about nothing. By playacting, pretending dislike, the two manage for much of the play to conceal their love before ardently protesting it: "And Benedick, love on: I will requite thee, taming my wild heart to thy loving hand."

I sit in the third row among the undergraduates, laughing with the rest, thinking how different this knowing lovemaking is from Romeo and Juliet's innocent and tragic passion. And all at once it comes to me! I'm not really here at all. For a moment I'm back in the 1920s, an undergraduate at this university, and everything is exactly the same — same room in Cobb Hall, same play — except that I am eighteen years old listening to the man up front, a young professor named David — David Stevens. Nothing's changed, nothing at all, except that this other David is my son, teaching the class while the merry war rages on between Beatrice and Benedick, unaware of the incredible experience it is to return to this room and find him here.

Blue Sheep and Snow Leopards. George Schaller is a writer who makes you believe in his extraordinary way of life and wish he'd take you with him. Among the many scientific expeditions he has made as a zoologist — studying tigers in India, lions in the Serengeti of Tanzania, and pandas in the Sichuan province of China—the grandest journeys must have been in the Himalayas, where he spent four years altogether climbing the sheerest mountains to study wild sheep and goats. "Poets may praise the deer and nightingale," he wrote in his notebook. "I celebrate the wild goat." And the wild sheep, he might add, most persistently the blue sheep called bharal, a little-known breed partway between a sheep and a goat. Schaller gathered careful data about them, noting the curls in their horns, examining their droppings to learn what they ate, observing their rut and mating season, most of all trying to discover what hope they had of escaping extinction. In the mountains of central Asia—Kashmir, Pakistan, India—at altitudes up to 18,000 feet, he would walk alone for hours and days, apart from his porters. In deep snows and icy winds, up snow peaks and over glaciers, he tested the limits of his strength and skill to stay alive, filled sometimes he says "with quiet ecstasy." "I like solitude," he reflected alone in the immense stillness, "not loneliness." He liked for their silence the company of yaks.

The book Schaller wrote about these Himalayan journeys, *Stones of Silence,* is by a man in love with his work. Before I came across it, I had read with pleasure Peter Matthiessen's *The Snow Leopard* about the remarkable adventure he had in the fall of 1973 when Schaller took him along on one of his mountain journeys, this time in Nepal near the Tibetan frontier. On a walk of two hundred miles, Peter declared it his personal mission to catch a glimpse of the snow leopard, an extremely rare and elusive beast that inhabits the region, while Schaller, who was an old hand at spotting snow leopards, pursued the wild blue sheep to be found in the neighborhood when not eaten by snow leopards. Peter was first to publish his book, a highly entertaining account of the quest, which was also an inner search that, as a Zen Buddhist, absorbed him and took up much of his time in meditation and the chanting of Buddhist mantras. By the end of the journey, in spite of his goal, Peter had never once laid eyes on a snow leopard. He had mystical feelings about the beast and thinks he may have felt its presence, just as once he almost glimpsed the dark shadow of the abominable snowman springing behind a rock.

The final chapter of Schaller's book describes from his point of view this same journey with Peter that took them to the Crystal Mountain and the remote Land of Dolpo on the Tibetan Plateau. Four years earlier, he and Peter had met in the Serengeti where they shared daylong excursions among the plentiful lions, and where his easy charm, Schaller said, made him a pleasant companion. Neither had reckoned, it seems, on the profound difference in their natures (and in their quests); or that in the punishing hardships and anxieties ahead they would occasionally get on each other's nerves — as when Peter tried to persuade Schaller to spend the nights by the campfire composing haiku. Fortunately each man traveled at his own speed while the porters straggled behind, though it's unclear to me what kept Schaller from getting lost in the white wilderness or losing Peter completely as he wandered off in the snowdrifts or sat in a tree to meditate; or why nobody was ever attacked by a stray yeti or wild sheep.

Patient and steady as Schaller was, he had certain qualities that might alarm or upset a meditator. "I am teutonically punctual," he wrote. "I leap out of bed at dawn and in ten minutes am washed, packed, and ready to go (and that is in weather where washing is possible). I find contentment in physical exertion and happily race over hills." At the sight of whole herds of blue sheep, plainly ready to show off their mating habits poised on the highest rocks and sharpest peaks, he could barely contain his joy: "I watch voraciously, elated over every new observation. . . . I want to miss nothing."

After two months of rugged travel, on November 18 Peter, grown suddenly restless, packed up and departed in haste from the mountains, taking with him two guides. Schaller, puzzled but not offended, stayed on, watching his sheep till the December storms and furious winds, plus the danger of being trapped till spring without provisions, obliged him to give up the quest. It had been a good trip, he told himself. He had learned much about the bharal, convinced by now it really was a sheep that in some ways resembled a goat. But a day came of raging blizzards when he and his porters were barely able to make their way down from the heights escaping through a narrow pass to safety beyond the thickening walls of ice. Up there at the last minute Schaller turned and saw something that gave him particular satisfaction, something white and nearly invisible as it stood watching him in the falling snow.

It was a snow leopard.

Islands. Ask a Southerner if he has been to the Thousand Islands, and he will say, "Never heard of them" or "Oh, you mean the Everglades." But the Florida Everglades are called the Ten Thousand Islands to describe those swampy half-submerged hammocks covered with mangrove trees, whose tangled white roots rise out of the mud soup of a shallow inland sea. On a clear day, the claim is, you can see ten thousand birds, though on a boat trip I took through the Everglades I caught sight at most of some white pelicans, a great blue heron flapping overhead, an ibis wading, black cormorant perching, terns flying, a couple of snowy egrets, and young ospreys on their nests in the treetops gaping like baby eagles. Maybe they mean ten thousand seagulls. Except for a sudden bird squawk, nothing broke the stillness of this dense wilderness fifty to seventy miles wide that used to be home to Seminole Indians. As we twisted among the little nameless islands, a single manatee sunned itself like a beached mermaid resting on the saw grass.

Southerners are, however, acquainted with Thousand Island Dressing (mayonnaise with chili sauce), which was invented by a millionaire who, early in the century, built an immense Gothic castle on one of the Thousand Islands. They are incredibly numerous — these endless isles in the St. Lawrence River — spectacular enough to be one of the world's wonders. Before I saw them this summer, I assumed the number was grossly exaggerated — a thousand, I thought, would obliterate the river completely — only to discover there were closer to *two* thousand islands visible for about fifty-two miles downstream from Lake Ontario.

Two friends of mine, Chuck and Bertha Osbourn, have a summer home on Wellesley Island, one of the largest and most populous, most extensively wooded, most beautiful, big enough to contain a village — Thousand Islands Park — as well as outlying farms, handsome estates beside the water, too many golf courses to count. The International Bridge, opened in 1938 between the U.S. and Canada, crosses over this island.

The Osbourn house on the village green facing the St. Lawrence was formerly a hotel with ornately carved balconies, which they bought years ago because they had six daughters and needed room, and because they are naturally hospitable. Now with the daughters grown and married, some of the bedrooms are equipped with cribs. Not mine, though. Mine was a spacious room and bath, with a view of the river and the sign No. 21 on the door. For forty years Chuck and Bertha have kept the house filled with guests, who are given blueberry pancakes for breakfast and made to feel so much at home that they dream, like me, of staying on and buying a hotel themselves or an entire island. Up there where an island is an island if it has a tree on it, some are for sale, many are privately owned. It was tempting to think about, a whole island, a kingdom to oneself.

Since Chuck's motorboat was anchored in the marina below the house, we spent the warm days speeding up and down the scenic river while David or Sarah (my granddaughter) waterskied behind us, making lordly sweeps across our wake. Sooner or later Chuck would pick out an island he fancied on either the Canadian or the New York State side of the river and anchor there while we explored the place. The one I loved was Camelot, as idyllic as its name and uninhabited, where we climbed for hours along the steep rock face till we had completely circled the island. We would then eat Bertha's enormous picnic lunch and after a while set out for another island, perhaps Endymion. Chuck seemed to know them all separately, as if he were a man who spent his life discovering islands.

One day he took us by boat to Boldt Castle, owned by the millionaire George Boldt, who as a young immigrant from Prussia worked in the kitchens of the Waldorf Astoria and eventually bought the hotel (besides inventing Waldorf Salad). He built the medieval castle on Heart Island in 1904 for his adored wife Louise — a massive, many-towered mock-Gothic pile of 120 rooms suggesting immense luxury, with thick granite walls, an Italian garden, a pond for swans, an arched watergate down by the river for his three yachts and anchored houseboat. It was still under construction when one day Louise suddenly died. A few hours later a telegram arrived from New York signed by Boldt, saying "Stop!" and all work on the castle instantly ceased, to be abandoned for good. Three hundred workmen were out of a job. The empty rooms stayed as they were, unpainted, unfurnished, the tapestries, mantelpieces, fine furniture, marble statuary from all over Europe left unopened in their crates. For nearly seventy-five years the forsaken castle stood alone on its island, never once visited by Boldt in his grief, gradually decaying, despoiled by vandals who tore it apart and spread graffiti over the bare walls.

Now Boldt's castle is being slowly repaired and restored, while tourists wander in a daze through its huge desolate rooms and vast halls, climbing the stately staircase, imagining the splendor that never was. Yet what a monument it remains, after all, to a man's despair, the loss of the one thing in life he wanted to keep.

A Quick Trip to Arizona. When my friend H.C. retired, he made a list of seventy-five ways to spend the rest of his life, such as going to Mardi Gras and the Rose Bowl parade, and reading *Look Homeward, Angel.* In six months he had polished off thirty-five of them and was looking round for more.

I like H.C.'s style. He reminded me of a list I made on retirement, which included the Khyber Pass, Arizona, and Saint Augustine's *Confessions.* I added them up the other day and found at least half attended to, though Antarctica and the Oxford English Dictionary in ten volumes were taking a little longer.

It seemed time to get going, what with the world changing so fast, with England having retired the shilling and Leningrad calling itself St. Petersburg. Besides, there was Arizona. My friend Marian asked me to accompany her to her son's wedding in Phoenix in November. "Afterward," she said, "we can rent a car and drive around the Southwest for a week or two." It sounded good, a chance to dance at Peter's wedding and look for Apaches and Frank Lloyd Wright's spread down there. I began to read the story of Coronado's search for the Seven Golden Cities, which somewhat resembled the California gold rush three centuries before the Forty-Niners got to it.

Then I heard a new rock number on the radio, "By the Time I Get to Phoenix." That would be the day after tomorrow.

We flew to Phoenix. And the streets were lined with immensely tall cacti—a modern city with a desert air, risen from the ashes of an earlier Indian civilization. At the airport Marian and I rented a brand new four-door Dodge Dynasty that we would take off in after the wedding. We were staying in Tempe, where Peter and Diana live, a suburb of Phoenix named for the Vale of Tempe near Mt. Olympus. From our rooms at the Mission Palms Hotel, we gazed down on gardens of palm trees and poinsettias—a summery inn now in November, whose only flaw was it charged a dollar for a cup of hot water and a tea bag.

This morning Peter and Diana waked, like the rest of us, to the sound of pouring rain. It was the day of their wedding, to be performed in their backyard beside the pool. I'd looked forward to the ceremony, since Peter was a dear friend who wrote me letters in praise of English literature when he was a student at Yale. Now he was a Ph.D. whose specialty was hummingbirds. His bride, also a Ph.D., was into lizards, with a three-year grant to study their gonads, for which purpose she caught the lizards alive. When asked what items they would need to live as man and wife, Diana listed "a nice set of fine glass tumblers to drink Scotch from, champagne glasses, a cappuccino maker, a camp stove, and an electric drill."

Though Marian considered hiring a hall in the hotel if the driving rain continued, by four this afternoon we were gathered under clear skies, thirty of us, in the small backyard where a lone hummingbird darted to and fro above our heads, officiating as Peter's bird. Trees of oranges hung over the fence. We sat huddled together on wooden benches trying not to shiver in the sudden wintry cold. On a porch bare as a meetinghouse, without music since the hummingbird didn't sing, Peter and Diana were wed by a magistrate in a black robe who pushed them around a bit to improve the arrangement. Diana wore a crown of flowers and a white lace gown that left her shoulders bare and roused our pity till we could plainly see how warmed she was by Peter's presence. It looked like a commitment for life.

Afterward we got in our cars and drove to the Desert Botanical Gardens where the reception was to be held among the cacti. But the cold hurried us into the Webster Center where we gradually unfroze with the help of champagne, and margaritas drawn from a spigot. After dinner when the four-piece rock band started up, so did the dancing, while appropriate among us was John O'Neill, the famous painter of hummingbirds, Peter's friend, who really should have married them.

Next morning Marian and I lit out for Taliesen. Only ten miles from town in the suburb of Scottsdale, it occupies six hundred acres of the Sonoran desert that Frank Lloyd Wright shaped out of desert stone. He and his apprentices in 1937 gathered huge rocks to build his desert sculpture that he said "belonged to the Arizona desert as though it had stood there during creation."

From a distance Taliesen looked like a long red abandoned railway car against the McDowell Mountains, but when we drew near it became an astonishing array of flat buildings with low overhang. It was Wright's western home where as "resident deity" he lived with his third wife, Olgivanna, and a commune of twenty-three young men and women whom he put into tents and allowed no pepper with their meals. We walked through Taliesen with a guide who had been a student there under Wright and loudly praised the egocentricity and imagination of the old man — who had planned a mile-high skyscraper for Chicago, had built "Fallingwater" over a waterfall, had created the spectacular Guggenheim Museum in New York of one continuous spiral ramp, and had made Taliesen into a thing of beauty, with its horizontal lines and projecting eaves. I told him what I liked about Wright, that he had changed ordinary little houses into areas without walls or doors, attics or basements, letting in air and light. I liked him for getting rid of clutter.

Coming back to the hotel that night, we drove through streets lined with cacti turned into Christmas trees, trimmed with hundreds of light bulbs glittering in the dark.

From there we planned to look for Apaches. But in desert country beyond Tucson we were sidetracked by the immense outdoor Arizona Sonora Desert Museum. As a sight it was irresistible, more visible than the desert itself, furiously alive with assorted desert spiders, centipedes, scorpions, chuckwallas, rattlesnakes, and venomous gila monsters (named for the Gila River), which I hoped Diana wasn't in the habit of bringing home. *The New York Times* called it one of the ten best museums in the world, a picture of a desert twice the size of North Carolina, containing only the plants and animals that actually live in the Sonora.

The acres of cacti made a tremendous spectacle, some like prehistoric beasts, some like towering malevolent giants fifty feet tall, weighing tons, and two hundred years old. Till now I'd thought a cactus was a cactus, but here were endless varieties: the majestic saguaro whose arms curve upward like a pitchfork, the totem pole, organ pipe, strawberry hedgehog, claret cup, prickly pear—cacti that would blossom in the spring with brilliant gaudy flowers, cacti in which the cactus wren lived and tiny creatures hid themselves. Mesquite grew in thorny thickets, strange yuccas flourished—the Joshua tree that seemed to pray, the boojum tree that resembled a carrot twenty feet tall.

There were the desert birds, the desert trees, the desert animals, even the mountain lion and the Sonora bighorn. But totally unexpected in that place were the Sonora hummingbirds. In a desert! They seemed to be members of the wedding who had followed us here, darting about their tree-lined house—fifty at least we counted, though the docent said twenty, each conspicuously different from the rest: blue-throated, violet-eared, black-chinned hummingbirds. Had they been more than three inches long, they would have terrified us with their piercing beak and wild unpredictable flight. One bad-tempered fellow, a rufous, was shut in a fine-meshed cage to keep him from attacking the world and eliminating it.

I'd never have believed a rainless desert world could be so populous and so alive, abundant with hummingbirds.

Arizona is the Apache state. A thousand years ago the Apaches came down from the north—a ruthless, warlike people who for three centuries fought the white man for possession of land and sky they thought their own. Since the sixteenth century they had resisted the Spaniards, who arrived soon after Columbus, they had battled the Mexicans, who in 1821 freed themselves from Spain, but most of all, savagely and persistently, they had fought the Americans—especially after 1848 when we won the war with Mexico and took over the territory of the Southwest. Till the final struggle in 1886, when the Apaches led by Geronimo were conquered and put into reservations, they warred with cruelty and cunning to drive us from their homeland. During the gold rush of 1849 when the stampede began through Apache country to the gold fields of California, from their hiding places in the mountains they swept down to plunder and raid, murder and destroy. One of them was the famous Apache chief Cochise, leader of his people, who swore never to surrender to the white man.

We were now in the Dragoon Mountains, in what was the Cochise Stronghold. He was born in 1812 in these mountains from which he fought, and in them he died. We stopped the car in the lonely snow-covered forest wilderness beside Cochise's monument, a large tombstone that bore the inscription: "Chief Cochise, greatest of Apache warriors, died June 8, 1874 in this his favorite stronghold, interred secretly by his followers."

Then at last we found what we were looking for, a marker beside the road that said "Fort Bowie, 1 ½ miles"—that is, 1 ½ miles *up*. Fort Bowie had been the major military post in this area of the Dragoon Mountains called the Apache Pass. In 1861 Cochise with 700 warriors had briefly commanded the heights of the pass, dislodged only after an all-day fight. In 1862 there at the summit Captain Roberts and his Union soldiers stationed at the fort tried to wipe out Cochise and his close friend, Mangas Coloradas, till in the skirmish Mangas Coloradas was wounded, hit in the chest by a bullet. Cochise didn't try to fight on without him, the Apaches slipped away. A month or two later, Mangas Coloradas walked alone into an American camp saying he came to make a lasting peace. Instead, he was brutally murdered by the soldiers, his body thrown into a gulley, his head shipped to the Smithsonian. In bitter fury Cochise resumed his war that became a new, twenty-year struggle against the enemy from his stronghold in these mountains. A dozen years later he was stricken and died. After him came the celebrated Apache chief Geronimo, seventeen years younger, who fiercely led his people in their last stand for freedom.

These were the years the Americans fought for freedom themselves in the Civil War while waging battle to destroy the Apaches. Arizona wanted only to exterminate them; General Sherman strongly advised just leaving Arizona to the Indians.

Marian parked the car and started up the footpath of the Apache Pass. "You can wait down here if you like," she said. I stared round me at an empty, silent world; we had seen nobody all day, it was getting on in the afternoon. I decided to stay close to Marian in this business if we were to be overtaken by night. She was better at scaling mountains than I — a fearless traveler who had recently camped out in the Himalayas, ridden the rapids down the Colorado River, canoed for a week in the forty-mile-long Okefenokee Swamp.

"Wait for me," I shouted after her.

Together we climbed the pass, straight up the mountain on a rocky path covered with snow. I kept Marian's red jacket in view (though it reminded me of a stop sign), struggling in icy ruts to reach the summit or more likely die in the attempt. Halfway we came to a little fenced-in cemetery, stark and neglected, where among soldiers' graves a weathered stone marked that of a two-year-old son of Geronimo — Little Robe, buried here in 1885, not however killed by the white man as, earlier, Geronimo's mother, his first wife, and other children had been.

At Fort Bowie the American flag still waved, but the ranger's station was closed for the winter, not a soul stirred in this godforgotten place. Nothing remained but the scattered ruins of the old military fort and the memory of bloodshed. It was growing terribly cold and late. Shivering, we turned and ran, pursued by dead men, down the pass, and silent in the face of such bloody history drove on in the dark.

Besides Apaches, there were the mining towns. Bisbee was a famous one that, with the working of the Copper Queen Lode in 1877, became the largest mining town in the world, crammed into Mule Pass Gulch on the steep sides of a ravine. With the Copper Queen Mine long since abandoned, Bisbee was a quiet, emptied little place where we spent the night at the Copper Queen Hotel that claims to have "45 gracious rooms and a long saloon." In the saloon was a huge painting over the bar of an outstretched naked Venus with a dazzling white body peered at by a baby Cupid. Bisbee was understandably proud of this grand old hotel where Teddy Roosevelt, General Pershing, and John Wayne slept. I imagined John Wayne swaggering into the saloon and staring fixedly at the Venus.

Twenty-five miles farther was Tombstone, where silver was discovered in 1877. Left over from the old Wild West, Tombstone consisted of a main street, a covered boardwalk, and a row of one-story saloons still open for business. There was Big Nose Kate's, once run by Katie Fisher, a frontier barroom prostitute and Doc Holliday's mistress. There was the O.K. Corral, the Longhorn (formerly the Bucket of Blood), the Lucky Cuss, and so on. The silver rush in 1881 had made Tombstone the worst of Arizona's boomtowns, the most violent and lawless. Till 1889 when the mines were flooded, well-known gunfighters and outlaws lived here—the consumptive Doc Holliday, Johnny Ringo, Bat Masterson, the Earp brothers. The O.K. Corral was the scene of a gunfight made historic by the Earps—Wyatt, Virgil, Morgan—plus Holliday, who on October 26, 1881, shot it out with five members of the Clanton gang. Within sixty seconds three Clantons were dead, and Wyatt Earp, like Geronimo, became an American folk hero.

But the wickedest spot in town was the Bird Cage—a combination theater, saloon, dance hall, gambling den, and bordello—that never closed its doors for nine years, the bawdiest nightspot from coast to coast. We wandered freely about this faded sink of iniquity, sorry to find missing the fourteen bird cages with their red velvet curtains for the use of the prostitutes. Wyatt Earp met his third wife here, Virgil was shot to death on the second floor. Gone too were the flashy entertainers from New York, such as Eddie Foy and Lotta Crabtree, who performed on the real stage and sang to the customers the popular song, "She's Only a Bird in a Gilded Cage."

Tombstone is called "the town too tough to die," kept alive and flourishing by us tourists.

Down at the Mexican border we found the Coronado Memorial that marks the point of entry, four centuries ago, of Coronado when he left Mexico in search of the Seven Golden Cities. He was a Spaniard who came to the new world in 1535. When his friend Mendoza, the Viceroy of Mexico, heard rumors of riches to the north — towns, streams, mountains of gold — he formed an expedition to search for the Seven Cities of Ćibola and asked Coronado to lead it. Coronado, thirty years old, set forth in 1540 with a glorious army of some thousand Spanish soldiers, friendly Mexican-Indians, four priests, strings of mules to carry equipment, and fifteen hundred sheep, pigs, goats, cattle to feed them all. His horsemen wore gilded armor with plumed helmets and carried shields, swords, daggers, lances, plus a half-dozen cannon. They nearly perished on the way from the heat alone.

After five months of travel, at the Gila River Coronado turned northeast to enter what is now New Mexico, and on July 7, 1540, came to Ćibola, the reputed region of the seven cities. But the Ćibola before his eyes was only a few poor Zuni pueblos, wretched sunbaked Indian villages made of sticks and mud. During two years of occupation among these miserable towns, Coronado and his men captured and drove the Indians from their homes, ate their food, and kept up a desperate search for gold. The pursuit took them as far north as Kansas, but they found *nada,* nothing. In 1542 he led the straggling expedition back to a cold reception in Mexico. The golden dream had ended in disgrace.

It was a long stretch north to the Grand Canyon. When one day we reached the final spectacle, I thought of my old professor at Columbia,

Joseph Wood Krutch, who was brave enough to write a book titled simply *Grand Canyon*. The need to find sufficient adjectives for such an enterprise would have finished me, but Professor Krutch had no problem with it. He stuck to the facts, poetry enough for him — that the Canyon is a billion years old, growing wider and deeper, though nowhere on earth is there a chasm so wide and deep, so incomprehensible. It began, Krutch said, as a flat plain of two hundred miles along the Colorado River, and in a few more eons would probably through erosion become a flat plain again. The population of the earth, he guessed, could be all but lost in it. The distance across the gorge from rim to rim was a good ten to eighteen miles. To me it seemed as large as the solar system.

As an abyss the Grand Canyon was said, not by Krutch, to humble the soul. People were apt to respond to its awful mightiness by doing something heroic they would soon repent, like riding a mule the mile down the narrow Bright Angel Trail to the bottom and back again, or climbing alone down the canyon wall. People regularly got into trouble, as I read in the newspaper circulated by the Park Service, which reported 750 rescue operations in the past year of hikers who had to be hauled back up to the top. Others succumbed to fatigue and dehydration, or from leaning too far over the edge.

Marian and I were in no immediate danger. You had to book a mule a year in advance. We signed in at El Tovar, a hotel with a view of the Canyon and the look of a hunting lodge. All day we walked enrapt along the lookout points of South Rim till the shifting winter light and changing hues — old gold, bronze, copper, topaz, tinges of lavender — faded and ravens swooped in the deepening sky. Indians used to live in caves a mile down there beside the Colorado River, but I wouldn't go in search of them even if they were Apaches. Anyway, on this sunny day we had come to the end of a thousand-mile journey, and this was the magnificence we found.

Amazing state, Arizona.

It had taken time, into December. Next night in Phoenix before our plane left, we had Peter and Diana to dinner at our hotel and were happy to see what an old married pair they had become.

The Laughter Must Be Kept

Fontenelle wasn't known to laugh. Described with malice by Voltaire as "le discret Fontenelle," he lived to be one hundred (1657–1757) and left behind a recipe for longevity: keep the heart cold and the stomach warm. This he did by detaching himself from passion, staying unruffled, untroubled, unmarried. They called him revoltingly heartless, neither laughing nor weeping. His curiosity led him to a profound scepticism of people, their faith, their morality. He was a thinker to a fault. His friend Madame de Tencin placed her hand on his heart and said, "You have nothing there but brain."

Alexander Pope never laughed. Sir Isaac Newton is thought to have laughed once in his life. A glacial Chesterfield warned his son against laughter as illiberal and ill-bred, distorting the face and making a disagreeable noise. Lord Halifax objected to a smile; he told his daughter to guard against merriment, "few things are more offensive." She was Chesterfield's mother.

Rabelais, drunk on laughter, said he drank no more than a sponge. Sydney Smith, who liked noise and frolic, was laughter holding both his sides. A sidesplitter. He laughed, wrote Hesketh Pearson, "when a comic idea came into his head; he laughed as he put it into words; he joined in the laughter with which it was received." In our time the Czech writer Milan Kundera calls his unhappy, sex-ridden novel *A Book of Laughter and Forgetting*. E. B. White writes, "I must read the Book of Job, for laughs."

Recently I was invited to join the Fellowship of the Merry Heart, headquarters in Cedar Rapids, Iowa. It is an honor that I dream not of, perhaps because the word merry goes so far in claiming a heart full of mirth and elation that it sounds slightly archaic, out of tune with our time and with life itself. It used to be a good, understandable word. In the fifteenth century the seesaw was the merry-totter. A wishbone was a merrythought. A festival was a merrimake. A bastard was a merry begot. Shakespeare used the word more than a hundred times in his plays:

Falstaff: "There's a merry heart! Good Master Silence . . .

Silence: "Who, I? I have been merry twice, and once ere now."

But of Fontenelle the rumor isn't strictly true. "Quelquefois," he said, "j'ai dit ha ha."

La Vie

La vie est telle
Que Fontenelle
Quelquefois
A dit "ha ha,"
Lui et moi.

The Anatomy of Melancholy. In his great study of melancholy, Robert Burton lists the main causes of depression, gloom, misery, and a sinking heart. They are: God, bad angels and devils, witches and magicians, stars, old age, parents, and bad diet. To them he adds the pain of love, love melancholy, a common cause of sorrow and despair. According to Burton, the amiable vicar of St. Thomas's in Oxford, this thing called melancholy is universally present in mankind, a malady in each of us, since "all the world is melancholy or mad." "Go to Bedlam for examples," he said. As a collector of notions and oddities, he began his famous and only book, first published in 1621, as a way of lifting his own depression, to escape being "silent, sedentary, solitary." Finding the subject utterly intoxicating, he then spent the rest of his bachelor life, twenty more years, in elaborating it, rummaging through dusty shelves at Oxford to find more causes of melancholy, more symptoms, and more cures. As a lifework it not only lifted his spirits, but proved to him that the greatest cause of all was idleness or sloth, and the most dependable cure, besides fresh air and country living, was keeping busy. The last words he uttered before he died were, "Be not solitary, be not idle."

By those who knew him, Burton was said to be lively company, even frisky, even humorous. At least he intended to be. "To play the fool now and then," he wrote, "is not amiss." He called himself Democritus Junior, the son of Democritus, the Laughing Philosopher, to whom the true end of life was happiness, and laughter the remedy for the thorn in the flesh. You don't necessarily die of melancholy but you suffer. Believing this to be what really ails the world, Democritus wore a laughing face. He retired to his garden, where throughout a very long life, according to Juvenal, he was constantly amused by the frailties and follies of humankind. Burton contrasted the laughter of Democritus with the incurable tears of Heraclitus, known as the Weeping Philosopher from the dismal view he took of the same follies. And it must be said that Heraclitus, the mourner to whom life was no laughing matter, has generally been considered the more observant, the more accurate of the two. (Bertrand Russell: "I find that of all the men that ever lived Heraclitus is the most intimate to me.") Like Democritus, he retired from the marketplace, not to a sunny garden but to a bleak mountaintop where he fed on grass, then went to live on a dunghill.

It's easy to imagine how often Robert Burton laughed, and chose to laugh, as instructive thoughts on the subject came to him, and how diligently he hastened to celebrate them in *The Anatomy of Melancholy.* Such as:

All poets are mad.
What Pythagoras said to his scholars of old may be applied to melancholy
    men: eat no beans.
One madness is to live like a wretch and die rich.
Women wear the britches.
Wine and women go together, those two main plagues and dotages that
    infatuate and besot people.
England is a paradise for women and hell for horses.

The Rejoicers

For laughter, look to Master Rabelais,
The blithe Montaigne, the rollicking John Gay,
And look to Chaucer, affable and mellow,
To genial Horace, that lighthearted fellow—
The revelers. I love a cheerful man,
Content with fortune and with rhymes that scan
To praise retirement or the gaudy town,
Or quick with prose to set a pleasure down,
Above whose disquisition I can hear
Consoling answer in the atmosphere
For you and me, my darling. Look to them
Who wore no sorrow like a diadem.

Postscript: End of Story

"We are poor passing facts," said Robert Lowell in almost his last poem. As one of these facts, I recently wrote what I intended to be my last book, *The World and the Bo Tree*. That wasn't the original title, which was more ambitious: I meant to call it *By the Look of Things*. From the eminence where I sat, though the visibility was poor, I planned to take one more quick look at existence to see what I thought of it. For one thing, had I lived in vain? Would one actually want to live it again? "To judge whether life itself is or is not worth the trouble of being lived," said Camus, "that is the basic question of philosophy." But philosophy's answer? Hard to say. I only know I barely got through this one alive.

Santayana was a philosopher. "That life is worth living is the most necessary of assumptions," he wrote, "and, were it not assumed, would be the most improbable of conclusions." And yet the simplest and truest philosophy is perhaps found written on ancient Greek tombs: "I was not. I came to be. I am not. I care not."

My first title for the book proved to be a large order, so exhaustive it ran me out of words and I settled for the more modest approach of inspecting just one world and one bo tree. Isaac Asimov, who died not long ago, was an example of the tireless investigator of multiple worlds who never for a moment stops looking and telling you what he finds out. Once when Barbara Walters asked Asimov what he would do if he knew he had but six months to live, "Type faster," he said. Poor man, he died at seventy-two with barely five hundred books written and things by the thousand yet unexamined.

There were other reminders of mortality, like an appalling item that appeared lately in the *Times Literary Supplement* to keep me from aspiring further to sum things up. In a piece about wild animals and the need for proper zoos to preserve them in, it said, "We know that half of all living species are about to be wiped out *right now*"—which included mass extinction of African elephants, mountain gorillas, Manchurian tigers, Sichuan pandas, Madagascar lemurs, New Zealand kiwis, Bangladesh frogs, plus millions of beetles and might as well include mankind. A bad day too for bananafish.

Besides, with a failing memory and a growing tendency to dwell less on the eternities than on passing facts — such as the weather, the evening news and anchor man Peter Jennings' splendid taste in neckties (a new one each night) — it wasn't easy to say what I was looking *at*. In an interview with Dick Cavett, the poet John Ashbery claimed not to know what he was looking at or what, in fact, he thought when he did look because of an absent mind befuddled by the smell of frying sausages or where he had to be in the next hour. Confusion amounting to a breach of the peace resulted. Doesn't one want a poet to look where he's going?

Just the other day, still seeking a clearer field of vision I asked at the florist's for a fig tree to take home and sit under — not in the hope it would bear a fig or provide me a fig leaf, but because I find the need in the wilderness of the world, and at this hour, to look for something to sit under (contrary to Robert Graves' opinion: "to sit / Always beneath the same small tree / Argues a certain lack of wit." And Mae West's advice, "There's no future under a fig tree.")

Yet what better place?

The man had plenty of fig trees in stock, but he warned me about the *ficus,* which I see is specifically recommended in Micah 4:4, "Every man shall sit under his fig tree," as the bo tree itself is, *Ficus religiosa.* While being hardy and long-lived as they come, it is also temperamental, at least as a house plant, and if not content with your company will drop its leaves and play dead. This is the kind of threat the Buddha never faced while sitting under the bo tree when he said, "For me the world no longer matters"; it might have changed the look of nirvana if he had. Nevertheless, I chose a fig tree about five feet tall with shiny green leaves and just room for sitting, not for daliance or entertaining friends. And the man said, "What it wants is *light.* Give it plenty of *light.*" That being coincidentally what I too am after, my tree and I will have to look for illumination in the noonday sun, or drop our leaves together.

In the end, said Wallace Stevens, there is the necessary fiction—the way the world is, and the way you see it; the way things are and the way they seem—for such a little while. There can be at best only hurried glimpses, a version of the thing—people to know scarcely at all, houses to live only temporarily in, windows to polish to brighten the outlook, this earth to learn so little about, the sense of having lived and not lived, the unbearable loss of those we love.

In the end, he said, "perhaps the truth depends upon a walk around a lake." Show me the way.

And Things Are As I Think They Are

I wouldn't claim we're deep in clover
Or fit as fiddles, you and I,
Fond, but scarcely fond as pigeons,
Young, but not to passersby,
Weak in the loins, it's true, diminished
To mere handwavings, nonetheless
Beyond all this the sweet illusion
Of love unchanged, enduring. Yes.

Helen Bevington has published many books, including *Doctor Johnson's Waterfall, Nineteen Million Elephants, A Change of Sky, When Found, Make A Verse Of, Charley Smith's Girl, A Book and a Love Affair, The House Was Quiet and the World Was Calm, Beautiful Lofty People, Along Came the Witch, The Journey Is Everything,* and *The World and the Bo Tree.* She has written regularly for the *New York Times Book Review,* has published light verse in the *New Yorker,* and has contributed to *Atlantic Monthly* and *American Scholar,* among other periodicals. For many years she taught at Duke University, as did her late husband, Merle. She is now Professor Emeritus of English at Duke.

Library of Congress Cataloging-in-Publication Data

Bevington, Helen

The third and only way / Helen Bevington.

p.   cm.

ISBN 0-8223-1850-4 (acid-free paper)

1. Bevington, Helen Smith — Biography.   2. Women authors, American — 20th

century — Biography.   3. Aged — Conduct of life.   I. Title.

PS3503.F924Z474   1996

811'.54 — dc20

[B]   96-14208   CIP